AF614095

THE PRIVATE EQUITY GAMEPLAN

The Operator's Playbook for Optimizing and Sequencing Value Creation in PE-backed Companies

Book Three of the Private Equity Theater Trilogy

First Edition

Mohamad Chahine

MeritIP Publishing

Copyright

Gender Neutrality

This book uses gender-neutral language throughout. All references to leaders, executives, and practitioners are intended to be inclusive of all genders. The examples and guidance herein celebrate the diverse leadership qualities found in private equity and across all business contexts.

Disclaimer

The strategies, frameworks, and examples in this book are based on the author's experience and research. They are intended as educational guidance, not as specific investment, legal, or financial advice. Results will vary based on circumstances, execution, and market conditions. The author and publisher disclaim any liability for decisions made based on this content.

Dedication

To my wife, son and daughters.

To every operator who builds value in the trenches.

Contents

The Private Equity Trilogy

This is the third book in the Private Equity Leadership Trilogy. Before you turn another page, understand where it fits.

The Trilogy

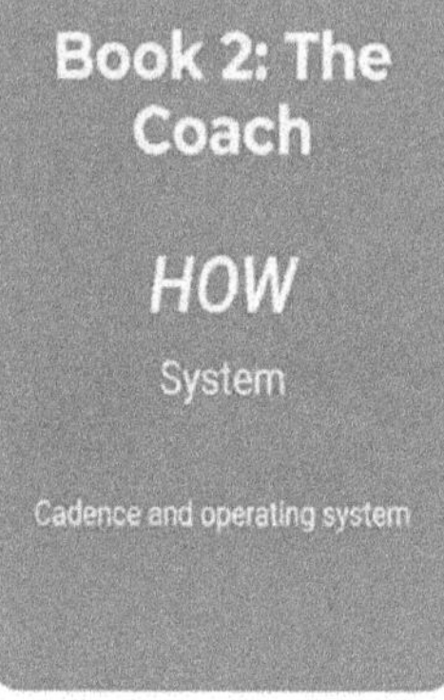

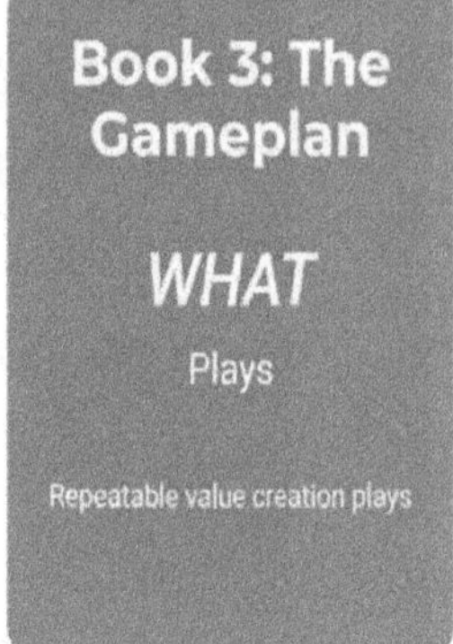

The PE Quarterback answers the question: *Who?*

It addresses the leader. The mindset. The stakeholder dynamics. The psychology of operating under pressure with investor capital at stake. If you need to understand what kind of person thrives in the chief executive seat of a sponsor-backed company, read that book.

The PE Coach answers the question: *How?*

It addresses the system. The governance. The cadence. The operating rhythm that keeps a company aligned and accountable. Meetings, metrics, dashboards, decision velocity, and the architecture of execution. If you need to install a repeatable operating system that translates strategy into weekly behavior, read that book.

The PE Gameplan answers the question: *What?*

It addresses the patterns. The specific tactical combinations that change the numbers on the value bridge. Not philosophy. Not process. The precise sequence of actions that move operating earnings, shift enterprise value, and expand equity outcomes. If you need to know which levers to pull and in what order, you are holding the right book.

The Litmus Test

If a chapter explains how to hold a meeting, it belongs in the Coach. If a chapter explains how to raise prices by ten percent without losing volume, it belongs here.

This book is a pattern library. Each gambit is a repeatable combination that produces a recognizable shape on the value bridge. Read it front to back for the full architecture. Or flip directly to a specific section when facing a specific problem.

The gambits are designed to stack. Mix them. Sequence them. Build your custom bridge from the catalog.

Three books. Three questions. One outcome: equity value created through disciplined execution.

How to Use This Book

This book is built differently from the first two volumes. It is a reference, not a narrative. Read it cover to cover for the architecture. Or treat it as a field manual, opening to the pattern you need when you need it.

The Visual Alphabet

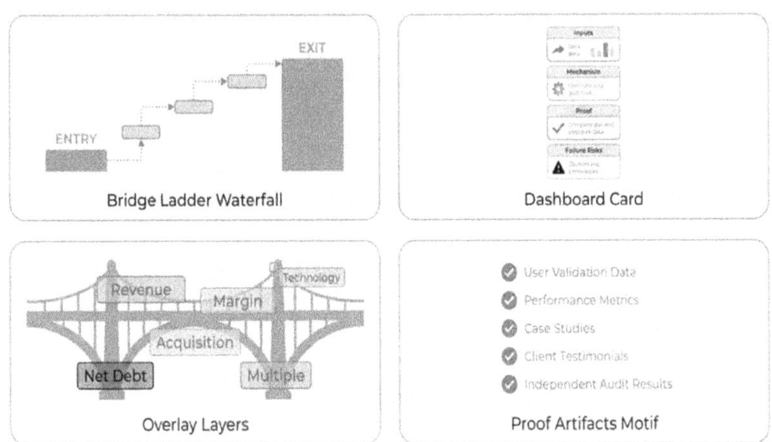

Step One: Find Your Starting Position

Before selecting gambits, diagnose where you are. Most portfolio companies fall into one of five starting positions:

The Growth Problem. Revenue is flat or declining. The market exists, but the company is not capturing it. The investment thesis depends on top-line expansion. The expansion is not happening.

The Margin Problem. Revenue is acceptable, but profitability is weak. Costs are bloated or poorly understood. Operating earnings lag where they should be given business scale.

The Cash Problem. The profit and loss statement looks fine, but cash is tight. Working capital consumes value. Debt reduction is slower than planned. The equity story suffers because cash conversion is broken.

The Platform Build. The thesis is inorganic. The company is meant to acquire, integrate, and consolidate. The challenge is making acquisitions accretive and capturing the synergies promised in the model.

The Re-Rate Need. Operating earnings are growing, but the exit multiple is stuck. The company has not built the proof points, the narrative, or the quality signals that command premium valuation.

Step Two: Select Three to Five Gambits

Resist the temptation to run twelve initiatives at once. The best value creation plans focus on a small number of high-impact patterns executed with discipline. Choose three to five gambits for the next twelve to eighteen months. Assign owners. Set milestones. Track progress weekly.

Step Three: Stack Them Into a Custom Bridge

The gambits in this book are not isolated tips. They are designed to combine. A pricing gambit plus a working capital gambit plus a multiple expansion gambit creates a compound effect that exceeds the sum of the parts. Think of each gambit as a building block. Your job is to assemble them into a bridge that connects entry value to exit value.

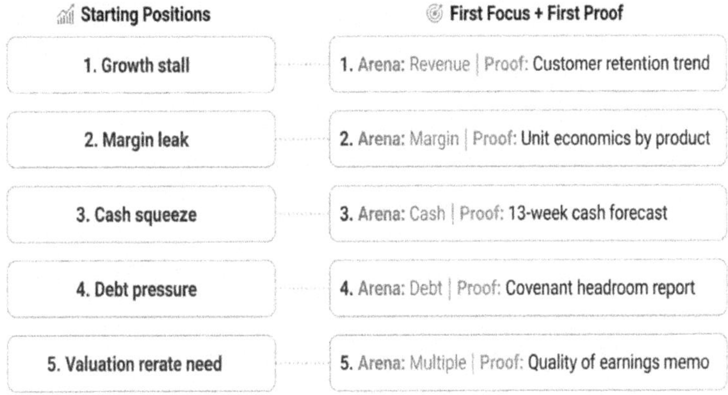

The Structure of Each Gambit

Every gambit follows the same format. This consistency allows you to compare patterns, evaluate trade-offs, and make decisions quickly.

The Name. A memorable label that captures the essence of the pattern.

Bridge Target. Which of the three bridges does this gambit affect: operating earnings, enterprise value, or equity value?

Time to Impact. Fast (under six months), medium (six to eighteen months), or long (eighteen months or more).

The Pattern. What it is in plain language.

The Sacrifice. What you give up or risk in the short term. Every gambit involves a trade-off.

The Sequence. Step-by-step execution. No more than twelve steps.

Preconditions. When it works. Not every gambit fits every situation.

The Trap. How it fails. Every pattern has a failure mode.

The Proof. Buyer-grade metrics and artifacts. What evidence does this gambit produce that a buyer will pay for?

Variants. Two or three common adaptations of the pattern.

Disqualifiers. When not to pursue it. Conditions that make the gambit wrong for your situation.

The One Equation

Every gambit in this book serves one purpose: to change the variables in the equation that determines what equity owners receive at exit.

Equity Value = (Operating Earnings × Multiple) − Net Debt

This is the arithmetic of private equity. Simple to state. Difficult to execute. Everything else is commentary.

Operating Earnings

Operating earnings measures profit generated by the business before financing and accounting adjustments. It is the numerator of enterprise value. Grow it sustainably, and enterprise value expands. Grow it unsustainably, and buyers will discount it during diligence.

The Multiple

The multiple is the market's judgment of quality. Two companies with identical operating earnings can have vastly different enterprise values if one trades at six times and the other at twelve times. The difference is perceived quality: durability of revenue, predictability of cash flow, strength of market position, clarity of growth runway, reduction of risk. Multiples are earned during the hold period, not negotiated at exit.

Net Debt

Net debt is the claim satisfied before equity holders receive value. Funded debt minus cash on hand. Every dollar of net debt reduction translates directly into equity value. Cash conversion, working capital discipline, and debt paydown are not secondary concerns. They are direct contributors to the outcome.

The Three Bridges

Throughout this book, we work with three bridges that flow from this equation:

The Operating Earnings Bridge shows how profit moves from entry to exit through revenue growth, margin expansion, and operational improvement.

The Enterprise Value Bridge shows how total business value changes by combining operating earnings growth with multiple expansion or contraction.

The Equity Value Bridge shows what remains for equity holders after deducting net debt from enterprise value.

Every gambit targets one or more of these bridges. Some gambits grow operating earnings. Some expand the multiple. Some accelerate debt reduction. The most powerful gambits affect multiple bridges simultaneously.

The Equation Is Unforgiving

The equation does not care about your effort. It does not reward activity. It responds only to changes in operating earnings, the multiple, or net debt. A hundred initiatives that do not move these variables are worth less than a single gambit that does.

Keep this equation visible. Print it. Post it. Reference it weekly. When evaluating any initiative, ask: which variable does this change, and by how much? If the answer is unclear, reconsider the initiative.

The rest of this book shows you exactly how to move the equation in your favor.

Author's Note

I have spent twenty-five years watching value creation plans succeed and fail. I have sat in boardrooms where elegant strategies collapsed under execution pressure. I have seen simple, disciplined patterns compound into extraordinary outcomes. The difference was rarely sophistication of the idea. It was precision of execution.

This book captures what I have learned about patterns that work. Not theories. Not frameworks. Patterns. Repeatable combinations that produce recognizable results on the value bridge.

I call them gambits because the term captures something essential. A gambit in chess involves a calculated sacrifice to gain a later advantage. In private equity, the sacrifice is rarely a pawn. It is usually short-term comfort, short-term profit, or short-term simplicity. The advantage is compounding value that appears in the equity bridge at exit.

The forty gambits in this book are not the only patterns that create value. They are patterns I have seen work repeatedly across industries, geographies, and market conditions. Specific enough to be actionable. General enough to adapt to your context.

A word of caution. No gambit works in isolation. The best results come from stacking patterns intelligently, sequencing them correctly, and executing with relentless discipline. A pricing gambit without commercial capability will fail. A working capital gambit without operational discipline will revert. Context matters. Execution matters more.

Use this book as a reference. Return to it when facing a specific challenge. Mark the pages. Argue with the ideas. Adapt them to your reality. The goal is not to follow patterns blindly but to understand them deeply enough to know when to apply them and when to modify them.

The bridge from entry to exit is not built by hope. It is built by patterns.

Let us begin.

Book Infographic

The Book-at-a-Glance

What This Book Is

A field manual for value creation

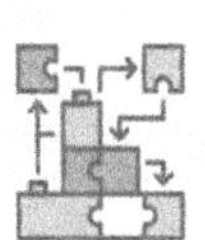
A pattern library you can reuse

A bridge-first way to explain results

A proof-first way to earn credibility

Designed for practitioners.

What This Book Is Not

Not a deal sourcing book

Not a leadership book

Not a meeting playbook

Not theory without action

Who This Is For

- Private equity professionals
- Operating partners
- Portfolio leaders
- Finance leaders
- Board members

Who it's not for

- Deal sourcing teams
- Early-stage founders

One-Page Summary

What the book gives you	What you can do with it
• 40 proven value creation patterns	• Pick plays that fit your constraint
• A bridge-first attribution method	• Explain results with clarity
• Proof-before-narrative discipline	• Stack patterns without conflict
• Stacking and sequencing rules	• Build buyer-grade proof artifacts
• Anti-pattern recognition library	• Avoid common value traps
• Exit-ready proof pack builder	• Accelerate exit readiness

[Author bio line]

The Book Map

Navigate the gameplan

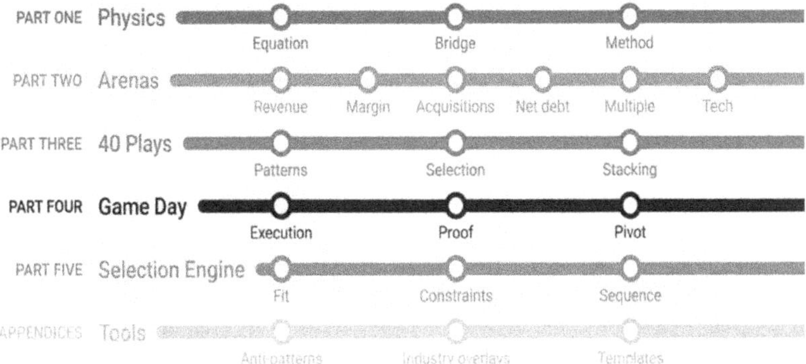

Five Arenas

Where value is created

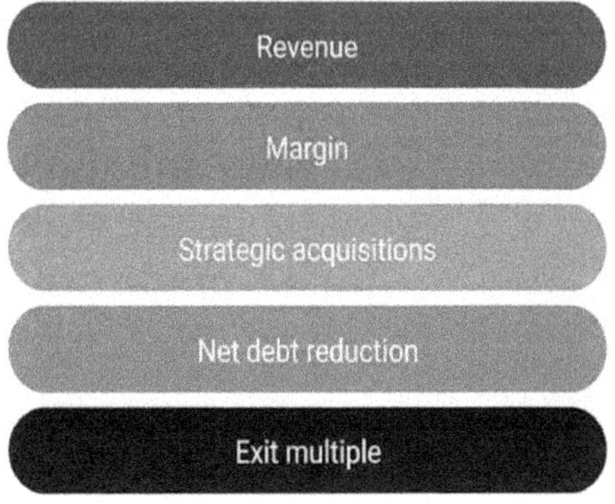

Technology accelerant applies to all

The Problem

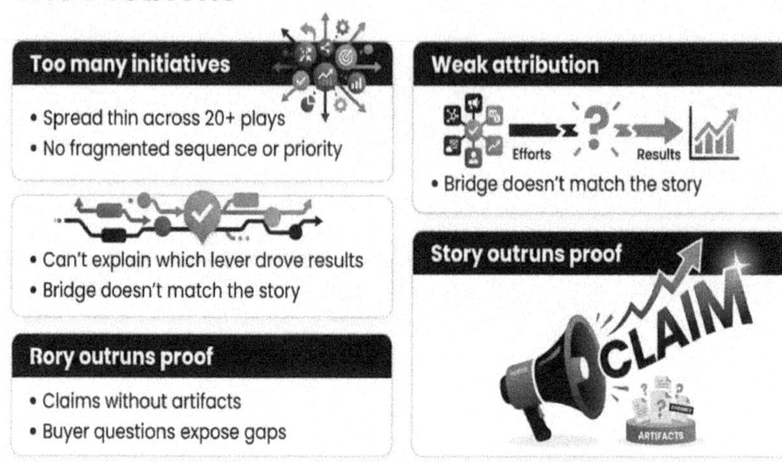

The Promise

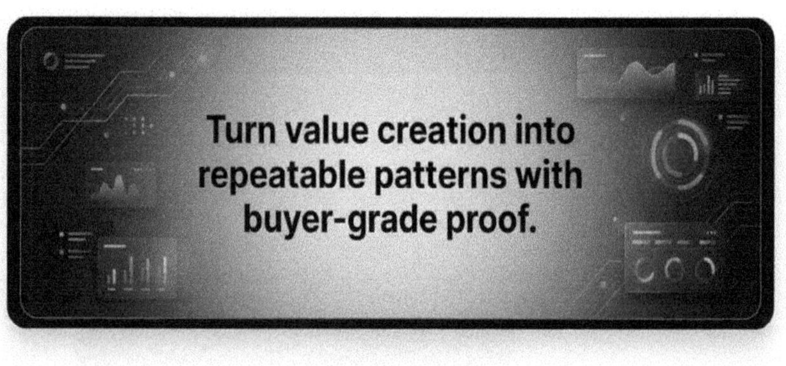

● Pattern recognition over reinvention ● Proof before narrative ● Built for stacking and sequencing

The Library

Built for stacking.

Select the Right Plays

Constraint-first selection

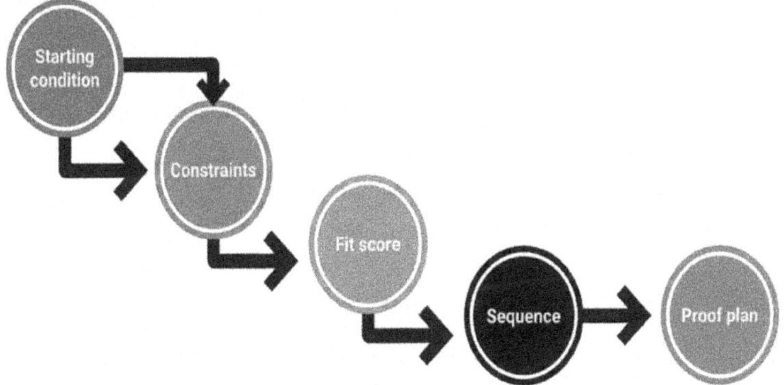

The Format

How each play is structured

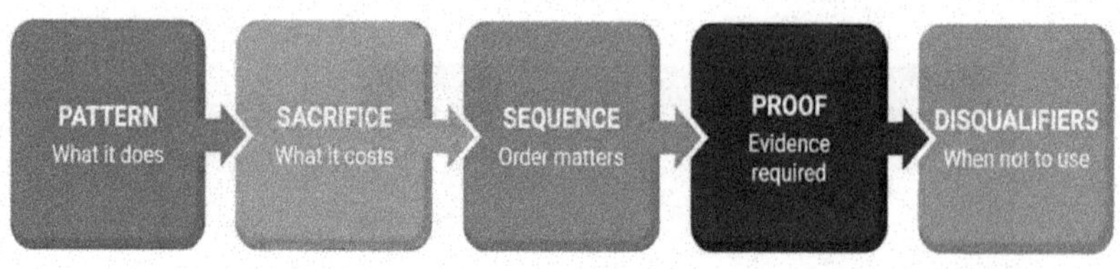

Proof Pack

Exit-ready documentation

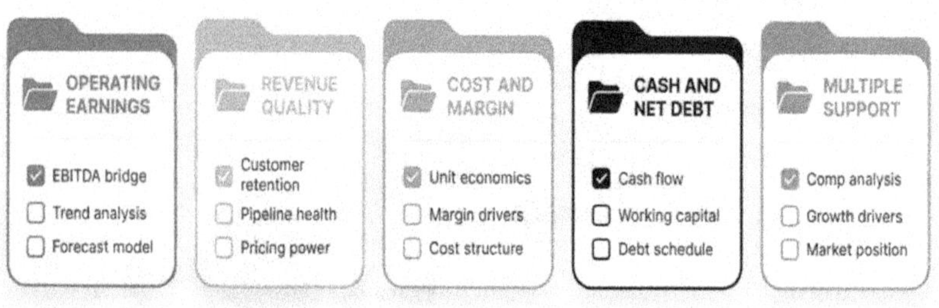

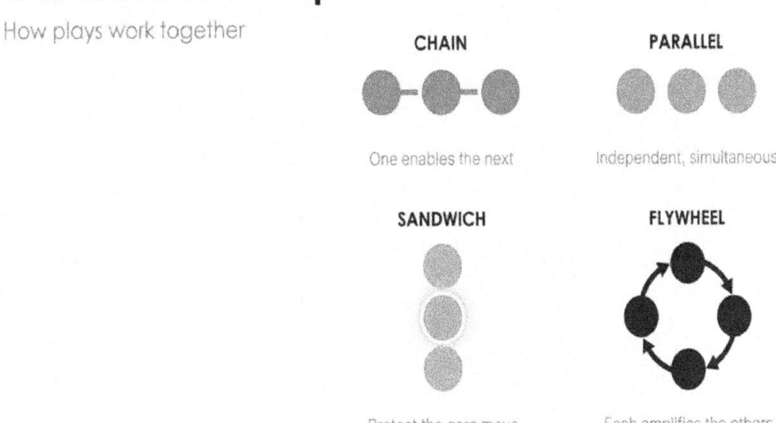
Combination Shapes
How plays work together
CHAIN
One enables the next
PARALLEL
Independent, simultaneous
SANDWICH
Protect the core move
FLYWHEEL
Each amplifies the others

Evidence Strength
Build proof that buyers trust
MARKET VALIDATION
Buyer-grade evidence
AUDITABLE PROOF
Third-party validated
VERIFIED TREND
Consistent pattern
INTERNAL TRACKING
Self-reported metrics
ASSERTION
Claim without data

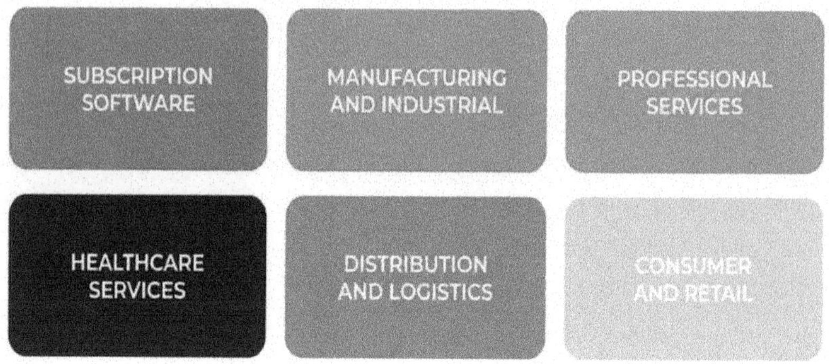
Industry Overlays
Same bridge, different sensitivities
SUBSCRIPTION SOFTWARE
MANUFACTURING AND INDUSTRIAL
PROFESSIONAL SERVICES
HEALTHCARE SERVICES
DISTRIBUTION AND LOGISTICS
CONSUMER AND RETAIL
Same bridge, different sensitivities.

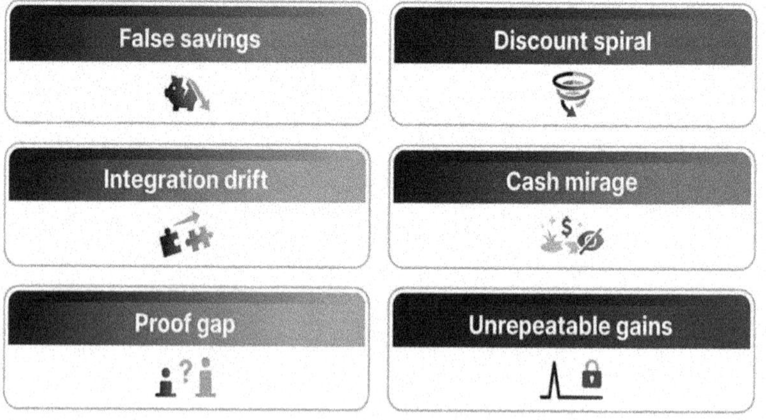
Common Traps
False savings
Discount spiral
Integration drift
Cash mirage
Proof gap
Unrepeatable gains

Test Before Rollout

Sandbox testing canvas

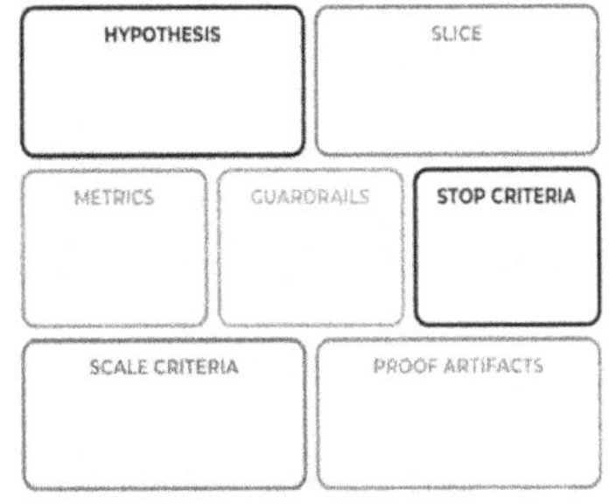

Use It in Three Steps

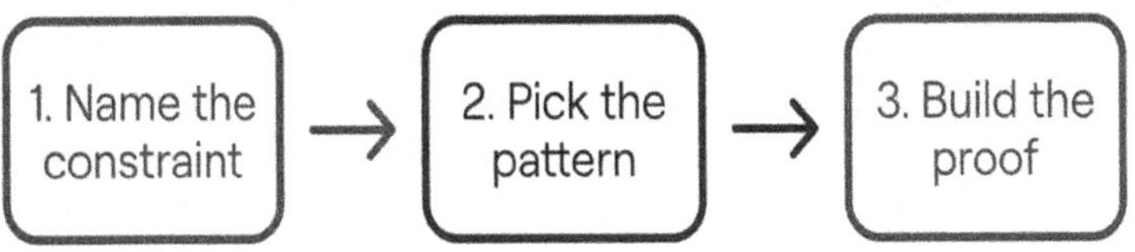

Proof Before Narrative

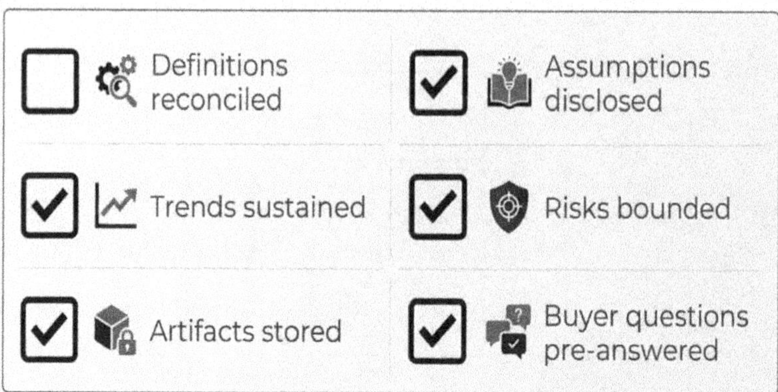

Your Next 30 Days

Getting started

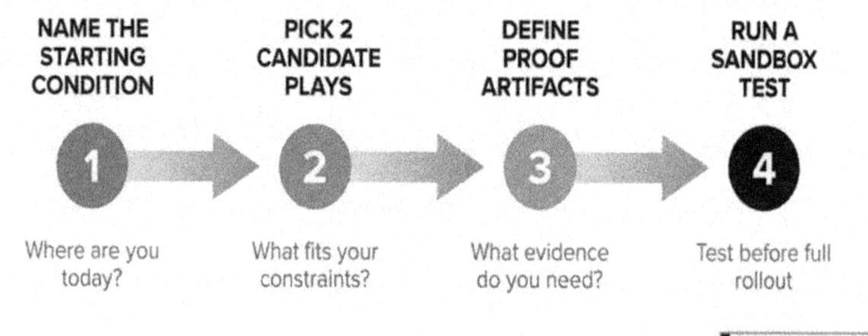

DELIVERABLE
A buyer-grade proof trail

PART ONE

THE PHYSICS OF VALUE CREATION

Understanding How Equity Value Actually Changes

Chapter 1

Why Equity Value Moves

A portfolio company enters ownership at one value and exits at another. The distance between those two numbers determines whether the investment succeeds or fails. Everything in private equity reduces to this gap.

Yet most operators cannot explain precisely why the gap widened or narrowed. They point to revenue growth. They mention cost reductions. They reference market conditions. These explanations are true but incomplete. They describe symptoms without revealing the underlying mechanics.

Understanding why equity value moves requires understanding the physics of private equity. Not the philosophy. Not the strategy. The physics. The fundamental forces that cause value to increase, decrease, or remain stuck.

The One Equation

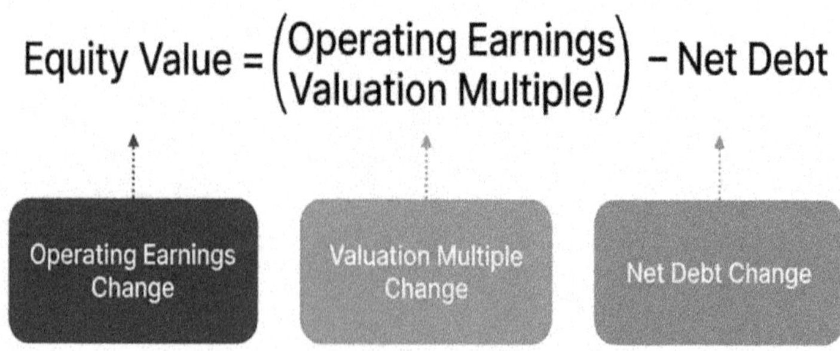

Every bridge ladder explains one or more of these changes.

The Three Bridges

Value creation operates across three connected bridges. Each bridge measures something different. Each responds to different actions. Confusing them leads to misallocated effort and missed targets.

The Operating Earnings Bridge tracks how profit changes over the hold period. It starts with entry operating earnings and ends with exit operating earnings. The steps in between represent the sources of profit growth or decline: revenue expansion, margin improvement, cost reduction, mix shift, and operational efficiency. This bridge answers the question: did the business become more profitable?

The Enterprise Value Bridge tracks how the total value of the business changes. Enterprise value equals operating earnings multiplied by the valuation multiple. This bridge combines two forces: changes in operating earnings and changes in the multiple. A company can grow operating earnings and still see enterprise value decline if the multiple compresses. A company can hold operating earnings flat and still see enterprise value expand if the multiple improves. This bridge answers the question: did the business become more valuable to all capital providers?

The Equity Value Bridge tracks what remains for equity holders after satisfying prior claims. Equity value equals enterprise value minus net debt. This bridge incorporates everything from the first two bridges plus the effect of debt paydown, cash generation, and changes in the balance sheet.

This bridge answers the question: did the owners actually capture value?

The three bridges are connected but not identical. An operator can succeed on the operating earnings bridge while failing on the equity value bridge. If operating earnings grow but debt balloons, equity holders may receive less at exit than at entry. An operator can succeed on the enterprise value bridge while the equity value bridge lags. If the multiple expands but cash conversion is poor, the theoretical value never translates into actual returns.

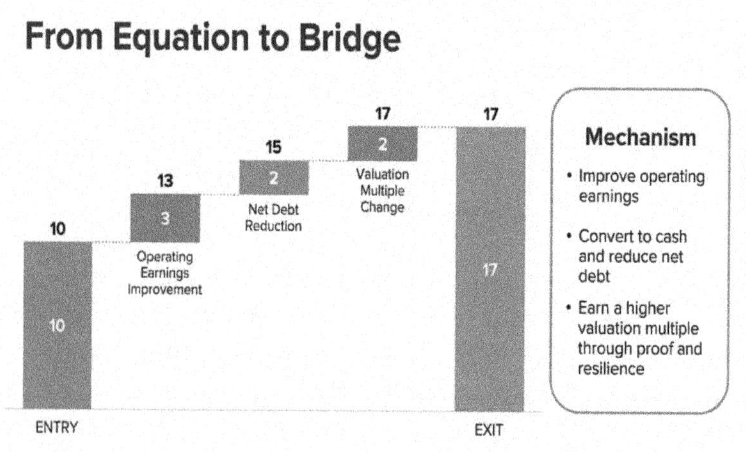

Why Teams Confuse Enterprise Value and Equity Value

In weekly operations meetings, teams focus on revenue and margin. They track operating earnings because it appears on the monthly report. They celebrate when operating earnings beats budget. This focus is understandable but incomplete.

Operating earnings is not equity value. A business can generate strong operating earnings while destroying equity value through poor cash management, excessive capital expenditure, or deteriorating quality metrics that compress the multiple.

Consider a scenario. A manufacturing business grows operating earnings from twelve million to eighteen million over three years. The team celebrates a fifty percent improvement. But during the same period, the company invests heavily in new equipment, increasing net debt from twenty million to thirty-five million. Working capital deteriorates as inventory builds. The exit multiple compresses from seven times to five and a half times because buyers see customer concentration risk.

The math at entry: twelve million in operating earnings times seven equals eighty-four million enterprise value, minus twenty million net debt equals sixty-four million equity value.

The math at exit: eighteen million in operating earnings times five and a half equals ninety-nine million enterprise value, minus thirty-five million net debt equals sixty-four million equity value.

Operating earnings grew fifty percent. Equity value stayed flat. The team won the wrong game.

Why Cash Is Not Optional

Net debt is not a financing detail. It is a direct subtraction from equity value. Every dollar of debt that remains at exit is a dollar that equity holders do not receive.

Cash conversion is the link between operating earnings and net debt reduction. A business generates operating earnings. Those earnings either convert to cash or they do not. If they convert, the cash can pay down debt. If they do not convert, the debt remains.

The enemies of cash conversion are familiar: growing receivables that customers do not pay on time, inventory that accumulates faster than it sells, capital expenditures that exceed depreciation, and one-time items that consume operating cash. Each of these erodes the link between profit and equity value.

The best operators track cash conversion with the same intensity they track revenue. They know their collection days. They know their inventory turns. They know how many cents of free cash flow they generate for each dollar of operating earnings. When cash conversion weakens, they treat it as seriously as a revenue miss.

Why the Multiple Is Not Random

Many operators treat the valuation multiple as a market phenomenon beyond their control. They believe multiples rise and fall with interest rates, buyer appetite, and sector trends. This belief is partially true and mostly limiting.

Multiples are not random. They are judgments about quality. A buyer pays a higher multiple for a business they perceive as more predictable, more durable, and less risky. A buyer pays a lower multiple for a business they perceive as volatile, concentrated, or dependent on factors outside management control.

The components of quality are specific:

Revenue durability. Is the revenue recurring or transactional? Does it come from contracts or from one-time orders? Are customers sticky or price-sensitive? A business with eighty percent recurring revenue trades at a different multiple than a business with eighty percent project revenue.

Customer concentration. Does the top customer represent five percent of revenue or thirty percent? Concentration is risk. Buyers discount for it.

Earnings predictability. How accurately does the company forecast? Do results match projections? A company that consistently meets or exceeds guidance signals operational control. A company that regularly misses signals chaos.

Growth runway. Is there visible opportunity for continued expansion? Buyers pay premiums for growth potential they can underwrite with confidence.

Management depth. Is the business dependent on one or two individuals, or is there a capable team? Key-person risk compresses multiples.

Operational maturity. Are systems professional? Is reporting reliable? Are processes documented? Buyers pay more for businesses that look like institutions than for businesses that look like projects.

These factors are not fixed at entry. They can be changed during the hold period. A business can shift from transactional revenue to recurring revenue. A business can reduce customer concentration. A business can improve forecast accuracy. Each improvement is an investment in multiple expansion.

Bridge Blindness

Bridge blindness is the inability to see where value is actually coming from. It is surprisingly common, even among experienced operators.

A team suffering from bridge blindness attributes results to effort rather than to specific sources. They say "we worked hard" instead of "price realization improved by three percent while volume held steady." They say "the market was strong" instead of "customer retention increased from eighty-two percent to ninety-one percent." They say "we cut costs" instead of "procurement consolidation reduced direct material expense by four hundred basis points."

Bridge blindness is dangerous because it prevents learning. If you do not know which actions caused which results, you cannot repeat the actions that worked or avoid the actions that failed. You are operating on intuition instead of evidence.

The cure for bridge blindness is rigorous bridge attribution. Every quarter, build a waterfall that shows exactly where operating earnings came from. Break it down by source: price, volume, mix, cost reduction by category, and one-time items. Do the same for enterprise value and equity value. Make the bridges visible. Discuss them in leadership meetings. Hold owners accountable for the steps they control.

The Five Forces That Move the Equation

Value creation at the equity level comes from five primary forces. These are not categories of activity. They are categories of impact. Every initiative, every project, every operational change should ultimately connect to one or more of these forces.

Revenue Growth. Increasing the top line through price, volume, mix, retention, expansion, new products, new channels, or new markets. Revenue growth matters for its direct contribution to operating earnings and for its effect on the multiple. Companies that demonstrate sustainable growth command higher valuations.

Margin Expansion. Improving gross and operating margins through cost reduction, productivity improvement, mix optimization, and complexity simplification. Margin improvement often has an outsized effect on equity value because it flows directly to operating earnings without requiring additional revenue.

Strategic Acquisitions. Adding value through disciplined acquisition and integration. Acquisitions can accelerate growth, add capabilities, consolidate markets, and capture synergies. They can also destroy value if integration fails or if purchase prices exceed the value created.

Debt Reduction. Converting operating earnings to cash and using that cash to reduce net debt. Every dollar of debt repaid translates directly into equity value. Working capital improvement is particularly powerful because it generates cash without reducing operating earnings.

Multiple Expansion. Enhancing the quality and strategic attractiveness of the business to justify a higher exit multiple. This includes improving revenue durability, reducing risk, building proof points, and constructing a compelling narrative for buyers.

These five forces are not independent. They interact. Revenue growth can fund margin improvement. Margin improvement can accelerate debt reduction. Debt reduction can create capacity for acquisitions. Acquisitions can support multiple expansion. The best value creation plans sequence these forces intentionally.

The Physics in Practice

Understanding why equity value moves is the foundation for everything that follows in this book. The gambits in later chapters are specific patterns for changing the variables in the equation. But patterns without physics are just tricks. They work sometimes and fail other times without explanation.

When you understand the physics, you can diagnose why a gambit is working or failing. You can adapt patterns to your specific context. You can combine patterns in ways that compound rather than conflict.

Keep the three bridges visible. Track operating earnings, enterprise value, and equity value separately. Know where your value is coming from. Know which forces are contributing and which are detracting. The equation is unforgiving. Respect it.

Chapter 2

The Bridge as a Battle Map

A military commander studies terrain before committing forces. The shape of the land determines where to attack, where to defend, and where to maneuver. Ignoring terrain leads to avoidable losses.

The value bridge is the terrain of private equity. It shows where value can be captured, where it is leaking, and where the obstacles lie. Reading the bridge correctly determines which gambits to deploy and in what sequence.

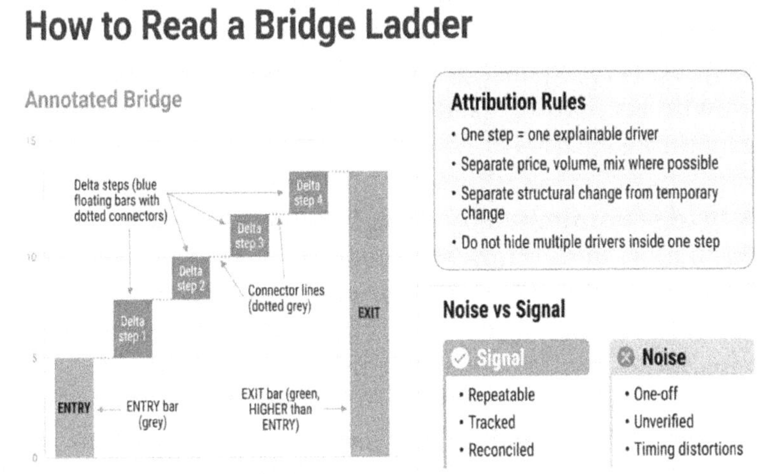

How to Read a Value Bridge

A value bridge is a waterfall chart that shows how value changes from one state to another. The left bar represents the starting point. The right bar represents the ending point. The steps in between represent the sources of change, with positive contributions stepping up and negative contributions stepping down.

Most teams build bridges for board presentations. They show the bridge once per quarter, explain the variance, and move on. This is a waste of a powerful tool.

A bridge should be studied, not just presented. Study the shape. Note which steps are largest. Identify which steps are within management control and which are driven by external factors. Look for patterns across multiple periods. Ask what the bridge reveals about the underlying business.

The shape of the bridge tells a story:

A bridge dominated by revenue growth suggests the business is in expansion mode. The question becomes: is the growth profitable? Is it sustainable? Is it consuming or generating cash?

A bridge dominated by margin improvement suggests the business is in optimization mode. The question becomes: is there more margin to capture? Is the improvement sustainable or one-time? Has cost cutting damaged capability?

A bridge with offsetting positive and negative steps suggests the business is churning. Growth in one area is being consumed by decline in another. The net result masks the underlying volatility.

A bridge with large "other" or "one-time" categories suggests poor attribution. If significant value changes cannot be traced to specific sources, the team does not truly understand what is driving results.

The Gap Between Current and Full Potential

Every business operates below its full potential. The gap between current performance and full potential is where value creation lives.

Estimating full potential requires honest assessment:

Revenue potential. If pricing were optimized, if retention were maximized, if expansion revenue were captured, if the sales team performed at top-quartile levels, what would revenue be?

Margin potential. If procurement were consolidated, if operational waste were eliminated, if the product mix were optimized, if overhead were right-sized, what would margins be?

Cash potential. If working capital were managed to best-in-class levels, if capital expenditure were disciplined, if collections were accelerated, what would cash conversion be?

Multiple potential. If revenue quality improved, if concentration decreased, if systems were professionalized, if the story were compelling, what multiple would buyers pay?

The full potential bridge shows what the business could achieve if all levers were pulled successfully. Comparing the current bridge to the full potential bridge reveals the value gap. This gap is the prize. The gambits in this book are the tools for capturing it.

Finding the Constraint

Not all steps on the bridge are equally important. In most businesses, one or two constraints control the entire system. Identifying these constraints is the most valuable use of bridge analysis.

A constraint is a factor that limits overall performance. Improving anything other than the constraint produces limited results. Improving the constraint creates disproportionate value.

Consider a distribution business. The bridge shows moderate revenue growth but declining margins. Digging deeper reveals that gross margin is stable, but logistics costs are escalating. Further investigation shows that the warehouse network was designed for a smaller footprint. As the business grew, it added facilities without optimizing the network. The constraint is the warehouse footprint. No amount of revenue growth or procurement savings will fix the margin problem until the footprint is rationalized.

Consider a software business. The bridge shows strong new customer acquisition but weak revenue retention. Expansion revenue is low. Churn is elevated. The constraint is customer success. The sales engine is working, but customers are not realizing value after purchase. No amount of additional marketing spend will fix the retention problem until customer success is rebuilt.

Finding the constraint requires asking the right questions: What is preventing the next step of improvement? If we could change only one thing, what would have the largest impact? Where does the system break down?

Building Multiple Versions of the Bridge

Effective bridge analysis requires multiple views:

The historical bridge shows what actually happened. It compares entry to current state and attributes the change to specific sources. This bridge reveals patterns and identifies what is working.

The budget bridge shows what was planned. It compares budget to actual and highlights variance by source. This bridge reveals execution gaps and forecast accuracy.

The full potential bridge shows what is possible. It estimates the maximum achievable value if all initiatives succeed. This bridge defines the prize.

The exit bridge shows the path to target. It works backward from the required exit value and identifies what must be true for that value to be achieved. This bridge tests whether the plan is realistic.

The scenario bridges show alternative paths. They model what happens if key assumptions change: slower growth, margin pressure, multiple compression, or delayed initiatives. These bridges stress-test the plan.

Teams that maintain multiple bridge versions make better decisions. They see options. They understand trade-offs. They can adjust course when reality diverges from plan.

Using the Bridge to Prioritize

Every portfolio company faces more opportunities than capacity. The bridge provides a framework for prioritization.

For any proposed initiative, ask: which step on the bridge does this affect? By how much? With what confidence? In what timeframe?

Initiatives that affect large steps deserve more attention than initiatives that affect small steps. Initiatives with high confidence deserve more attention than speculative bets. Initiatives with near-term impact deserve attention before initiatives with distant payoffs.

This sounds obvious. In practice, it is rare. Most prioritization discussions devolve into advocacy for pet projects, debates about strategic importance, or deference to the loudest voice in the room. The bridge cuts through this noise. It provides an objective frame for comparing unlike alternatives.

One chief executive told me: "Every time someone proposes a new initiative, I make them show me where it appears on the bridge. If they cannot point to a specific step and quantify the impact, the initiative does not get approved." This discipline eliminated most low-value projects without extended debate.

The Bridge as Communication Tool

The bridge is not just an analytical tool. It is a communication tool that aligns stakeholders around a shared understanding of value creation.

In board meetings, the bridge provides structure for performance discussions. Instead of reviewing slides filled with numbers, the board can focus on the few steps that matter. Where are we ahead of plan? Where are we behind? What is driving the variance? What are we doing about it?

In leadership team meetings, the bridge creates accountability. Each step on the bridge should have an owner. That owner is responsible for the initiatives that drive that step. Progress is visible. Excuses are harder to sustain.

In exit preparation, the bridge tells the story buyers need to hear. It shows where value came from during the hold period. It demonstrates operational capability. It provides evidence that the improvements are sustainable rather than one-time.

A well-constructed bridge is worth more than a hundred pages of management presentation. It compresses complexity into a single visual that anyone can understand.

Chapter 3

What Buyers Actually Pay For

The ultimate test of value creation is the exit. A buyer writes a check. That check reflects their judgment of what the business is worth. Understanding what drives that judgment is essential for creating value that translates into returns.

Many operators believe they are creating value but are surprised when buyers discount their work. The initiatives that felt important during the hold period turn out to be irrelevant at exit. The improvements that seemed significant receive skeptical scrutiny.

The disconnect stems from a fundamental misunderstanding. Operators optimize for operating earnings. Buyers optimize for risk-adjusted future cash flows. These are related but not identical.

What Buyers Pay For

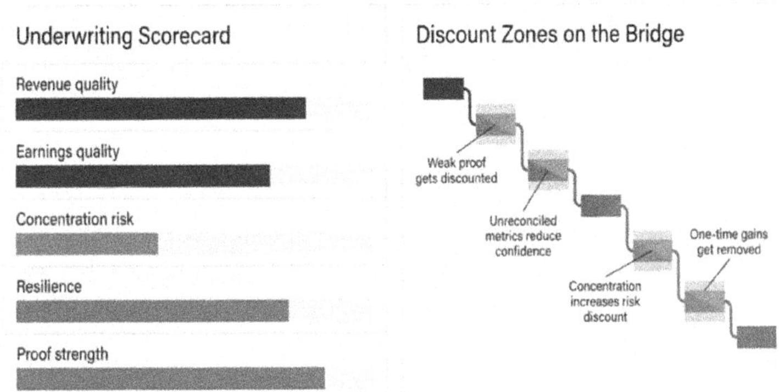

Durable Revenue Versus Fragile Revenue

Not all revenue is created equal. A dollar of durable revenue is worth more than a dollar of fragile revenue.

Durable revenue has characteristics that make it likely to persist and grow:

Contractual commitment. Revenue backed by multi-year contracts is more durable than revenue requiring continuous reselling. A three-year services agreement provides visibility that a month-to-month arrangement does not.

Recurring nature. Revenue that renews automatically is more durable than revenue requiring active renewal decisions. Subscription models create structural durability.

Switching costs. Revenue protected by high switching costs is more durable than revenue vulnerable to easy substitution.

When changing suppliers requires significant investment or operational disruption, customers stay.

Mission criticality. Revenue from products or services essential to customer operations is more durable than revenue from discretionary purchases. Customers cut discretionary spending first.

Diversification. Revenue spread across many customers is more durable than revenue concentrated in a few accounts. Concentration creates vulnerability to single-customer decisions.

Fragile revenue has opposite characteristics: project-based, non-recurring, easily substituted, discretionary, and concentrated. Buyers discount fragile revenue because they cannot rely on it persisting after the transaction.

The implication for value creation is clear. Initiatives that convert fragile revenue to durable revenue create more value than initiatives that simply grow fragile revenue. A business that shifts from fifty percent recurring to seventy percent recurring will command a higher multiple, even if total revenue stays flat.

Proven Cash Flow Versus Projected Synergies

Buyers pay full price for proven cash flow. They discount projections.

The distinction matters enormously. A business generating fifteen million in operating earnings with clear evidence of sustainability will receive a different valuation than a business generating twelve million with projections showing fifteen million next year. Even if both have the same "run rate," the proven cash flow commands a premium.

This principle applies to all forms of value creation. A cost reduction that has been implemented and verified is worth more than a cost reduction that has been identified but not yet captured. A price increase that has been rolled out and accepted by customers is worth more than a price increase that is still in negotiation.

The implication is timing. Value creation initiatives should be completed, not just started, before exit. A buyer will not pay full credit for initiatives still in flight. They will apply their own probability adjustment and typically be conservative.

Some sellers argue for "pro forma" adjustments: showing operating earnings as if planned initiatives had already been completed. Sophisticated buyers see through this. They discount pro forma heavily and sometimes penalize sellers for appearing to manipulate the presentation.

The path to full credit is execution. Complete the initiative. Run it for multiple quarters. Generate verifiable results. Then present it as proven cash flow rather than projected improvement.

Predictability as a Premium Driver

Buyers pay premiums for predictability. The ability to forecast accurately signals operational control and reduces buyer risk.

Predictability shows up in several dimensions:

Forecast accuracy. Does the company hit its numbers? A business that consistently delivers within five percent of forecast demonstrates control. A business that regularly misses by twenty percent raises questions about what else management does not understand.

Revenue visibility. How much of next quarter's revenue is already contracted or highly probable? High visibility reduces uncertainty.

Seasonality understanding. Does management understand the seasonal patterns and plan accordingly? Businesses with choppy quarterly results that surprise management signal weak planning.

Cohort behavior. Do customer cohorts behave consistently? If customers acquired in similar periods show similar retention and expansion patterns, the business is predictable. If cohort behavior is erratic, forecasting becomes guesswork.

Building predictability is not glamorous work. It requires rigorous forecasting processes, honest variance analysis, and willingness to adjust when predictions prove wrong. But the payoff at exit is significant. Buyers trust predictable businesses and pay accordingly.

Risk Factors That Compress Multiples

While some factors expand multiples, others compress them. Identifying and addressing these risk factors during the hold period prevents unpleasant surprises at exit.

Customer concentration. When the top customer represents more than fifteen percent of revenue, buyers worry. When the top customer represents more than twenty-five percent, they apply significant discounts. The reasoning is simple: losing that customer would materially damage the business, and the buyer cannot control whether the customer stays.

Key-person dependency. If critical relationships, knowledge, or capabilities reside in one or two individuals, the business is fragile. Buyers discount for the risk that these individuals leave after the transaction.

Deferred maintenance. If the business has underinvested in technology, infrastructure, or capability to inflate short-term profits, buyers will discover this in diligence. They will either walk away or extract price concessions to fund the required catch-up investment.

Earnings quality issues. Aggressive accounting, unusual adjustments, or earnings that rely on non-recurring items trigger skepticism. Buyers will normalize earnings downward and question management credibility.

Compliance and legal exposure. Unresolved legal matters, regulatory risks, or compliance gaps create uncertainty that buyers price into their offer.

Technology debt. Legacy systems that require replacement, cybersecurity vulnerabilities, or outdated infrastructure represent future costs that reduce present value.

Each of these risk factors can be addressed during the hold period. Customer concentration can be reduced through focused acquisition of new accounts. Key-person dependency can be mitigated through hiring and documentation. Deferred maintenance can be caught up. Earnings quality can be cleaned. The best time to address these issues is before starting an exit process, when there is time to demonstrate sustained improvement.

The Proof Package

Claims without evidence receive discounts. Buyers trust data over assertions.

A proof package is the collection of metrics, artifacts, and documentation that substantiates the value creation story. Building the proof package should begin at deal entry, not at exit preparation.

The components of a strong proof package include:

Cohort retention curves. Showing how customer cohorts retain and expand over time. Strong retention curves justify revenue durability claims. This is Level 4 or Level 5 evidence on the Evidence Standard Ladder.

Price realization tracking. Demonstrating actual price versus list price over time. Strong realization supports margin sustainability.

Customer concentration trend. Showing how concentration has decreased over the hold period. Declining concentration demonstrates deliberate risk reduction.

Contribution margin by segment. Breaking down profitability by product, customer type, or geography. Granular visibility demonstrates operational sophistication.

Run-rate reconciliation. Showing how reported operating earnings reconciles to sustainable run-rate after adjustments. Clean reconciliation builds buyer confidence.

Cash conversion history. Demonstrating consistent conversion of operating earnings to free cash flow. Strong conversion supports the claim that profits are real.

Contract quality summary. Showing contract lengths, renewal rates, and escalation clauses. Strong contract quality supports revenue durability.

The proof package should be assembled progressively. Every quarter, update the key metrics. Every major initiative, document the results. By the time exit preparation begins, the proof package should be largely complete.

Proof Checklist Template

Operating Earnings Proof	Cash and Net Debt Proof	Multiple Support Proof
☐ [Item 1]	☐ [Item 1]	☐ [Item 1]
☐ [Item 2]	☐ [Item 2]	☐ [Item 2]
☐ [Item 3]	☐ [Item 3]	☐ [Item 3]
☐ [Item 4]	☐ [Item 4]	☐ [Item 4]
☐ [Item 5]	☐ [Item 5]	☐ [Item 5]

Chapter 4

The Gambit Method

In chess, a gambit is a deliberate sacrifice to gain strategic advantage. The player gives up material, usually a pawn, to achieve better position, faster development, or attacking opportunities. The sacrifice is calculated. The advantage is earned through superior play after the opening.

Value creation in private equity follows the same logic. Every significant improvement requires a sacrifice. Understanding this trade-off structure separates effective operators from those who chase improvements without recognizing their costs.

The Method

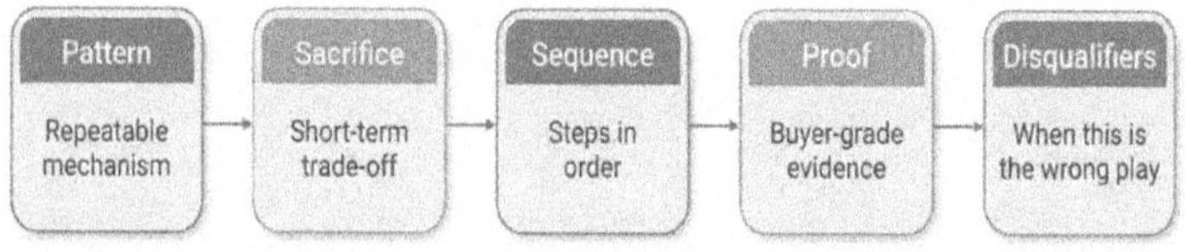

The book is a library of plays written in this format.

What Makes a Pattern a Gambit

A gambit is not a tip, a best practice, or a general recommendation. It is a specific pattern with defined components:

A sacrifice. Something must be given up or risked. This could be short-term profit, short-term growth, organizational comfort, or management attention. Without sacrifice, there is no gambit, just wishful thinking.

An advantage. Something specific must be gained. The advantage should be measurable and should appear on one of the three bridges. Vague benefits like "improved morale" or "better alignment" do not qualify unless they translate to financial impact.

A sequence. The pattern must have defined steps that can be followed. Order matters. Skipping steps or reversing sequence typically causes failure.

A proof. The gambit must produce evidence that buyers will accept. If the improvement cannot be demonstrated through metrics or artifacts, it will not translate to value at exit. The goal is to reach Level 4 or Level 5 on the Evidence Standard Ladder before exit.

The Four Phases of Every Gambit

Regardless of category, every gambit moves through four phases. Understanding these phases helps with planning, execution, and troubleshooting.

Phase One: Set-Up

The set-up phase establishes the conditions required for the gambit to succeed. This includes gathering data, building capability, aligning stakeholders, and removing obstacles. Many gambits fail because operators skip the set-up and rush to execution.

For a pricing gambit, set-up might include: analyzing price sensitivity by segment, documenting competitive pricing, training the sales team on value communication, and updating systems to support new price structures.

For a working capital gambit, set-up might include: establishing baseline metrics, identifying root causes of poor performance, designing new processes, and securing executive sponsorship for the changes.

The set-up phase often takes longer than operators expect. Rushing through it creates problems that compound during execution.

Phase Two: Strike

The strike phase is the active intervention. This is where the change happens: prices increase, costs decrease, processes change, or acquisitions close. The strike should be decisive and well-timed.

Timing matters enormously. A price increase implemented during contract renewal is different from a price increase imposed mid-contract. A cost reduction announced during a growth period is received differently than one announced during decline. The best operators choose their moments carefully.

The strike phase should be fast once it begins. Prolonged transitions create uncertainty and invite resistance. Make the change. Communicate clearly. Move forward.

Phase Three: Lock-In

The lock-in phase prevents reversion. Without lock-in, improvements decay. Prices drift back down through discounting. Costs creep back up through exceptions. Processes deteriorate through neglect.

Lock-in mechanisms vary by gambit type:

For pricing gambits: discount approval processes, compensation alignment, contract language, and regular price realization tracking.

For cost gambits: budget controls, headcount governance, procurement policies, and expense monitoring.

For process gambits: documentation, training, system enforcement, and audit routines.

Lock-in is where many gambits fail. The initial improvement looks promising, but without reinforcement, it fades. Sustaining the lock-in requires ongoing attention and periodic reinforcement.

Phase Four: Prove

The prove phase generates evidence that the improvement is real and sustainable. This evidence becomes part of the proof package discussed in the previous chapter.

Proving requires time. A single quarter of improved performance is not proof. Multiple quarters showing sustained improvement is proof. The prove phase should run for at least three to four quarters before the improvement can be credibly claimed.

Proving also requires clean attribution. The improvement should be traceable to the specific gambit, not to confounding factors like market tailwinds or one-time events. Clean attribution requires rigorous tracking from the beginning.

Why Sequencing Matters

Gambits interact. The order in which they are deployed affects their success. Some sequences compound value. Other sequences create conflict.

Consider two common sequences:

Margin before growth. When a business has weak unit economics, fixing margins before investing in growth is essential. Growing a business with negative contribution margin accelerates losses. Fixing contribution margin first ensures that growth investments pay off.

Retention before acquisition. When a business has high customer churn, fixing retention before investing in customer acquisition is essential. Acquiring new customers into a leaky bucket is inefficient. Fixing the bucket first ensures that acquisition investments accumulate.

Poor sequencing is a common cause of value creation failure. Teams launch multiple initiatives simultaneously without considering dependencies. They invest in growth while unit economics are broken. They acquire companies before integration capability exists. They pursue multiple expansion while fundamental operating issues remain unresolved.

The discipline of sequencing requires honest assessment of current state. What must be true before this gambit can succeed? What other gambits need to complete first? What capacity constraints limit parallel execution?

Common Sequencing Conflicts

Some gambit combinations create friction. Recognizing these conflicts before committing prevents wasted effort.

Cost reduction plus growth investment. Aggressive cost cutting can remove the capability needed for growth. If the same initiative promises both thirty percent cost reduction and twenty percent revenue growth, test the assumptions carefully. One often undermines the other.

Acquisition plus operational improvement. Integrating an acquisition consumes bandwidth that could go to operational improvement. If both are priorities, the operational improvement often stalls while integration absorbs attention. Sequence them or accept that one will suffer.

Pricing improvement plus market share expansion. Raising prices and growing market share simultaneously is difficult. Higher prices typically slow volume growth. If both are targets, be explicit about which takes priority when they conflict.

The Gambit Catalog as a Pattern Library

The forty gambits presented in the following chapters form a pattern library. Each pattern has been observed working in real portfolio companies across different industries and market conditions. The patterns are specific enough to be actionable and general enough to be adapted.

The patterns are organized by category: revenue, margin, acquisition, cash, multiple, and technology. Within each category, the patterns address different starting conditions and objectives.

Use the library as a reference. When facing a specific challenge, review the relevant category. Identify patterns that match your situation. Assess the preconditions and traps. Adapt the sequence to your context. Execute with discipline.

The gambits are not recipes to follow blindly. They are patterns to understand and adapt. Context matters. Execution matters more. A gambit that works brilliantly in one situation may fail in another. The value is not in mechanical application but in understanding the underlying logic well enough to know when and how to deploy each pattern.

Before diving into the catalog, spend time with Part Two, which describes the five arenas where value creation happens. Understanding the arenas provides context for the individual patterns. It helps you see how the pieces fit together and how to build a coherent value creation plan from the available patterns.

The bridge is built one pattern at a time. Choose wisely. Execute relentlessly. Prove continuously.

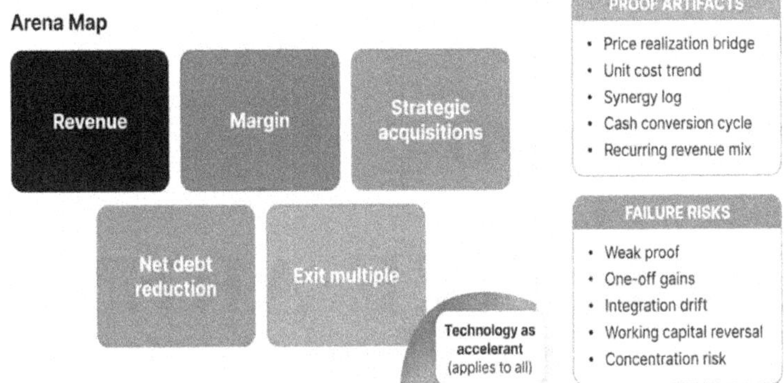
The Five Arenas of Value Creation
Arena Map
Revenue
Margin
Strategic acquisitions
Net debt reduction
Exit multiple
Technology as accelerant (applies to all)
PROOF ARTIFACTS
Price realization bridge
Unit cost trend
Synergy log
Cash conversion cycle
Recurring revenue mix
FAILURE RISKS
Weak proof
One-off gains
Integration drift
Working capital reversal
Concentration risk

PART TWO

THE FIVE ARENAS OF VALUE

Where Enterprise Value Is Actually Created

Chapter 5

Growing Revenue

Revenue is the lifeblood of enterprise value. Without revenue, there is no business to value. With growing revenue, buyers see potential. The top line is the first number every investor examines and the foundation on which all other value creation rests.

Yet revenue growth is the most misunderstood arena of value creation. Teams chase volume without examining economics. They celebrate bookings without tracking retention. They expand geographies before proving unit economics. The result is growth that consumes cash rather than generating it, growth that buyers discount rather than reward.

Understanding revenue as an arena means understanding that not all growth is equal. Some revenue strengthens the business. Some revenue weakens it. The difference lies in the quality, durability, and economics of the growth.

Revenue Arena: How Growth Shows Up on the Bridge

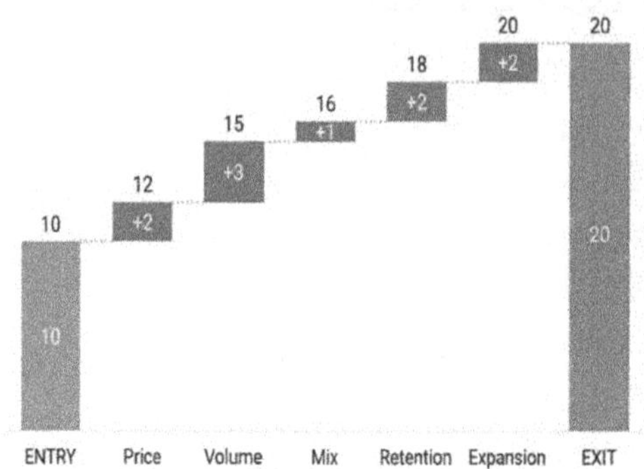

PROOF ARTIFACTS

- Price realization
- Cohort retention
- Pipeline conversion
- Churn
- Contribution margin by segment

FAILURE RISKS

- Discounting hides weak demand
- Mix shifts lower margin
- Churn spike post-price
- Channel conflict

The Components of Revenue Growth

Revenue growth decomposes into distinct components. Each component responds to different actions and produces different value outcomes.

Price. Increasing the amount charged for existing products or services. Price improvements flow directly to profit without requiring additional cost. A three percent price increase on a business with twenty percent operating margins improves operating earnings by fifteen percent. Price is often the most powerful and most underutilized lever.

Volume. Selling more units to existing or new customers. Volume growth requires capacity to deliver and often requires proportional increase in cost. The value of volume growth depends on contribution margin. Growing volume in a negative-margin product destroys value.

Mix. Shifting the composition of revenue toward higher-margin products, services, or customer segments. Mix improvement can increase revenue and margin simultaneously. A business that shifts from fifty percent services to sixty percent services, where services carry higher margins, improves profitability without necessarily growing the top line.

Retention. Keeping existing customers and their revenue. Retention is often more valuable than acquisition. Acquiring a new customer costs five to seven times more than retaining an existing one. A business that improves retention from eighty-five percent to ninety-two percent dramatically changes its growth trajectory without additional sales investment.

Expansion. Growing revenue within existing customer relationships. Expansion revenue is the highest quality growth. The customer already trusts the business. The cost to serve is already absorbed. Expansion revenue typically carries higher margins and lower risk than new customer acquisition.

New Customers. Acquiring entirely new accounts. New customer acquisition is necessary for long-term growth but expensive in the short term. Acquisition cost must be recovered through lifetime value. If the payback period exceeds twenty-four months, or if churn erodes lifetime value, new customer acquisition may destroy rather than create value.

The Bad Revenue Paradox

Not all revenue is good revenue. Some revenue costs more to deliver than it generates in contribution. Some revenue distracts from higher-value opportunities. Some revenue creates complexity that drags down the entire organization.

Bad revenue typically exhibits one or more warning signs:

Negative contribution margin. When the direct costs of serving a customer exceed the revenue generated, every additional sale increases losses. This situation is more common than executives admit, particularly when cost-to-serve is poorly understood.

Excessive service burden. Some customers consume disproportionate support, customization, or management attention. Even if technically profitable, these customers may crowd out capacity that could serve more valuable relationships.

Strategic distraction. Revenue from products or markets outside the core strategy dilutes focus. The organization chases opportunities that will never reach scale instead of deepening positions that could become dominant.

Complexity multiplication. Every product variant, pricing exception, and custom solution adds complexity. Complexity has hidden costs: slower decision-making, increased errors, training burden, and system overhead. Revenue that multiplies complexity often costs more than it appears.

The paradox is that eliminating bad revenue can improve both profitability and growth. Resources freed from unprofitable activities can be redirected to profitable ones. Complexity reduction improves execution speed. Focus enables excellence.

The gambits in the revenue section include patterns for identifying and exiting bad revenue as well as patterns for growing good revenue. Both are essential.

Revenue Quality and the Multiple

Revenue quality directly affects the valuation multiple. Buyers assess not just how much revenue exists but how reliable, durable, and expandable that revenue is.

High-quality revenue characteristics include:

Recurring structure. Revenue that automatically renews commands premiums over revenue requiring active reselling. Subscription models, maintenance contracts, and licensing arrangements all create structural recurrence.

High retention. Gross revenue retention above ninety percent signals that customers value the product and are unlikely to leave. Net revenue retention above one hundred percent signals that existing customers are growing, not just staying.

Diversified base. Revenue spread across many customers reduces concentration risk. Buyers are wary of businesses where losing one or two customers would materially damage performance.

Visible pipeline. A healthy pipeline of qualified opportunities provides confidence in future growth. Buyers want to see that growth is not dependent on heroic efforts or lucky breaks.

Pricing power. The ability to raise prices without losing customers indicates differentiation and value delivery. Commoditized businesses lacking pricing power face margin pressure that erodes value over time.

Revenue growth initiatives should be evaluated not just for their impact on the top line but for their impact on revenue quality. A slower growth strategy that improves quality may create more value than a faster growth strategy that degrades it.

The Revenue Arena in Practice

The revenue gambits in Part Three address the full spectrum of revenue challenges:

Pricing patterns for capturing value that is currently left on the table through undisciplined discounting, outdated price lists, or failure to communicate value.

Mix patterns for shifting toward higher-margin segments, products, and customer types without losing scale.

Retention patterns for identifying at-risk customers early and intervening before they leave.

Expansion patterns for systematically growing revenue within existing customer relationships.

Channel patterns for reaching customers more efficiently through redesigned routes to market.

Exit patterns for identifying and eliminating bad revenue that drags down overall performance.

Each pattern includes the specific sequence, the preconditions for success, the common failure modes, and the proof metrics that demonstrate impact. The revenue arena is where most value creation stories begin.

Revenue Attribution Template

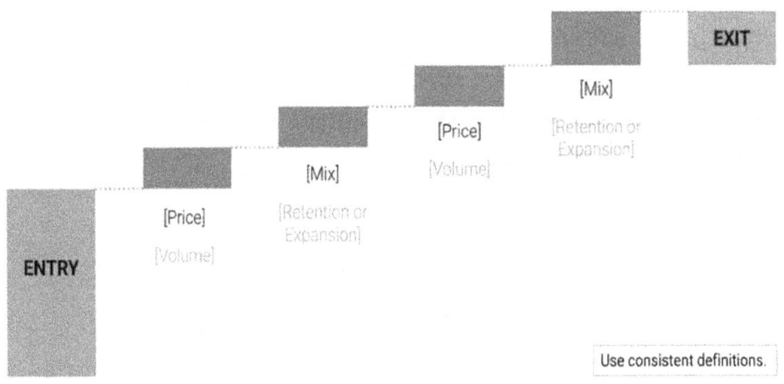

Chapter 6

Expanding Margins

Margin expansion is often misunderstood as cost cutting. Teams approach margins with a scalpel, trimming expenses line by line, squeezing suppliers, and reducing headcount. These actions can improve margins in the short term. They rarely create sustainable value.

True margin expansion is about work quality. Margins rise when companies reduce friction, stabilize workflows, eliminate unnecessary variation, and strengthen decision-making. They fall when processes are inconsistent, information is unreliable, and teams spend more time reacting than executing.

The strongest margin improvements happen when operational and cultural changes reinforce each other. A procurement initiative that merely pressures suppliers yields temporary savings that erode over time. A procurement transformation that consolidates spend, standardizes specifications, and builds supplier partnerships yields sustainable improvement.

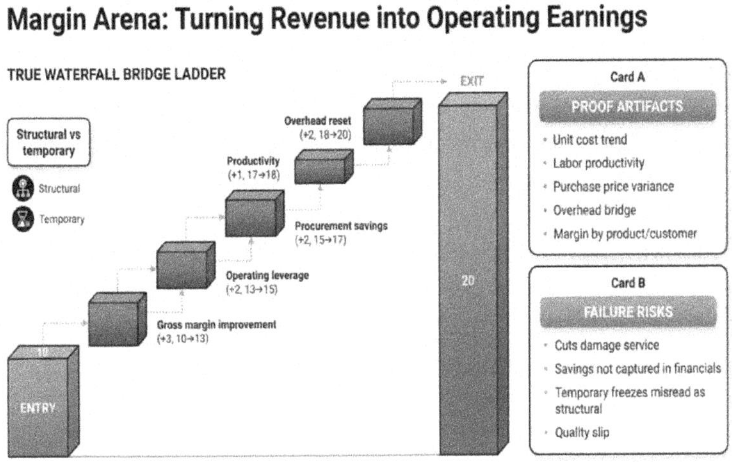

The Layers of Margin

Margin analysis requires understanding different layers, each responding to different actions.

Gross margin measures the difference between revenue and the direct costs of delivering products or services. Gross margin improvement comes from better pricing, lower input costs, improved yields, reduced waste, and more efficient production or service delivery. Gross margin is the first filter: if gross margin is weak, no amount of overhead reduction will create a healthy business.

Contribution margin measures gross profit minus variable costs directly attributable to sales, such as commissions and shipping. Contribution margin reveals the true profitability of each product line, customer segment, or channel. Many businesses do not calculate contribution margin, which means they cannot identify which parts of their business actually make money.

Operating margin measures contribution minus overhead costs such as sales management, general administration, research, and corporate functions. Operating margin improvement comes from contribution margin improvement plus overhead efficiency. The healthiest businesses improve both simultaneously.

Understanding which layer contains the problem is essential for choosing the right gambit. A gross margin problem requires different interventions than an overhead problem. Treating all margin issues as "cost reduction" leads to misallocated effort.

Operating Leverage as a Designed Outcome

Operating leverage is the degree to which operating earnings grow faster than revenue. A business with high operating leverage can grow revenue by ten percent and see operating earnings grow by twenty percent. A business with low operating leverage sees operating earnings grow in line with or slower than revenue.

Operating leverage comes from the relationship between fixed and variable costs. When a business has high fixed costs and low variable costs, incremental revenue flows largely to profit. When a business has low fixed costs and high variable costs, incremental revenue requires proportional cost increases.

Many operators treat cost structure as given. The best operators treat it as a design choice. They deliberately invest in fixed costs that create leverage: systems that scale without proportional headcount, processes that handle volume without proportional labor, and capabilities that serve many customers simultaneously.

The gambits in the margin section include patterns for redesigning cost structure to create operating leverage. These patterns often require upfront investment but generate compounding returns as the business grows.

The Productivity Imperative

Productivity measures output per unit of input. Revenue per employee. Units per labor hour. Transactions per system. Productivity improvement is the sustainable path to margin expansion.

Productivity improvement comes from several sources:

Process improvement. Eliminating unnecessary steps, reducing handoffs, and streamlining workflows. Process improvement does not require technology investment. It requires honest examination of how work actually gets done.

Automation. Using technology to perform tasks previously done manually. Automation works best for repetitive, rule-based activities with high volume. It works poorly for judgment-intensive activities requiring human expertise.

Capacity utilization. Making better use of existing resources. A factory running at sixty percent utilization has different economics than one running at eighty-five percent. Utilization improvement requires both volume growth and operational discipline.

Skill development. Improving the capability of people to perform their work. Skilled workers produce more output with fewer errors. Training investment often has higher returns than technology investment.

Productivity gains compound over time. A business that improves productivity by five percent annually for four years will have twenty percent higher output per input than when it started. This compounding is the engine of sustainable margin expansion.

Cost Structure Visibility

Many margin problems stem from poor visibility. Teams do not know what activities actually cost. They do not know which customers are profitable and which are not. They do not know where waste occurs or where efficiency opportunities exist.

Building cost visibility requires investment in measurement:

Activity-based costing allocates overhead to activities based on actual consumption rather than arbitrary allocation. It reveals the true cost of serving different customers, products, and channels.

Cost-to-serve analysis calculates the full cost of serving each customer segment, including sales, support, customization, and logistics. It often reveals that the largest customers are not the most profitable.

Variance analysis compares actual costs to standards and investigates the reasons for differences. Systematic variance analysis surfaces problems early and builds organizational cost consciousness.

The gambits in the margin section include patterns for building cost visibility as a foundation for improvement. Without visibility, margin initiatives are shots in the dark.

The Margin Arena in Practice

The margin gambits in Part Three address the full spectrum of profitability challenges:

Procurement patterns for consolidating spend, renegotiating supplier agreements, and reducing input costs sustainably.

Structural patterns for redesigning how work gets done to eliminate waste and create operating leverage.

Complexity patterns for simplifying product lines, service offerings, and organizational structures that have grown unwieldy.

Footprint patterns for rationalizing facilities, geography, and physical infrastructure.

Variable cost patterns for understanding and managing costs that fluctuate with volume.

Each pattern carries risk. Aggressive cost cutting can damage capability. Structural changes can disrupt operations. The gambits include guardrails and warning signs to prevent common mistakes.

The margin arena rewards discipline over drama. The biggest improvements come not from heroic one-time efforts but from systematic attention to how work gets done, week after week, quarter after quarter.

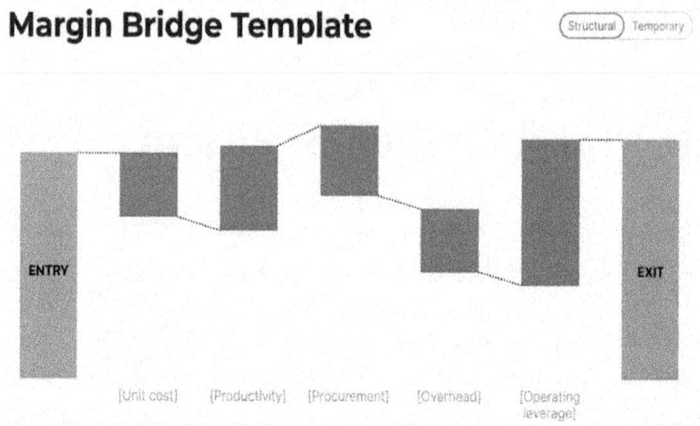

Margin Bridge Template

Structural
Temporary

ENTRY
[Unit cost]
[Productivity]
[Procurement]
[Overhead]
[Operating leverage]
EXIT

Chapter 7

Strategic Acquisitions

Acquisitions are the highest-leverage and highest-risk arena of value creation. A well-executed acquisition can transform a company's trajectory, adding capabilities, customers, and scale that would take years to build organically. A poorly-executed acquisition can destroy value, distract management, and burden the balance sheet with assets that never perform.

The private equity model often relies on acquisitions. Platform strategies, roll-up theses, and buy-and-build approaches all depend on successful acquisition and integration. Yet the track record of acquisitions across industries is sobering. Most studies suggest that the majority of acquisitions fail to deliver their projected value.

The difference between success and failure lies not in deal-making but in execution. Identifying targets, negotiating terms, and closing transactions are necessary but insufficient. The real work, and the real value creation, happens after the deal closes.

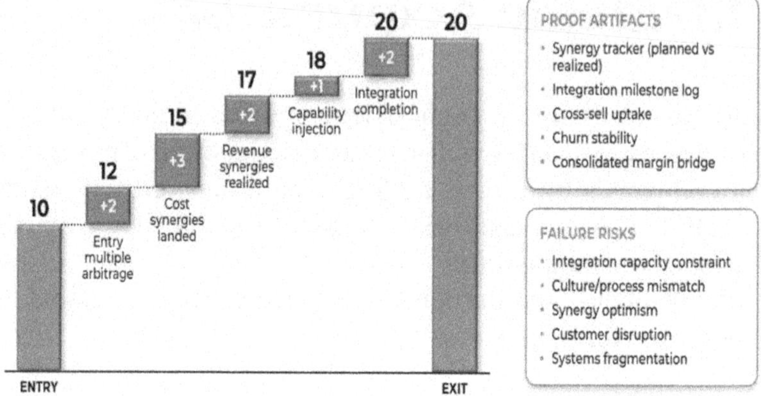

The Logic of Inorganic Growth

Acquisitions create value through several mechanisms:

Scale economies. Combining two businesses can reduce unit costs through purchasing leverage, shared overhead, and capacity utilization. The combined entity can achieve efficiency that neither business could achieve alone.

Revenue synergies. Cross-selling products to combined customer bases, entering new geographies with established infrastructure, or bundling offerings can accelerate revenue growth beyond what either business could achieve independently.

Capability addition. Acquiring technology, talent, or expertise that would take years to develop internally. The acquisition buys time and reduces execution risk.

Market consolidation. Reducing competition, gaining pricing power, and improving industry structure. Consolidation strategies can create value industry-wide, though they require careful navigation of regulatory constraints.

Multiple arbitrage. Buying at a lower multiple than the combined entity will command at exit. Small companies often trade at lower multiples than larger ones. A platform that acquires multiple small businesses and integrates them into a single larger entity may capture multiple expansion through size alone.

Each mechanism has different requirements and different risk profiles. Scale economies require operational integration. Revenue synergies require commercial coordination. Capability addition requires cultural integration. Market consolidation requires strategic discipline. Multiple arbitrage requires execution credibility.

Why Integration Determines Value

Synergies projected in deal models rarely materialize automatically. They require deliberate action, sustained attention, and organizational capability to capture.

Cost synergies are the most concrete and the most achievable. Eliminating duplicate functions, consolidating facilities, and leveraging combined purchasing power are straightforward conceptually. Yet even cost synergies frequently underperform because integration is slower than planned, severance and transition costs exceed estimates, or productivity drops during the transition period.

Revenue synergies are more speculative and more difficult to capture. Cross-selling requires sales teams to learn new products and new customer relationships. Bundling requires pricing strategies that do not cannibalize existing revenue. Geographic expansion requires local adaptation. Most revenue synergy projections should be heavily discounted.

Integration discipline means having a clear plan before closing, dedicated resources for integration execution, aggressive timelines with accountability, and honest tracking of synergy capture. It means treating integration as a project with the same rigor applied to operating the base business.

Platform Versus Bolt-On

Acquisition strategies differ based on the role of each acquisition in the overall thesis.

A platform acquisition establishes the foundation for a buy-and-build strategy. The platform provides the management team, the systems infrastructure, the customer base, and the operational capability to absorb future acquisitions. Platform selection is critical: the wrong platform constrains everything that follows.

Bolt-on acquisitions add to an existing platform. They may bring customers, geography, products, or capabilities. Bolt-ons should be easier to integrate than standalone acquisitions because the platform provides the absorption capacity. In practice, bolt-ons often stumble because the platform is not as capable as assumed.

The distinction matters for integration planning. Platform integrations require building capability. Bolt-on integrations require deploying existing capability. Confusing these leads to underinvestment in platform-building and overconfidence in bolt-on execution.

Synergy Landing Tracker

Planned Synergies

[Category]	[Value]	[Timing]

Realized Synergies

[Category]	[Value]	[Timing]

Variance Bridge

ENTRY

[Timing]

[Scope]

[Execution]

EXIT

The Acquisition Arena in Practice

The acquisition gambits in Part Three address both platform development and bolt-on execution:

Roll-up patterns for building scale through serial acquisition in fragmented markets.

Adjacency patterns for expanding into related markets, products, or geographies.

Synergy patterns for systematically capturing the cost and revenue benefits promised in deal models.

Cross-sell patterns for activating revenue synergies across combined customer bases.

Capability patterns for acquiring and integrating specific skills, technologies, or talent.

Standardization patterns for bringing consistency to multi-site or multi-brand portfolios.

Each pattern includes integration requirements, timeline expectations, and warning signs that synergies are slipping. The acquisition arena rewards preparation and discipline. Speed and optimism are poor substitutes.

Chapter 8

Accelerating Debt Reduction

Debt reduction is the most direct path from operating performance to equity value. Every dollar of debt repaid translates directly into a dollar of equity value. Unlike operating earnings improvement, which depends on the multiple, debt reduction has a one-to-one relationship with value.

Yet debt reduction is often treated as a financial concern, delegated to the finance leader and discussed only in the context of covenant compliance. This is a mistake. Debt reduction is an operating concern. It depends on cash generation, which depends on operational discipline across the entire organization.

Cash and Net Debt: Converting Improvement into Equity Value

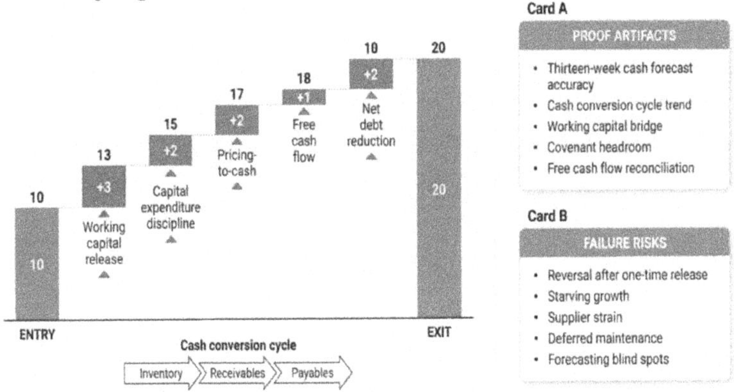

The Cash Conversion Challenge

The link between operating earnings and cash is not automatic. Many businesses generate strong operating earnings while struggling with cash. The difference is cash conversion.

Cash conversion measures how much of operating earnings translates to free cash flow. A business with one hundred percent cash conversion generates one dollar of cash for every dollar of operating earnings. A business with fifty percent cash conversion generates only fifty cents.

The enemies of cash conversion are familiar:

Working capital growth. As revenue grows, receivables and inventory often grow faster. If customers pay slowly or inventory builds ahead of demand, cash is consumed rather than generated.

Capital expenditure. Investment in plant, equipment, and technology consumes cash. When capital expenditure consistently exceeds depreciation, operating earnings overstate cash generation.

One-time items. Restructuring charges, transaction costs, and unusual items that are excluded from adjusted operating earnings still consume cash. Businesses with frequent "one-time" items often have chronically weak cash conversion.

Working Capital as a System

Working capital includes accounts receivable, inventory, and accounts payable. These components interact as a system. Optimizing one component while ignoring others often shifts the problem rather than solving it.

Days sales outstanding measures how quickly customers pay. Reducing days sales outstanding accelerates cash collection. The levers include tighter credit policies, more aggressive collection, early payment incentives, and addressing root causes of disputed invoices.

Days inventory outstanding measures how long inventory sits before being sold. Reducing inventory days frees cash. The levers include demand forecasting improvement, supplier lead time reduction, product portfolio simplification, and obsolete inventory disposition.

Days payables outstanding measures how quickly the company pays suppliers. Extending payables conserves cash. The levers include payment term negotiation, supplier consolidation for leverage, and payment timing optimization.

The cash conversion cycle combines these metrics: days sales outstanding plus days inventory outstanding minus days payables outstanding. A shorter cash conversion cycle means faster cash generation. Some businesses achieve negative cash conversion cycles, meaning they collect from customers before paying suppliers. These businesses generate cash as they grow rather than consuming it.

Capital Discipline

Capital expenditure decisions determine long-term cash flow. Every capital investment should generate returns that exceed the cost of capital. In practice, capital decisions are often made without rigorous analysis or post-investment tracking.

Capital discipline requires:

Investment criteria. Clear hurdle rates and payback requirements that all investments must meet. These criteria should reflect the cost of capital and the risk profile of the business.

Approval governance. Appropriate levels of approval based on investment size and type. Major investments should require board approval with documented analysis.

Post-investment review. Systematic tracking of whether investments delivered projected returns. Post-investment review creates accountability and improves future decision-making.

Maintenance versus growth distinction. Separating capital required to maintain current operations from capital invested for growth. Maintenance capital is a cost of doing business. Growth capital should generate incremental returns.

The Thirteen-Week Cash Forecast

The thirteen-week cash forecast is the most important financial tool for cash management. It projects cash receipts and disbursements week by week for the coming quarter, revealing exactly when cash will be needed and where it will come from.

Unlike annual budgets that can hide timing issues, the thirteen-week forecast exposes reality. It shows when customers actually pay, not when revenue is recognized. It reveals seasonal patterns and concentration risks. It highlights weeks when cash may be tight and forces proactive planning.

The best operators review the thirteen-week forecast weekly. They compare actual results to forecast, investigate variances, and update projections. Over time, forecast accuracy improves and cash surprises decrease. The forecast becomes a management discipline rather than just a reporting exercise.

The Cash Arena in Practice

The cash and debt gambits in Part Three include patterns for each component of the cash challenge:

Working capital patterns for systematically reducing the cash tied up in receivables, inventory, and payables.

Cash conversion patterns for improving the translation of operating earnings into free cash flow.

Capital discipline patterns for making better investment decisions and tracking their outcomes.

Debt paydown patterns for accelerating the reduction of net debt and the corresponding increase in equity value.

Visibility patterns for building the forecasting capability that enables proactive cash management.

Covenant patterns for managing lender relationships and maintaining financial flexibility.

Cash is the bridge between operating performance and equity value. Strong operations with weak cash conversion leave value trapped in the business. The cash gambits ensure that operating improvements translate into returns that equity holders actually receive.

Cash Conversion Template

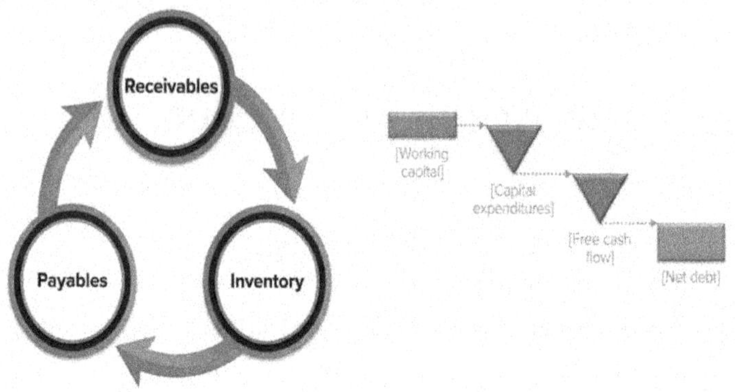

Chapter 9

Expanding the Exit Multiple

The exit multiple is the ultimate measure of business quality. It reflects how buyers The exit multiple is the ultimate measure of business quality. It reflects how buyers perceive the durability, predictability, and attractiveness of future cash flows. A business trading at twelve times operating earnings is fundamentally different from one trading at six times, even if both generate the same current profit.

Multiple expansion is often dismissed as market-driven and outside management control. This view is partially true and mostly limiting. Market conditions set the overall environment, but company-specific factors determine whether a business trades at a premium or discount to the market.

The best operators treat multiple expansion as a deliberate outcome. They identify the factors that drive premiums in their sector. They invest in building those factors throughout the hold period. They arrive at exit with a company that looks institutionally mature rather than founder-dependent, predictable rather than volatile, positioned for growth rather than optimized for current profit.

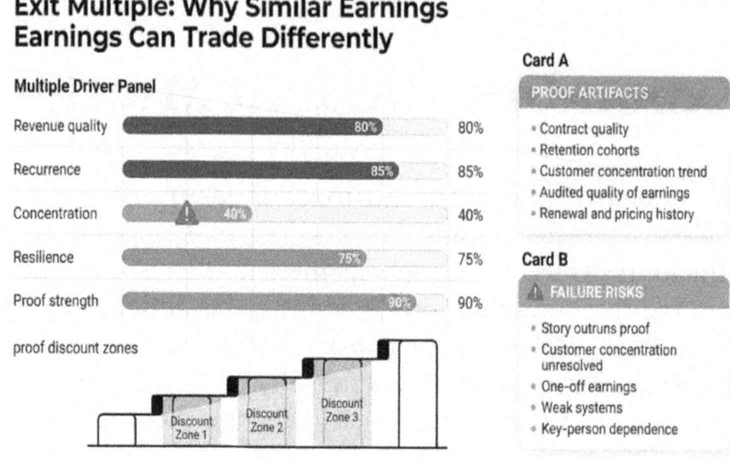

What Drives Premium Multiples

Premium multiples reflect reduced risk and enhanced potential. Buyers pay more when they have confidence in the future.

Revenue quality. Recurring revenue commands higher multiples than transactional revenue. Diversified customer bases command higher multiples than concentrated ones. Contractually committed revenue commands higher multiples than at-will arrangements.

Growth visibility. A clear growth runway commands premium. Buyers want to see where future growth will come from and have confidence in the company's ability to capture it. Addressable market, competitive position, and historical growth trajectory all contribute to growth visibility.

Margin sustainability. Margins that appear sustainable command higher multiples than margins that seem fragile.

Cost structures that scale, pricing power that endures, and efficiency gains that persist all support margin sustainability.

Management depth. A capable leadership team with clear succession commands premium. Buyers discount businesses dependent on key individuals who may not continue post-transaction.

Operational maturity. Professional systems, documented processes, and reliable reporting command premium. Buyers want to acquire a business, not a project that requires significant investment to professionalize.

Strategic positioning. Market leadership, defensible competitive advantages, and barriers to entry command premium. Businesses that can articulate why they are difficult to replicate receive higher valuations.

Building Proof Points

Claims without evidence receive discounts. Assertions about quality, growth potential, or competitive position must be substantiated with data.

Building proof points is a continuous activity, not a pre-exit scramble. The most compelling proof points show sustained performance over multiple periods. A single quarter of strong retention proves nothing. Eight quarters of consistent retention above ninety percent proves capability.

Effective proof points include:

Cohort analysis showing how customer groups perform over time. Strong cohorts demonstrate predictable customer economics. This is Level 4 or Level 5 evidence on the Evidence Standard Ladder.

Trend data showing improvement in key metrics over the hold period. Trends demonstrate operational progress and suggest continued improvement.

Third-party validation from customers, industry analysts, or independent assessments. External voices carry more credibility than management claims. This represents Level 5 evidence.

Competitive comparisons showing outperformance relative to peers. Superior performance versus comparable companies justifies premium positioning.

The Exit Narrative

Buyers make decisions based on narratives as well as numbers. A compelling narrative explains why the business is special, why now is the right time to buy, and why the future is promising.

The exit narrative should be constructed deliberately:

The transformation story. What changed during the hold period? How is the business better, stronger, and more valuable than when ownership began? The transformation story demonstrates operational capability.

The market position story. Why does the business have a right to win in its market? What advantages does it possess? What barriers protect its position? The market position story justifies premium valuation.

The growth story. Where will future growth come from? What opportunities remain to be captured? What would a new owner do to accelerate growth? The growth story excites buyers about future potential.

The narrative must be consistent with the numbers. A transformation story that does not show up in the financials lacks credibility. A growth story that contradicts historical performance raises questions. The narrative and the data must reinforce each other.

The Multiple Arena in Practice

The multiple expansion gambits in Part Three include patterns for building each element of a premium-commanding profile:

Revenue quality patterns for upgrading the composition and durability of the revenue base.

Concentration patterns for reducing dependence on large customers, products, or markets.

Management patterns for building leadership depth and reducing key-person risk.

Recurring revenue patterns for converting transactional revenue into contractually recurring revenue.

Risk mitigation patterns for addressing the concerns that cause buyers to discount.

Narrative patterns for constructing and substantiating the story that supports premium valuation.

Multiple expansion is earned during the hold period, not negotiated at exit. The gambits show how to earn it.

Chapter 10

Technology and Automation as an Accelerant

Technology is not a sixth arena of value creation. It is an accelerant that amplifies the other five. Revenue grows faster with better sales tools. Margins expand more quickly with process automation. Acquisitions integrate more smoothly with unified systems. Cash converts more reliably with accurate forecasting. Multiples expand more readily with professional infrastructure.

Yet technology is also a trap. Investments in technology that do not connect to value creation are expensive distractions. Systems implementations that fail to achieve adoption waste resources and create organizational frustration. Technology initiatives launched without clear business cases consume capital that could be deployed elsewhere.

Understanding when technology accelerates value and when it becomes expensive theater is essential for deploying technology gambits effectively.

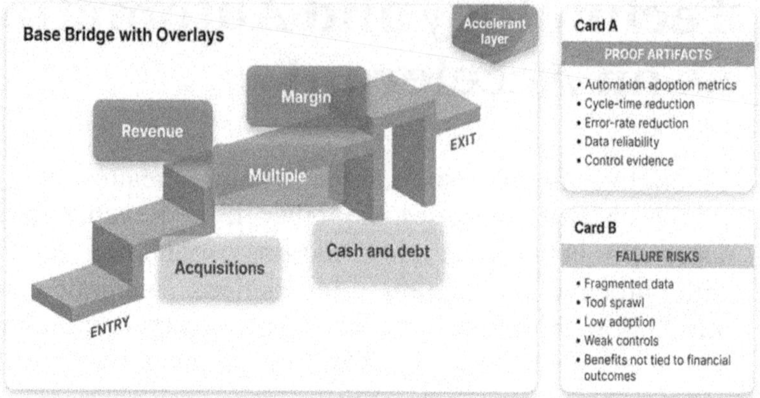
Technology as Accelerant:
It Multiplies the Other Arenas
Base Bridge with Overlays
Accelerant layer
Margin
Revenue
Multiple
EXIT
Acquisitions
Cash and debt
ENTRY
Card A
PROOF ARTIFACTS
• Automation adoption metrics
• Cycle-time reduction
• Error-rate reduction
• Data reliability
• Control evidence
Card B
FAILURE RISKS
• Fragmented data
• Tool sprawl
• Low adoption
• Weak controls
• Benefits not tied to financial outcomes

Technology That Creates Value

Technology creates value when it enables something that would otherwise be impossible or prohibitively expensive. The test is simple: what business outcome does this technology enable, and is that outcome worth the investment?

Revenue-enabling technology helps the company sell more effectively. This includes customer relationship management systems that improve pipeline visibility, digital commerce platforms that open new channels, and pricing tools that optimize price realization. The value is measurable in revenue growth and sales productivity.

Efficiency-enabling technology allows the company to do more with less. This includes automation of repetitive tasks, workflow systems that reduce handoffs, and analytics that improve decision-making. The value is measurable in cost reduction and productivity improvement.

Visibility-enabling technology provides information that improves management decisions. This includes business intelligence platforms, operational dashboards, and forecasting systems. The value is harder to measure but shows up in better decisions and faster responses to changing conditions.

Scale-enabling technology allows the company to grow without proportional cost increases. This includes infrastructure that handles increased volume, systems that serve additional customers without additional headcount, and platforms that support geographic expansion. The value is measurable in operating leverage.

Technology That Consumes Value

Technology consumes value when it costs more than it returns or when it creates problems that offset its benefits.

Technology without adoption is the most common failure mode. Systems are implemented but not used. Features are purchased but not deployed. Training is provided but not absorbed. The technology sits idle while the organization continues with old methods.

Technology without process change automates waste rather than eliminating it. Installing technology on top of broken processes locks in inefficiency. The technology makes it harder to fix the underlying problems.

Technology for its own sake pursues innovation without business purpose. New technologies are appealing, and technologists naturally want to experiment. But technology investment should serve business outcomes, not technological curiosity.

Technology that increases complexity adds systems without retiring old ones. The technology landscape becomes fragmented. Integration costs escalate. Data becomes scattered across systems. The organization spends more time managing technology than using it.

Machine-Supported Analysis as Accelerant

Machine-supported analysis and automation represent a particular category of technology with distinctive characteristics. These systems learn from data, improve with use, and can automate tasks requiring judgment rather than just rule-following.

The potential applications in value creation are significant:

Pricing optimization. Machine learning can analyze price sensitivity, competitive positioning, and demand patterns to recommend optimal prices. This application directly supports revenue gambits.

Demand forecasting. Automated analysis can improve forecast accuracy by identifying patterns in historical data and external factors. Better forecasts improve inventory management, production planning, and resource allocation.

Customer prediction. Models can predict which customers are likely to churn, which are likely to expand, and which offers will resonate. These predictions enable proactive intervention before problems occur.

Process automation. Intelligent automation can handle tasks previously requiring human judgment: document processing, exception handling, quality inspection, and customer service. This application directly supports margin gambits.

The caution with machine-supported analysis is proportional to its promise. Implementations require clean data, which many organizations lack. They require technical capability, which must be built or acquired. They require change management, as people adapt to working alongside automated systems. This technology is not a shortcut. It is an accelerant that works when the foundation is solid.

The Technology Foundation

Before deploying advanced technology gambits, most companies need to address foundational issues:

Data quality. Advanced analytics and automation require clean, consistent, accessible data. Many organizations have data scattered across systems, inconsistently defined, and difficult to access. Building a minimum viable data foundation is often prerequisite to technology acceleration.

System integration. Technology value often comes from connecting systems rather than deploying new ones. Customer data connected to financial data connected to operational data creates visibility impossible with isolated systems.

Process stability. Technology accelerates stable processes. It cannot fix unstable ones. Before investing in technology, ensure the underlying processes are sound.

Adoption capability. The organization must be able to absorb new technology. This requires training, change management, and often cultural adjustment. Technology implemented faster than the organization can absorb creates waste, not value.

The Technology Arena in Practice

The technology gambits in Part Three include patterns for building the foundation as well as patterns for deploying specific technologies:

Automation patterns for systematically identifying and automating high-volume, rule-based processes.

Data patterns for building the infrastructure that enables advanced analytics and machine-supported decision-making.

Deployment patterns for implementing machine learning and automation in ways that achieve adoption and deliver results.

Remediation patterns for addressing technical debt, legacy systems, and infrastructure limitations that constrain growth.

Enhancement patterns for using technology to improve products and services in ways customers value.

Service model patterns for redesigning how the company delivers value using technology as an enabler.

The foundation patterns are often less exciting but more valuable. A company with solid data, integrated systems, stable processes, and adoption capability can deploy any technology effectively. A company lacking these fundamentals will struggle regardless of which technology it chooses.

Technology is the accelerant. The gambits are the fuel. The five arenas are the destination. Part Three provides the specific patterns for creating value in each arena.

Proof Register: What Buyers Believe

Metrics	Artifacts	Buyer confidence
Revenue	Price/volume/mix	✓
Margin	Unit cost trend	✓
Acquisitions	Synergy tracker	✓
Cash/Debt	13-week forecast	✓
Multiple	Contract quality	✓

Card A PROOF ARTIFACTS

Top 10 buyer-grade exhibits

- Price realization bridge
- Unit cost trend
- Synergy tracker
- Cash forecast accuracy
- Retention cohorts
- Quality of earnings
- Working capital bridge
- Integration log
- Margin by segment
- Covenant headroom

Card B FAILURE RISKS

Top 8 proof-killers

- Weak proof
- One-off gains
- Unverified metrics
- Concentration risk
- Integration drift
- Forecasting blind spots
- Story outruns proof
- Key-person dependence

PART THREE

THE 40 GAMBITS

The Pattern Library for Engineering Equity Value

SECTION A

REVENUE GAMBITS

Gambits 1 through 8

Revenue is where value creation begins. The eight gambits in this section address the primary sources of top-line growth and quality improvement: pricing discipline, mix optimization, revenue quality, customer retention, expansion within existing relationships, channel effectiveness, conversion efficiency, and packaging architecture.

Each gambit targets the operating earnings bridge directly through revenue contribution and often influences the enterprise value bridge through improved revenue quality and durability. Select the gambits that match your starting position and sequence them for maximum impact.

GAMBITPLATE **#01**

THE PRICING RATCHET

BRIDGE: Operating Earnings **TIME:** 6 months

VALUE MECHANISM

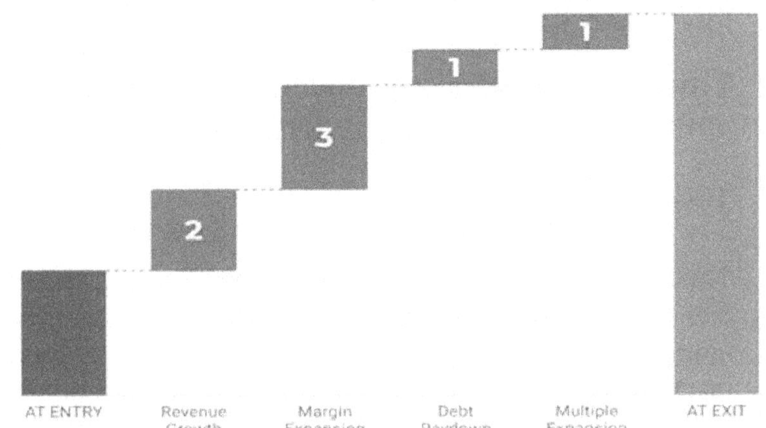

SCORE PANEL

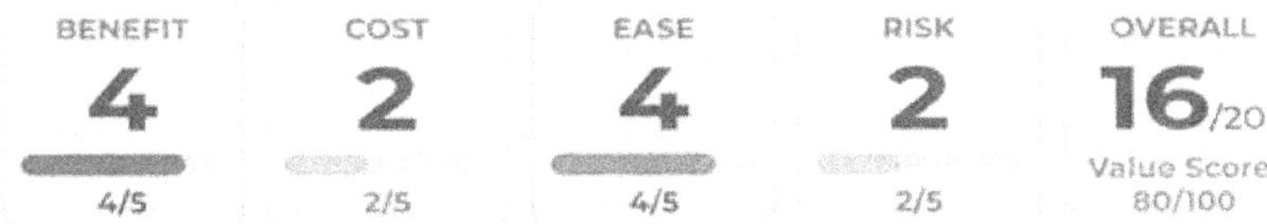

FIELD NOTES

TRIGGERS

- Gap between list and realized price exceeds 15%
- Sales discounting without approval governance

PROOF ARTIFACTS

- Price realization trend over 12+ months
- Volume retention during price increases

DISQUALIFIERS

- True commodity with no differentiation
- Contracts prohibit price changes during term

Systematically close the gap between list and realized price through value training, discount governance, and segment targeting.

Gambit 1

The Pricing Ratchet

Bridge Target: Operating Earnings Bridge (revenue line, direct flow-through to profit)

Time to Impact: Fast (under six months for initial impact, twelve months for full realization)

The Pattern

The Pricing Ratchet systematically captures price realization that is currently leaking through undisciplined discounting, outdated price lists, and failure to communicate value. It installs governance mechanisms that prevent reversion while building organizational capability for ongoing price optimization.

Most companies leave significant value on the table through pricing. Sales teams discount reflexively to close deals. Price lists lag cost increases. Value delivered to customers exceeds value captured. The Pricing Ratchet addresses each of these leaks through a structured program that improves price realization without triggering volume collapse.

The ratchet mechanism is essential. Prices are raised systematically across the customer base, with exceptions requiring approval and documentation. Each increase becomes the new floor. The ratchet only turns one direction.

The Sacrifice

Short-term sales friction. Sales teams accustomed to discounting will resist. Some deals will take longer to close. A small number of price-sensitive customers may leave. The sacrifice is temporary discomfort for permanent improvement.

The Sequence

1. Establish baseline price realization. Calculate the gap between list price and actual realized price by product, customer segment, and sales representative. Identify where the largest leakage occurs.

2. Segment customers by price sensitivity. Not all customers respond the same to price increases. Segment based on switching costs, competitive alternatives, and value received. Plan different approaches for different segments.

3. Update price lists to reflect current costs and value. Many price lists are years out of date. Bring them current before beginning realization improvement.

4. Train the sales team on value communication. Price increases stick when customers understand the value they receive. Equip the sales team with value documentation, comparison tools, and objection responses.

5. Implement discount approval governance. Establish thresholds requiring management approval. Track every exception. Review exceptions weekly to identify patterns.

6. Execute the first wave of increases. Begin with customers in low-sensitivity segments during natural renewal or reorder points. Document results and refine approach.

7. Roll out subsequent waves. Extend to medium-sensitivity segments. Customize messaging based on lessons from the first wave.

8. Align compensation to price realization. Adjust sales incentives to reward margin, not just volume. Remove incentives that encourage discounting.

9. Install ongoing tracking and reporting. Build a dashboard showing price realization by segment, representative, and product. Review monthly.

10. Institutionalize annual price reviews. Make pricing a recurring agenda item. Review competitive positioning, cost changes, and value delivery annually. Adjust prices proactively rather than reactively.

Preconditions

The Pricing Ratchet works when the company delivers genuine value that customers recognize, when there is meaningful differentiation from competitors, and when the sales organization has credibility with customers. It struggles in commodity markets with perfect price transparency, when customers have easy switching options, or when the sales team lacks the capability to communicate value.

The Trap

The most common trap is moving too fast without adequate preparation. Announcing price increases before training the sales team or updating value documentation creates chaos. Sales teams panic, customers complain, and management retreats. The retreat is worse than not starting because it signals that prices are negotiable.

The second trap is inconsistent enforcement. If some sales representatives can still discount freely while others cannot, resentment builds and the program loses credibility. Governance must be universal.

The Proof

Price realization trend. Quarterly tracking showing the gap between list and realized price narrowing over time. Target Level 3 or higher on the Evidence Standard Ladder.

Volume retention during increases. Evidence that price increases did not trigger proportional volume loss.

Discount exception tracking. Documentation of governance in action, showing exceptions decreasing over time.

Margin improvement attribution. Bridge analysis showing the specific contribution of pricing to operating earnings improvement.

Variants

Contract Escalator. For businesses with long-term contracts, focus on embedding annual escalation clauses tied to inflation or cost indices. Future price increases become automatic.

Surcharge Layer. For businesses facing volatile input costs, add surcharges (fuel, materials, energy) that adjust automatically. Base prices remain stable while surcharges absorb cost volatility.

Minimum Order Reset. For businesses with many small orders, increase minimum order sizes or add small order fees. This variant addresses profitability of the long tail without touching headline prices.

____
____
____

DISQUALIFIERS: When This Gambit Is Wrong

____
____
____

- The product is a true commodity with perfect price transparency and no differentiation
- Customer contracts prohibit price increases for the remaining term
- The sales organization lacks credibility with customers due to recent service failures
- No owner exists with authority to enforce pricing governance across the sales team

If disqualified, consider: Gambit 2 (The Mix Elevator) or Gambit 8 (The Value Packaging Reset)

____
____
____

GAMBITPLATE #02

THE MIX ELEVATOR

BRIDGE: Operating Earnings

TIME: 12 months

VALUE MECHANISM

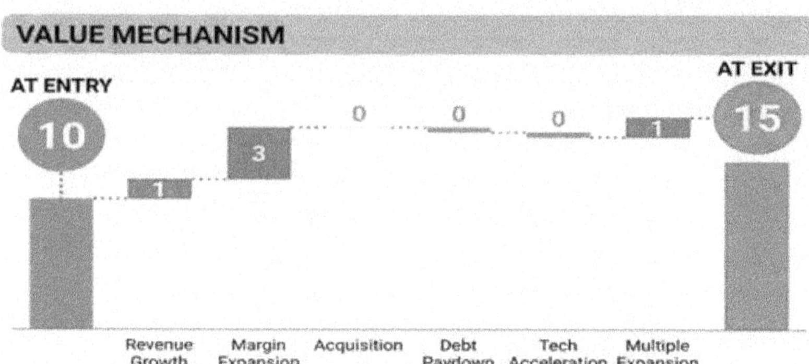

SCORE PANEL

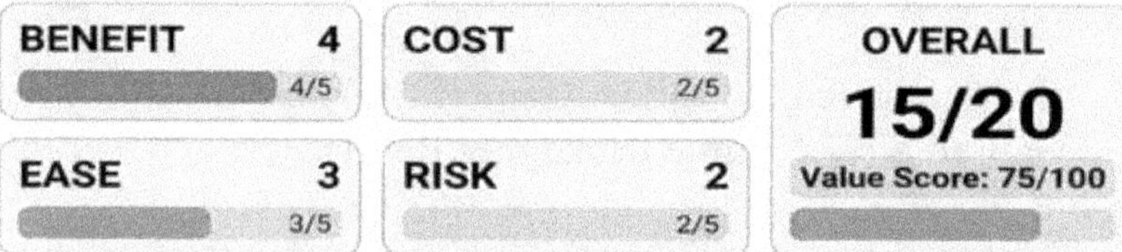

FIELD NOTES

TRIGGERS

- High-value segments under-penetrated
- Low-value segments over-served

PROOF ARTIFACTS

- Margin by segment over 12+ months
- Volume shift into premium tiers

DISQUALIFIERS

- No meaningful segment differentiation
- Customers locked into commodity pricing

Shift revenue mix toward higher-margin segments through targeted pricing, sales incentives, and product positioning.

Gambit 2

The Mix Elevator

Bridge Target: Operating Earnings Bridge (margin improvement through composition shift)

Time to Impact: Medium (six to eighteen months for meaningful shift)

The Pattern

The Mix Elevator shifts the composition of revenue toward higher-margin products, services, and customer segments. Rather than growing all revenue equally, it deliberately accelerates profitable segments while allowing unprofitable segments to shrink or hold steady.

The power of mix shift is often underestimated. A company with a forty percent gross margin overall might have segments ranging from twenty percent to sixty percent. Shifting ten percent of revenue from a twenty percent segment to a sixty percent segment improves blended margin by four percentage points without changing total revenue.

The Mix Elevator requires clear visibility into segment economics and deliberate commercial strategy. It often meets resistance because sales teams are compensated on revenue, not margin, and because low-margin segments may include historically important customers.

The Sacrifice

Potential short-term revenue decline if low-margin segments shrink faster than high-margin segments grow. Relationship strain with customers in deprioritized segments. Sales team frustration when asked to de-emphasize established accounts.

The Sequence

1. Build segment-level contribution margin visibility. Calculate fully-loaded contribution margin by product line, service type, customer segment, and channel. Identify the highest and lowest margin categories.

2. Define target mix. Establish the ideal revenue composition based on margin, growth potential, and strategic fit. Set explicit targets for the proportion of revenue from each segment.

3. Reallocate sales capacity. Shift sales resources toward high-margin segments. This may mean territory redesign, account reassignment, or hiring specialists for priority segments.

4. Adjust marketing investment. Redirect marketing spend toward high-margin segment acquisition. Reduce or eliminate marketing to segments targeted for de-emphasis.

5. Revise compensation structure. Align sales incentives with margin contribution, not just revenue. Introduce accelerators for high-margin products and decelerators for low-margin products.

6. Develop segment-specific offerings. Create products, bundles, or service levels designed specifically for high-margin segments. Make it easier for sales to sell what you want them to sell.

7. Implement segment tracking. Build reporting that shows mix evolution monthly. Track progress toward target mix. Identify segments drifting in the wrong direction.

8. Manage low-margin segment transition. For segments marked for de-emphasis, decide whether to maintain passively, reprice aggressively, or exit deliberately. Execute the chosen strategy.

9. Review and adjust quarterly. Mix shift is iterative. Review progress quarterly. Adjust tactics based on what is working and what is not.

Preconditions

The Mix Elevator works when there is meaningful margin variation across segments, when high-margin segments have growth capacity, and when the organization has the commercial capability to compete in priority segments. It struggles when all segments have similar margins, when high-margin segments are mature or shrinking, or when competitors dominate the attractive segments.

The Trap

The primary trap is shrinking low-margin revenue faster than growing high-margin revenue. The result is a better-looking margin percentage on a smaller revenue base, which may not improve absolute profit. Mix shift must be managed as a portfolio, ensuring that the net effect is positive.

The second trap is ignoring shared costs. Some overhead costs may not decline when low-margin segments shrink. If the same infrastructure serves all segments, mix shift may improve contribution margin without improving operating margin.

The Proof

Segment revenue composition trend. Quarterly tracking showing high-margin segments growing as a percentage of total revenue.

Blended margin improvement. Demonstration that overall margin improved through mix shift, with attribution analysis.

High-margin segment growth rate. Evidence that priority segments are growing faster than the overall business.

Variants

Product Portfolio Rationalization. Focus on eliminating low-margin products rather than just deprioritizing them. Simplify the portfolio to products that meet margin thresholds.

Services Attach. For product businesses, focus on increasing service attach rates. Services typically carry higher margins than products. Shift mix by growing the services wrapper around existing product sales.

Geographic Prioritization. When margin varies by geography due to competitive dynamics or cost-to-serve differences, shift investment toward high-margin regions.

____
____
____

DISQUALIFIERS: When This Gambit Is Wrong

____
____
____

- All segments have similar contribution margins within five percentage points
- High-margin segments are mature, declining, or already at capacity
- The business lacks the commercial capability to win in priority segments
- Shared cost infrastructure means segment shrinkage will not reduce total costs

If disqualified, consider: Gambit 9 (The Zero-Based Rebuild) or Gambit 11 (The Unit Economics Rewrite)

____
____
____

GAMBITPLATE **#03**

THE BAD REVENUE EXIT

BRIDGE: Operating Earnings TIME: 6 months

VALUE MECHANISM

SCORE PANEL

FIELD NOTES

TRIGGERS

- Negative-margin customers above 10% of revenue
- Chronic payment delays or disputes

PROOF ARTIFACTS

- Customer profitability analysis
- Margin improvement post-exit

DISQUALIFIERS

- Contractual lock-in with penalties
- Customer concentration risk

Systematically exit or reprice unprofitable customers to improve margin and free up capacity for better accounts.

Gambit 3

The Bad Revenue Exit

Bridge Target: Operating Earnings Bridge (margin improvement through elimination of negative contributors)

Time to Impact: Fast (under six months for cost relief, immediate margin improvement)

The Pattern

The Bad Revenue Exit identifies and eliminates customers, products, or contracts that generate negative contribution margin. This is not about deprioritizing low-margin revenue. It is about exiting revenue that loses money.

Negative-margin revenue is more common than most executives believe. When cost-to-serve is poorly understood, when pricing was set years ago under different cost structures, or when contracts include scope creep without price adjustment, revenue can become unprofitable without anyone noticing.

The counterintuitive truth is that eliminating bad revenue improves profitability even though revenue declines. The freed capacity can be redirected to profitable opportunities. The psychological burden of servicing unprofitable relationships is lifted. The organization focuses on what actually makes money.

The Sacrifice

Revenue decline that may concern stakeholders focused on top-line metrics. Relationship termination with long-standing customers. Internal resistance from teams who service these accounts. Potential reputation risk if exits are handled poorly.

The Sequence

1. Build complete cost-to-serve analysis. Calculate fully-loaded contribution margin for every customer or contract of meaningful size. Include direct costs, allocated costs, and an estimate of management attention consumed.

2. Identify the negative contributors. Flag every customer, product, or contract with negative contribution margin. Rank by magnitude of loss.

3. Assess remediation potential. For each negative contributor, evaluate whether repricing, scope reduction, or service level adjustment could restore profitability. Some relationships can be fixed. Others cannot.

4. Attempt remediation where feasible. Before exiting, attempt to fix salvageable relationships. Present customers with clear choices: accept new terms or transition to another provider.

5. Plan the exit sequence. For relationships that cannot be remediated, develop exit plans. Consider contract terms, notice requirements, and transition assistance.

Sequence exits to manage operational and reputational impact.

6. Communicate exits professionally. Handle every exit with respect and professionalism. Provide adequate notice. Offer transition support. Protect the company's reputation even while ending unprofitable relationships.

7. Reallocate freed resources. The capacity previously consumed by unprofitable relationships should be redirected to profitable opportunities. This reallocation captures the full value of the exit.

8. Install guardrails against future bad revenue. Update pricing approval processes, contract review requirements, and customer acceptance criteria to prevent future unprofitable relationships from forming.

9. Track margin improvement. Document the profit impact of each exit. Build the evidence base showing that revenue decline improved profitability.

Preconditions

The Bad Revenue Exit works when cost-to-serve data is reliable, when the organization has the commercial capability to replace exited revenue, and when stakeholders understand that revenue quality matters more than revenue quantity. It struggles when cost allocation is arbitrary, when there is no capacity to pursue replacement revenue, or when stakeholders judge performance purely on top-line growth.

The Trap

The primary trap is faulty cost-to-serve analysis. If costs are allocated arbitrarily rather than calculated accurately, profitable customers may be classified as unprofitable. Exiting the wrong customers destroys value rather than creating it. Invest in accurate cost analysis before making exit decisions.

The second trap is failing to reallocate freed capacity. If the resources previously serving unprofitable customers are not redirected to profitable activities, the cost base remains while revenue declines. The exit must be paired with reallocation.

The Proof

Margin improvement exceeding revenue decline. Demonstration that operating earnings increased even though revenue decreased.

Resource reallocation tracking. Evidence that freed capacity was redirected to profitable activities.

Customer portfolio quality metrics. Improvement in average contribution margin per customer, minimum contribution margin threshold compliance.

Variants

Product Line Exit. Rather than exiting customers, exit entire product lines that are structurally unprofitable. Simplify the portfolio to products that meet margin thresholds.

Geography Exit. For businesses operating in regions with structurally unfavorable economics, exit the geography entirely rather than trying to fix individual relationships.

Channel Exit. When certain channels consistently generate negative margins due to cost-to-serve or pricing dynamics, exit the channel while maintaining presence in profitable alternatives.

DISQUALIFIERS: When This Gambit Is Wrong

- Cost-to-serve analysis is unreliable or based on arbitrary cost allocations
- The "bad revenue" provides essential fixed cost absorption that cannot be replaced
- Exits would trigger contractual penalties exceeding the value of margin improvement
- No replacement revenue opportunity exists and freed capacity will become idle cost

If disqualified, consider: Gambit 1 (The Pricing Ratchet) to improve margin on existing relationships

GAMBITPLATE #04

THE EXPANSION LOOP

BRIDGE: Operating Earnings | **TIME:** 12 months

VALUE MECHANISM

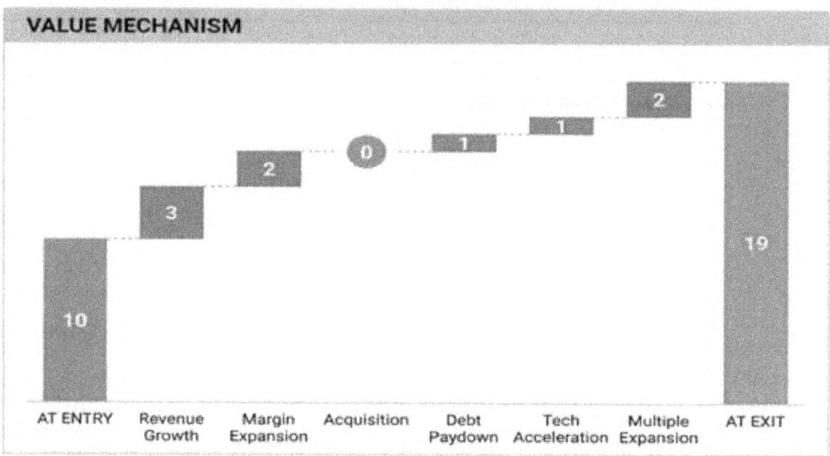

SCORE PANEL

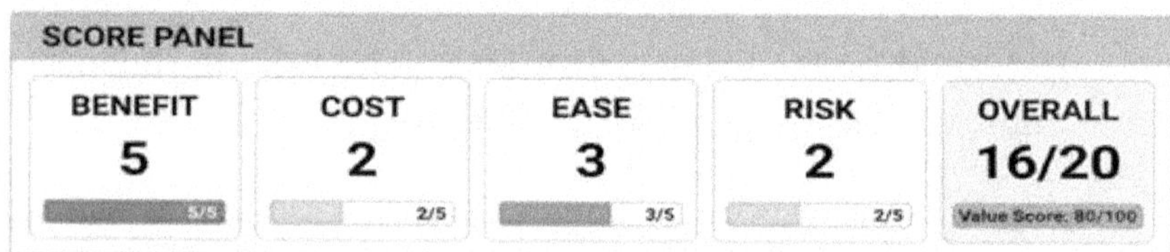

FIELD NOTES

TRIGGERS
- Land-and-expand model proven but underutilized
- High NRR but low initial ACV

PROOF ARTIFACTS
- Expansion revenue as % of total
- Time-to-expand cohort analysis

DISQUALIFIERS
- One-time transactional sales model
- No product modularity or upsell path

Build a repeatable expansion playbook that drives net revenue retention through cross-sell, upsell, and usage growth.

Gambit 4

The Expansion Loop

Bridge Target: Operating Earnings Bridge (high-margin revenue growth from existing customers)

Time to Impact: Medium (six to twelve months to build the system, ongoing compounding thereafter)

The Pattern

The Expansion Loop systematically grows revenue within existing customer relationships. This is the highest-quality growth available: lower acquisition cost, higher margins, and stronger retention when customers are more deeply embedded.

Most companies leave substantial expansion revenue on the table. Account teams focus on retention rather than growth. Cross-sell opportunities are identified but not pursued. Upsell conversations happen sporadically rather than systematically. The Expansion Loop installs the process, tools, and accountability to capture this latent revenue.

Net revenue retention is the key metric. A business with one hundred ten percent net revenue retention grows ten percent annually from existing customers alone, before any new customer acquisition. A business with ninety percent net revenue retention shrinks ten percent and must acquire new customers just to stay flat.

The Sacrifice

Sales team capacity redirected from new customer acquisition to expansion. Potential short-term slowdown in new customer acquisition while the expansion capability is built. Investment in customer success infrastructure.

The Sequence

1. Calculate current net revenue retention. Measure expansion, contraction, and churn within the existing customer base. Establish baseline and identify the primary drivers of each component.

2. Map expansion potential by account. For each significant customer, identify products or services they could purchase but do not. Quantify the whitespace in each relationship.

3. Develop expansion triggers. Identify the signals that indicate expansion readiness: usage thresholds, organizational changes, budget cycles, or satisfaction scores. Build these triggers into account monitoring.

4. Create expansion playbooks. Develop standard approaches for common expansion scenarios: adding users, upgrading tiers, purchasing additional products, or expanding to new departments. Make expansion repeatable.

5. Assign expansion ownership. Clarify who owns expansion for each account: the original sales representative, a dedicated account manager, or a customer success team. Eliminate ambiguity.

6. Build expansion into compensation. Include expansion targets in sales and account management incentives. Reward growing existing relationships, not just acquiring new ones.

7. Implement quarterly business reviews. Install a rhythm of strategic conversations with key accounts. Use these reviews to identify expansion opportunities and address barriers.

8. Track expansion pipeline separately. Build visibility into expansion opportunities distinct from new customer pipeline. Manage expansion with the same rigor applied to new business development.

9. Review and optimize monthly. Analyze expansion results monthly. Identify which playbooks work, which accounts are expanding, and where barriers remain. Continuously improve the expansion system.

Preconditions

The Expansion Loop works when customers are satisfied with current products or services, when there are additional products or services to sell, and when customer relationships support commercial conversations. It struggles when customer satisfaction is low, when the product portfolio is narrow, or when account teams lack commercial skills.

The Trap

The primary trap is pursuing expansion before stabilizing retention. If customers are churning, expansion conversations feel tone-deaf. Fix retention first. Then build the expansion engine.

The second trap is overloading account teams without clear prioritization. Not every account has equal expansion potential. Focus on accounts where the opportunity is large and the relationship is strong. Apply resources where they generate returns.

The Proof

Net revenue retention trend. Quarterly tracking showing net revenue retention improving toward or exceeding one hundred percent.

Expansion revenue as percentage of total growth. Demonstration that a meaningful share of revenue growth comes from existing customers.

Product adoption breadth. Tracking showing customers purchasing more products or services over time.

Variants

Usage-Based Expansion. For businesses with usage-based pricing, focus on driving usage growth within existing accounts. Create programs that encourage increased consumption.

Multi-Location Rollout. For businesses selling to multi-site customers, systematize the process of expanding from pilot locations to enterprise-wide deployment.

Adjacent Buyer Expansion. For businesses where different buyers within the same organization purchase separately, build programs to expand from the initial buyer to adjacent departments or functions.

DISQUALIFIERS: When This Gambit Is Wrong

- Gross revenue retention is below eighty percent (fix retention first)
- The product portfolio has no natural expansion paths or adjacent offerings
- Customer relationships are transactional with no strategic engagement
- Account teams lack commercial skills and cannot have expansion conversations

If disqualified, consider: Gambit 5 (The Retention Firewall) to stabilize the base first

GAMBITPLATE **#05**

THE RETENTION FIREWALL

BRIDGE: Operating Earnings

TIME: 6 months

VALUE MECHANISM

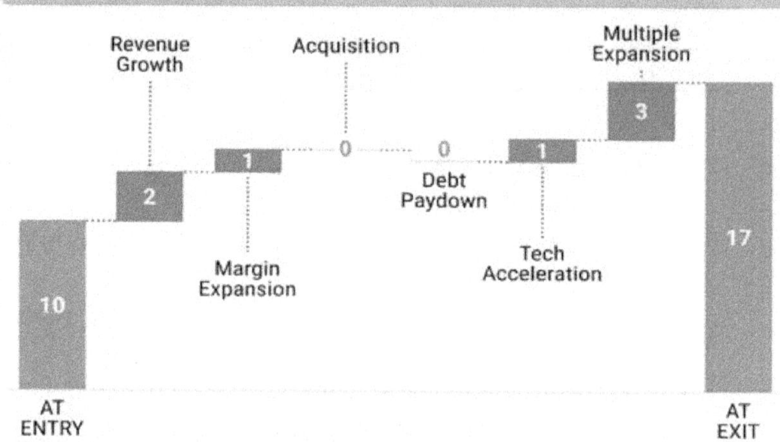

SCORE PANEL

BENEFIT: 5	COST: 3	EASE: 3	RISK: 2	OVERALL:
5/5	3/5	3/5	2/5	15/20 75/100

FIELD NOTES

TRIGGERS

- Churn above 8% annually
- No early warning system for at-risk accounts

PROOF ARTIFACTS

- Retention rate by cohort
- Churn reduction over 6+ months

DISQUALIFIERS

- Structural market decline
- Product obsolescence

Deploy proactive retention programs, health scoring, and customer success infrastructure to reduce churn and protect revenue base.

Gambit 5

The Retention Firewall

Bridge Target: Operating Earnings Bridge (revenue preservation) and Enterprise Value Bridge (durability improvement)

Time to Impact: Medium (three to six months to build the system, ongoing improvement in retention rates)

The Pattern

The Retention Firewall identifies at-risk customers before they leave and intervenes to save the relationship. Most churn is predictable if you know where to look. The firewall creates early warning systems, intervention protocols, and accountability for retention outcomes.

Customer retention is often more valuable than customer acquisition. Acquiring a new customer costs five to seven times more than retaining an existing one. A customer saved is a customer you do not have to replace. Improving retention from eighty-five percent to ninety-two percent has dramatic impact on growth trajectory and customer acquisition efficiency.

Retention also affects the exit multiple. Buyers pay premiums for businesses with high retention because high retention signals product value, customer satisfaction, and revenue durability. The firewall improves both current earnings and future valuation.

The Sacrifice

Investment in customer success infrastructure: people, systems, and processes. Management attention diverted from acquisition to retention. Potential margin impact from save offers or remediation actions.

The Sequence

1. Analyze historical churn. Study customers who left in the past two years. Identify common characteristics, warning signs, and the timeline from first signal to departure. Build the pattern library of churn indicators.

2. Define leading indicators. From the churn analysis, extract the signals that precede departure: declining usage, reduced engagement, support escalations, payment delays, or organizational changes at the customer.

3. Build the early warning system. Create automated tracking of leading indicators. Generate alerts when customers show warning signs. Prioritize alerts by customer value and risk severity.

4. Develop intervention playbooks. Create standard responses for each type of warning signal. Define who intervenes, what they offer, and how success is measured. Make retention intervention repeatable.

5. Assign retention ownership. Clarify accountability for retention outcomes. This may be account managers, customer success teams, or dedicated

retention specialists. Eliminate ambiguity about who saves at-risk customers.

6. Create save offer guidelines. Define what can be offered to save at-risk customers: discounts, service upgrades, extended terms, or remediation commitments. Set boundaries to prevent margin erosion.

7. Implement loss review process. When customers do leave, conduct systematic analysis. Understand why the firewall failed. Feed lessons back into indicator refinement and playbook improvement.

8. Track and report retention metrics. Build visibility into retention rates, intervention success rates, and time-to-save. Share metrics broadly to create organizational focus on retention.

9. Continuously improve the system. Retention is dynamic. Customer needs change. Competitors evolve. The firewall must evolve with them. Review and enhance quarterly.

Preconditions

The Retention Firewall works when churn has identifiable precursors, when the organization has capacity to intervene with at-risk customers, and when the product or service can be adapted to address customer concerns. It struggles when churn is driven by external factors beyond company control, when intervention capacity is limited, or when the product cannot be improved to meet customer needs.

The Trap

The primary trap is creating a save culture that rewards last-minute heroics instead of preventing the crisis. If teams are celebrated for dramatic saves, they have incentive to let situations deteriorate before intervening. The goal is prevention, not rescue.

The second trap is save offers that erode margin. If every at-risk customer receives a significant discount, the firewall becomes a margin leak. Save offers should be calibrated to customer value and used judiciously.

The Proof

Gross revenue retention trend. Quarterly tracking showing retention rates improving over time. Target Level 4 evidence with eight or more quarters of data.

Intervention success rate. Percentage of at-risk customers successfully retained after intervention.

Early detection rate. Percentage of churn that was identified by the warning system before the customer gave notice.

Cohort retention curves. Demonstration that newer cohorts retain better than older cohorts, showing system improvement over time.

Variants

Health Score Model. For businesses with rich customer data, build a predictive health score combining multiple indicators. Use the score to prioritize proactive outreach, not just reactive intervention.

Contract Renewal Engine. For businesses with annual contracts, build a structured renewal process beginning ninety days before expiration. Proactively manage every renewal rather than waiting for customer initiative.

Win-Back Program. For customers who do leave, build a structured program to win them back. Some customers can be recovered after departure, particularly if circumstances change or competitor experience disappoints.

DISQUALIFIERS: When This Gambit Is Wrong

- Churn is driven primarily by external factors (customer bankruptcy, market exit) not service issues
- No customer data exists to build early warning indicators
- The organization lacks capacity to intervene even when at-risk customers are identified
- The underlying product is fundamentally inferior and cannot be improved

If disqualified, consider: Addressing product or service fundamentals before building retention infrastructure

GAMBITPLATE **#06**

THE CHANNEL REDESIGN

BRIDGE: Operating Earnings | **TIME: 24 months**

VALUE MECHANISM

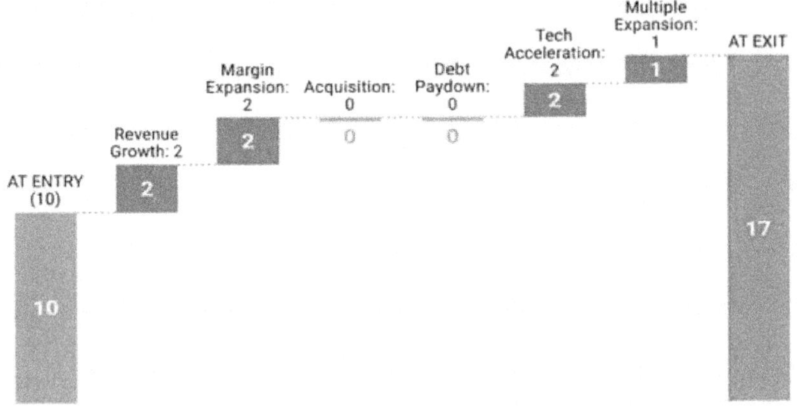

SCORE PANEL

BENEFIT: 4	COST: 4	EASE: 2	RISK: 4	OVERALL
4/5	4/5	2/5	4/5	**10/20** Value Score: 50/100

FIELD NOTES

TRIGGERS:
- Channel conflict or margin erosion
- Direct vs. indirect misalignment

PROOF ARTIFACTS:
- Channel economics model
- Pilot results in new channel

DISQUALIFIERS:
- Locked into long-term channel contracts
- No internal capability to go direct

Redesign go-to-market channels to optimize reach, margin, and customer experience through direct, partner, or hybrid models.

Gambit 6

The Channel Redesign

Bridge Target: Operating Earnings Bridge (revenue growth and margin improvement through route-to-market transformation)

Time to Impact: Long (twelve to twenty-four months for full transformation)

The Pattern

The Channel Redesign transforms how the company reaches customers. Channels that made sense at an earlier stage of growth may not optimize for scale. Direct sales may be too expensive for certain segments. Partners may not provide adequate coverage. Digital channels may be underdeveloped. The redesign realigns channels to growth strategy and cost structure.

Channel economics vary dramatically. The same product sold through direct sales, inside sales, partners, and digital commerce generates vastly different margins. The Channel Redesign matches each customer segment to the channel that balances reach, cost, and effectiveness.

This gambit is one of the highest-impact transformations available but also one of the highest-risk. Channel changes affect customer relationships, partner relationships, and sales team livelihoods. The execution must be carefully planned and communicated.

The Sacrifice

Disruption to existing channel relationships. Potential short-term revenue decline during transition. Sales team restructuring with associated severance and hiring costs. Partner conflict if transitioning business between partner and direct channels.

The Sequence

1. Map current channel economics. Calculate fully-loaded cost-to-serve for each channel. Include direct costs, channel margins, and overhead allocation. Understand the true profitability of each route to market.

2. Segment customers by channel fit. Analyze which customer types are best served by which channels. Consider transaction size, complexity, service requirements, and geographic distribution.

3. Design target channel architecture. Define the optimal channel mix for each customer segment. Specify where to invest, where to reduce, and where to transition between channels.

4. Build new channel capabilities. If the target architecture requires channels that do not exist or are underdeveloped, invest in building them. This may include hiring, training, technology, or partner development.

5. Plan the transition sequence. Determine which customer segments transition first, which transition

later, and how long the transition takes. Sequence to minimize revenue disruption.

6. Communicate with affected stakeholders. Inform sales teams, partners, and customers about changes. Provide rationale and timeline. Address concerns proactively.

7. Execute the transition. Move customers to new channels according to the plan. Monitor for retention issues. Intervene quickly when problems arise.

8. Restructure the sales organization. As channel responsibilities shift, adjust the sales organization accordingly. This may include role changes, territory adjustments, or workforce reduction.

9. Measure and optimize. Track the impact of channel changes on revenue, margin, and customer satisfaction. Adjust the model based on real-world results.

Preconditions

The Channel Redesign works when there is meaningful variation in channel economics, when alternative channels are viable for the customer segments in question, and when the organization has capacity to manage a complex transition. It struggles when customers have strong preferences for existing channels, when alternative channels lack credibility, or when transition execution is poor.

The Trap

The primary trap is transitioning customers to channels that cannot serve them effectively. Margin improvement is worthless if customers leave because the new channel provides inferior service. Test channel changes with pilot groups before broad rollout.

The second trap is partner conflict. If a redesign involves shifting business from partners to direct, partners may retaliate by directing customers to competitors. Manage partner relationships carefully during transitions.

The Proof

Channel cost-to-serve improvement. Demonstration that blended channel costs decreased through mix shift.

Customer retention during transition. Evidence that channel transitions did not trigger elevated churn.

Revenue growth post-transition. Showing that new channel architecture supports growth, not just cost reduction.

Variants

Digital First. Prioritize building digital and self-service channels for segments where transaction complexity is low. Use technology to enable self-service at scale.

Inside Sales Conversion. Transition field sales accounts to inside sales where appropriate. Inside sales typically costs forty to sixty percent less than field sales.

Partner Leverage. For businesses underinvesting in partner channels, build partner programs that extend reach without proportional cost increase.

____

DISQUALIFIERS: When This Gambit Is Wrong

- Customers have strong preferences for existing channels that will trigger churn if changed
- Alternative channels do not exist or cannot be built within the investment timeline
- The organization lacks change management capacity for a complex transition
- Partner contracts prohibit the channel shifts being contemplated

If disqualified, consider: Gambit 7 (The Conversion Rebuild) to optimize within existing channels

GAMBITPLATE **#07**

THE CONVERSION REBUILD

BRIDGE: Operating Earnings | **TIME:** 6 months

VALUE MECHANISM

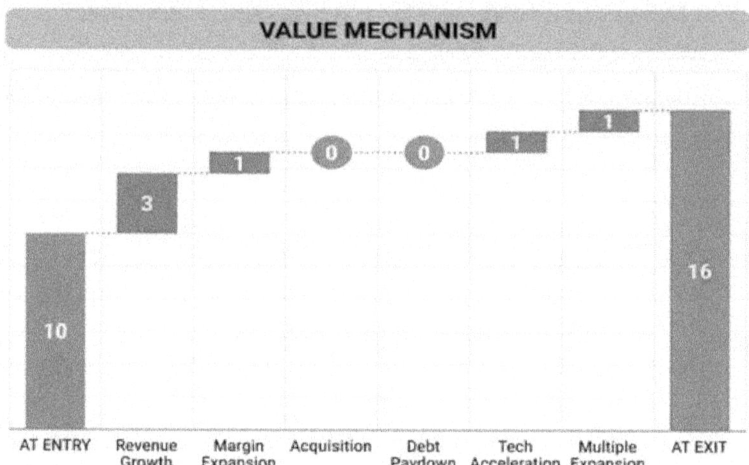

SCORE PANEL

BENEFIT: 4	COST: 2	EASE: 4	RISK: 2	OVERALL: 16/20
4/5	2/5	4/5	2/5	Value Score: 80/100

FIELD NOTES

TRIGGERS:
- Conversion rate below industry benchmark
- High traffic but low close rate

PROOF ARTIFACTS:
- Conversion funnel analysis
- A/B test results showing lift

DISQUALIFIERS:
- No digital presence or funnel
- Sales cycle too complex for quick wins

Redesign conversion funnels, landing pages, and sales processes to systematically improve lead-to-customer conversion rates.

Gambit 7

The Conversion Rebuild

Bridge Target: Operating Earnings Bridge (revenue growth through improved sales efficiency)

Time to Impact: Fast to Medium (three to nine months for measurable improvement)

The Pattern

The Conversion Rebuild optimizes the sales funnel from initial contact to closed deal. Most sales organizations lose significant opportunity at each stage of the funnel. Small improvements in conversion rates at each stage compound into major improvements in overall results.

Consider a funnel with four stages: lead to qualified opportunity, qualified opportunity to proposal, proposal to negotiation, negotiation to close. If each stage converts at fifty percent, only six percent of leads become customers. Improving each stage to sixty percent yields thirteen percent. The funnel output more than doubles from the same lead volume.

The Conversion Rebuild systematically identifies where the funnel leaks, diagnoses why prospects drop out, and implements targeted improvements to each stage. It is a diagnostic and execution discipline, not a single intervention.

The Sacrifice

Investment in funnel analysis and optimization. Changes to sales process that may initially feel uncomfortable. Possible short-term slowdown as new processes are learned. Transparency about conversion rates that may reveal uncomfortable truths.

The Sequence

1. Define funnel stages clearly. Establish precise definitions for each stage of the sales process. Ensure consistent classification across the organization.

2. Measure current conversion rates. Calculate the percentage of opportunities that advance from each stage to the next. Identify the stages with the largest drop-off.

3. Analyze lost opportunities. Study opportunities that stalled or were lost. Understand why they dropped out. Categorize reasons for loss.

4. Identify high-performer practices. Examine what top-performing sales representatives do differently. Extract best practices that can be taught to others.

5. Design stage-specific interventions. For each problematic stage, develop targeted improvements: better qualification criteria, improved collateral, stronger objection handling, or enhanced negotiation support.

6. Train the sales organization. Roll out new practices through training, coaching, and reinforcement. Ensure understanding and adoption.

7. Update sales tools. Improve collateral, proposals, and presentations based on conversion analysis. Remove friction from the buying process.

8. Implement ongoing tracking. Build dashboards showing conversion rates by stage, by representative, and over time. Make conversion visible and accountable.

9. Review and iterate monthly. Funnel optimization is ongoing. Review monthly. Identify new bottlenecks. Test new interventions. Continuously improve.

Preconditions

The Conversion Rebuild works when funnel data is available and reliable, when there is meaningful conversion improvement potential, and when the sales organization is capable of adopting new practices. It struggles when data is poor or inconsistent, when conversion rates are already optimized, or when the sales team resists process changes.

The Trap

The primary trap is optimizing for quantity over quality. Pushing more opportunities through the funnel by relaxing qualification standards fills the pipeline with deals that never close. Conversion improvement must maintain or improve deal quality.

The second trap is overcomplicating the sales process. Adding too many stages, requirements, or checkpoints can slow the sales cycle and frustrate both sales representatives and customers. Simplicity usually outperforms complexity.

The Proof

Stage-by-stage conversion improvement. Tracking showing conversion rates improving at targeted stages.

Overall funnel efficiency trend. Improvement in lead-to-close conversion rate over time.

Sales productivity improvement. More revenue per sales representative resulting from better conversion.

Variants

Qualification Tightening. Focus specifically on improving early-stage qualification. Better qualification means less time wasted on deals that will never close.

Proposal Optimization. Focus specifically on the proposal-to-close stage. Improve proposal quality, response time, and follow-up discipline.

Sales Cycle Compression. Focus on reducing the time opportunities spend at each stage. Faster cycles mean more throughput from the same capacity.

____

DISQUALIFIERS: When This Gambit Is Wrong

- Funnel data does not exist or is too unreliable to support analysis
- Conversion rates are already at or near best-in-class levels
- The sales team actively resists process changes and leadership lacks authority to enforce
- The problem is lead quality or volume, not conversion

If disqualified, consider: Marketing investment to improve lead quality before optimizing conversion

GAMBITPLATE #08

THE VALUE PACKAGING RESET

BRIDGE: Operating Earnings | **TIME:** 12 months

VALUE MECHANISM

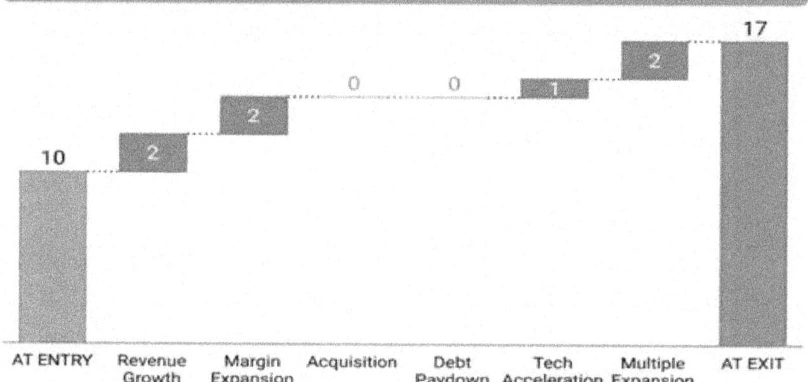

SCORE PANEL

BENEFIT	COST	EASE	RISK	OVERALL
4	3	3	3	13/20
4/5	3/5	3/5	3/5	Value Score: 65/100

FIELD NOTES

TRIGGERS

- Packaging misaligned with customer needs
- Value leakage through discounting

PROOF ARTIFACTS

- Willingness-to-pay research
- Package adoption and margin by tier

DISQUALIFIERS

- Commoditized product with no differentiation
- Regulatory constraints on pricing

Redesign product packaging and pricing architecture to capture more value through tiering, bundling, and feature alignment.

Gambit 8

The Value Packaging Reset

Bridge Target: Operating Earnings Bridge (revenue growth and margin improvement through packaging and pricing architecture)

Time to Impact: Medium (six to twelve months for design and rollout)

The Pattern

The Value Packaging Reset redesigns how products and services are bundled, tiered, and priced. Packaging architecture affects purchase decisions, customer segments served, competitive positioning, and margin capture. A well-designed packaging architecture makes it easier for customers to buy and easier for the company to profit.

Most packaging architectures evolve organically over time. Products are added. Bundles are created to close specific deals. Pricing tiers proliferate. The result is complexity that confuses customers, complicates sales, and leaves money on the table.

The Reset steps back and redesigns packaging from first principles. What customer segments exist? What value does each segment seek? What willingness to pay exists? How should products be bundled to capture value while maintaining simplicity? The output is a coherent architecture that aligns with customer needs and business objectives.

The Sacrifice

Disruption to existing customer arrangements. Transition complexity for customers moving to new packages. Sales team retraining on new architecture. Potential short-term friction during rollout.

The Sequence

1. Document current packaging complexity. Catalog all existing products, bundles, pricing tiers, and exceptions. Understand the full scope of what exists today.

2. Analyze customer purchasing patterns. Study how customers actually buy. Which bundles are popular? Which are rarely purchased? Where do customers ask for customization?

3. Research willingness to pay by segment. Conduct formal or informal research to understand price sensitivity and value perception across customer segments.

4. Design target packaging architecture. Create a simplified structure with clear tiers, logical bundles, and coherent pricing. Limit tiers to three or four to maintain simplicity.

5. Model financial impact. Project the revenue and margin impact of the new architecture. Identify which customers move to higher tiers, which move to lower, and the net effect.

6. Test with customer research. Validate the new architecture with customer feedback before committing. Test pricing, bundling, and tier definitions.

7. Prepare sales enablement. Develop materials that explain the new architecture, communicate value at each tier, and address objections. Train the sales team thoroughly.

8. Plan customer migration. Determine how existing customers transition to the new architecture. Grandfather selectively. Provide incentives for migration where appropriate.

9. Roll out to new customers first. Launch the new architecture with new customers before migrating existing ones. Refine based on initial experience.

10. Migrate existing customers. Execute the migration plan for existing customers. Monitor satisfaction and retention closely during transition.

Preconditions

The Value Packaging Reset works when current packaging is genuinely complex or suboptimal, when customer segments have differentiated needs and willingness to pay, and when the organization can execute a coordinated rollout. It struggles when current packaging is already optimized, when customer needs are homogeneous, or when sales and operations cannot support transition complexity.

The Trap

The primary trap is redesigning packaging without customer input. An architecture that seems elegant from the inside may not match how customers think about their needs. Customer research is essential, not optional.

The second trap is migrating existing customers too aggressively. Forcing customers into new packages that cost more or deliver less creates churn. Migration should be managed carefully with appropriate grandfathering and incentives.

The Proof

Average deal size improvement. Demonstration that new packaging drives larger initial purchases.

Tier mix optimization. Evidence that customers distribute across tiers as designed, with appropriate share at premium levels.

Sales cycle impact. Improvement in sales cycle time or conversion resulting from clearer packaging.

Migration retention. Evidence that existing customers migrated without elevated churn.

Variants

Good-Better-Best Tiering. Implement a classic three-tier structure with clear feature differentiation. This simple model works across many industries.

Usage-Based Conversion. Transition from fixed pricing to usage-based models that align price with value delivered. This works when usage correlates with customer value.

Platform Plus Add-Ons. Restructure around a core platform with optional add-on modules. This enables customers to start small and expand over time while creating natural expansion paths.

DISQUALIFIERS: When This Gambit Is Wrong

- Current packaging is already simple and well-aligned with customer needs
- Customer segments have homogeneous needs with no basis for differentiated tiers
- The organization lacks capacity to manage a coordinated redesign and rollout
- Existing contracts prevent migration for the majority of the customer base

If disqualified, consider: Gambit 1 (The Pricing Ratchet) to optimize within existing packaging structure

SECTION B

MARGIN GAMBITS

Gambits 9 through 16

Margin expansion is where discipline meets design. The eight gambits in this section address the primary sources of cost reduction and productivity improvement: overhead redesign, procurement optimization, unit economics clarity, throughput enhancement, service model alignment, organizational efficiency, footprint optimization, and variable cost management.

Each gambit targets the operating earnings bridge directly through cost reduction or productivity improvement. Unlike revenue gambits that depend on customer response, margin gambits are largely within management control. Select the gambits that match your cost structure and sequence them to build sustainable operating leverage.

GAMBITPLATE **#09**

THE ZERO-BASED REBUILD

BRIDGE: Operating Earnings | **TIME:** 12 months

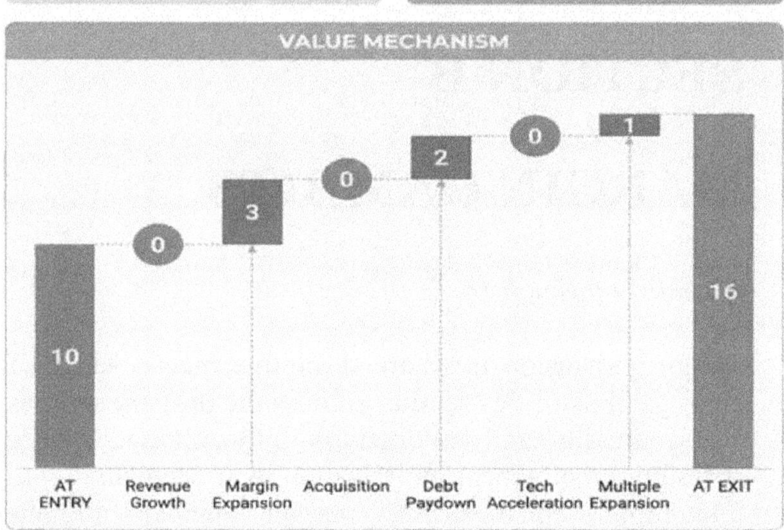

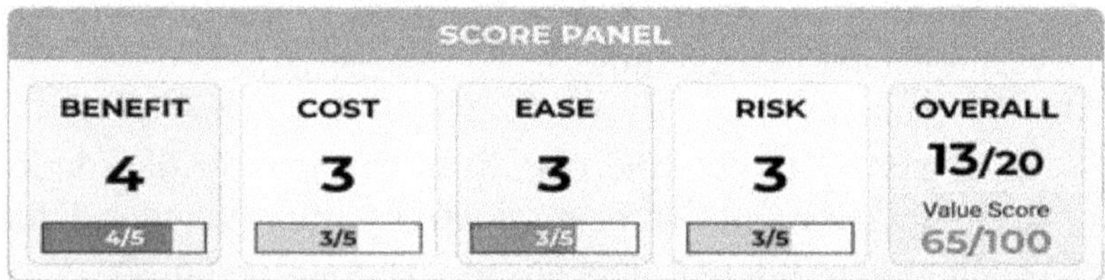

FIELD NOTES

TRIGGERS

- Cost structure bloated vs. peers
- No recent cost discipline exercise

PROOF ARTIFACTS

- Zero-based budget model
- Cost per unit trend over 12+ months

DISQUALIFIERS

- Recent restructuring already completed
- Union constraints on headcount

Rebuild cost structure from zero base to eliminate waste, right-size overhead, and align spending with strategic priorities.

Gambit 9

The Zero-Based Rebuild

Bridge Target: Operating Earnings Bridge (overhead cost reduction)

Time to Impact: Medium (six to twelve months for full implementation)

The Pattern

The Zero-Based Rebuild redesigns overhead from first principles rather than adjusting from last year's baseline. Traditional budgeting asks what we spent last year and how much more we need. Zero-based budgeting asks what we would spend if we were designing the function today, knowing what we know now.

Most overhead accumulates over time. Headcount grows as the business grows, but rarely shrinks when growth slows. Systems proliferate without rationalization. Processes add steps without removing old ones. The Zero-Based Rebuild cuts through accumulated inefficiency by requiring every expense to justify its existence against current needs, not historical precedent.

This is not across-the-board cost cutting. It is surgical redesign. Some areas may receive more resources. Others may be eliminated entirely. The goal is alignment between spending and value creation, not arbitrary reduction.

The Sacrifice

Management time and organizational disruption during the rebuild process. Workforce reduction with associated severance costs and morale impact. Short-term productivity decline as teams adapt to new structures. Political capital spent forcing difficult decisions.

The Sequence

1. Define the scope. Identify which functions will undergo zero-based review. Common targets include corporate overhead, shared services, administrative functions, and support staff. Exclude direct production costs, which require different approaches.

2. Document current state activities. For each function in scope, catalog every activity performed, the resources consumed, and the output produced. This inventory reveals what people actually do, which often differs from job descriptions.

3. Classify activities by value. Categorize each activity as essential, important, or discretionary. Essential activities are required for operations or compliance. Important activities add value but could be reduced. Discretionary activities could be eliminated without material impact.

4. Benchmark against alternatives. For each function, research external benchmarks: industry peers, best-

in-class operators, and outsourcing alternatives. Understand what is possible, not just what exists.

5. Design the target state. Define what each function would look like if designed from scratch for current needs. Specify staffing levels, organizational structure, and service delivery model. Be aggressive but realistic.

6. Calculate the gap. Quantify the difference between current state and target state in headcount, spending, and capability. Identify specific positions, activities, and expenses to eliminate or add.

7. Plan the transition. Develop implementation plans including timeline, workforce actions, process changes, and technology requirements. Account for severance costs and transition expenses.

8. Execute workforce changes. Implement headcount reductions with appropriate severance, communication, and support. Move quickly once decisions are made. Prolonged uncertainty damages morale more than decisive action.

9. Implement process changes. Redesign workflows to operate with the new structure. Eliminate activities that no longer have owners. Automate where possible.

10. Install controls to prevent regrowth. Establish headcount governance, spending approval requirements, and periodic reviews to prevent costs from creeping back. The rebuild is wasted if discipline does not persist.

Preconditions

The Zero-Based Rebuild works when overhead has grown faster than revenue, when there is meaningful accumulated inefficiency, and when leadership has the will to make difficult decisions. It struggles when the organization is already lean, when workforce reductions would damage critical capability, or when leadership cannot sustain focus through implementation.

The Trap

The primary trap is cutting too deeply in areas that affect revenue or customer experience. Overhead reduction that triggers customer defection or revenue decline destroys more value than it creates. Protect customer-facing and revenue-generating functions.

The second trap is failing to redesign processes before reducing headcount. Eliminating people without eliminating work creates burnout and quality problems. The rebuild must address work design, not just staffing levels.

The Proof

Overhead as percentage of revenue. Tracking showing sustained reduction in overhead ratio.

Headcount productivity metrics. Revenue per employee or similar metrics improving over time.

Service level maintenance. Evidence that customer service and internal support quality did not degrade despite cost reduction.

Variants

Function-Specific Zero-Basing. Apply zero-based methodology to a single function rather than the entire overhead base. Finance, human resources, and information technology are common starting points.

Shared Services Consolidation. Combine duplicate functions across business units into centralized shared services. Capture scale economies while standardizing processes.

Outsourcing Evaluation. Use the zero-based analysis to identify functions better performed by external providers. Compare internal cost to market alternatives.

DISQUALIFIERS: When This Gambit Is Wrong

- The organization is already lean with overhead below industry benchmarks
- Recent restructuring has exhausted organizational capacity for change
- Leadership lacks the will to make and sustain difficult workforce decisions
- Critical capability would be damaged and cannot be rebuilt

If disqualified, consider: Gambit 14 (The Organizational Flattening) for targeted layer removal

GAMBITPLATE **#10**

THE PROCUREMENT CONCENTRATION

BRIDGE: Operating Earnings | **TIME:** 6 months

VALUE MECHANISM

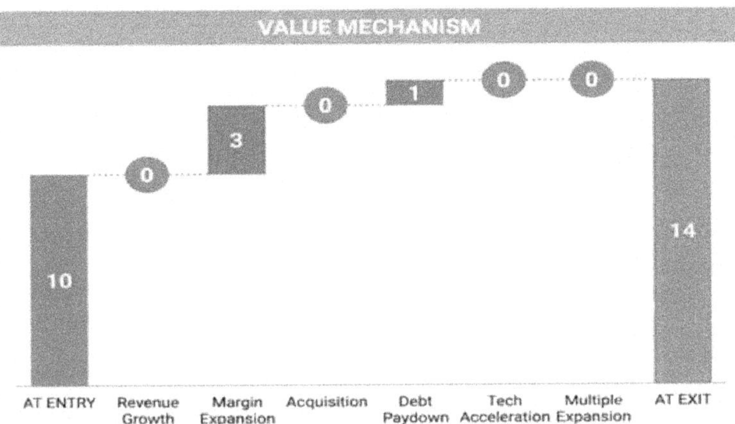

SCORE PANEL

BENEFIT	COST	EASE	RISK	OVERALL:
4	2	4	2	16/20
4/5	2/5	4/5	2/5	Value Score: 80/100

FIELD NOTES

TRIGGERS	PROOF ARTIFACTS	DISQUALIFIERS
• Fragmented supplier base • No volume leverage in purchasing	• Spend analysis by category • Savings from supplier consolidation	• Single-source dependencies • Long-term contracts locked in

Consolidate procurement across categories and suppliers to capture volume discounts, reduce admin cost, and improve terms.

Gambit 10

The Procurement Concentration

Bridge Target: Operating Earnings Bridge (direct cost reduction through purchasing leverage)

Time to Impact: Fast to Medium (three to nine months depending on contract cycles)

The Pattern

The Procurement Concentration consolidates purchasing across fewer suppliers, standardizes specifications, and leverages combined volume to negotiate better terms. Most companies buy the same categories from multiple suppliers at multiple prices with multiple specifications. Concentration eliminates this fragmentation.

The savings potential is often larger than executives expect. Spend fragmentation hides pricing variation, specification bloat, and administrative overhead. When spend is consolidated and made visible, the opportunities become clear. Three to five percent savings on direct materials flows directly to operating earnings.

Concentration requires discipline. Specifications must be standardized, which often meets resistance from engineering or operations. Supplier relationships must be managed strategically, not transactionally. Compliance must be enforced to prevent maverick buying that erodes savings.

The Sacrifice

Reduced flexibility in supplier selection. Potential supply chain risk from concentration. Internal resistance from teams that prefer current suppliers or specifications. Transition costs and effort during consolidation.

The Sequence

1. Build complete spend visibility. Aggregate all purchasing data across the organization. Categorize by commodity, supplier, business unit, and location. Identify total spend by category and the number of suppliers in each.

2. Identify concentration opportunities. Prioritize categories with high spend, multiple suppliers, and price variation. These categories offer the largest savings potential from consolidation.

3. Analyze specification variation. Within each category, examine specification differences across locations or business units. Identify opportunities to standardize without affecting quality or performance.

4. Develop category strategies. For each priority category, define the target state: number of suppliers, specification standards, contract terms, and pricing targets. Balance savings against supply security.

5. Conduct competitive bidding. Use consolidated volume to run competitive processes. Require suppliers to bid on total volume with standardized specifications. Create genuine competition.

6. Negotiate consolidated contracts. Award contracts to selected suppliers with volume commitments, pricing tiers, and performance requirements. Lock in savings through multi-year agreements where appropriate.

7. Implement compliance mechanisms. Create processes to ensure purchasing flows through contracted suppliers at contracted prices. Prevent maverick buying that circumvents negotiated agreements.

8. Monitor supplier performance. Track delivery, quality, and service levels from concentrated suppliers. Address problems quickly before they affect operations.

9. Repeat annually. Procurement concentration is not a one-time event. Review categories annually. Rebid where appropriate. Continuously improve specifications and terms.

Preconditions

The Procurement Concentration works when spend is currently fragmented across multiple suppliers, when specifications vary without operational necessity, and when the organization has the discipline to enforce compliance. It struggles when suppliers have monopoly positions, when specifications cannot be standardized for legitimate reasons, or when internal stakeholders successfully resist consolidation.

The Trap

The primary trap is over-concentration that creates supply chain vulnerability. Reducing to a single supplier for a critical input creates risk. Maintain backup options for essential categories, even if primary volume is concentrated.

The second trap is specification standardization that degrades quality. Not all variation is waste. Some specifications exist for legitimate operational reasons. Test standardization before broad rollout.

The Proof

Unit cost reduction by category. Tracking showing price per unit declining in concentrated categories.

Supplier count reduction. Demonstration of consolidation from many suppliers to few in priority categories.

Contract compliance rates. Evidence that purchasing flows through negotiated contracts rather than maverick channels.

Variants

Group Purchasing Organization. For smaller companies, join group purchasing organizations that aggregate volume across multiple companies to achieve scale that would be impossible alone.

Supplier Partnership Model. For strategic suppliers, move beyond transactional negotiation to partnership arrangements that share risk and reward. Joint improvement programs can generate savings beyond price negotiation.

Indirect Spend Focus. Apply concentration methodology to indirect categories like travel, professional services, and office supplies, which often receive less attention than direct materials.

DISQUALIFIERS: When This Gambit Is Wrong

- Suppliers have monopoly positions with no alternative sources
- Specifications genuinely cannot be standardized without affecting quality
- The organization lacks discipline to enforce compliance after negotiation
- Supply chain risk from concentration outweighs cost savings

If disqualified, consider: Gambit 16 (The Variable Cost Decomposition) for non-procurement cost reduction

GAMBITPLATE **#11**

THE UNIT ECONOMICS REWRITE

BRIDGE: Operating Earnings | **TIME:** 12 months

TRUE TLACK | **VALUE MECHANISM**

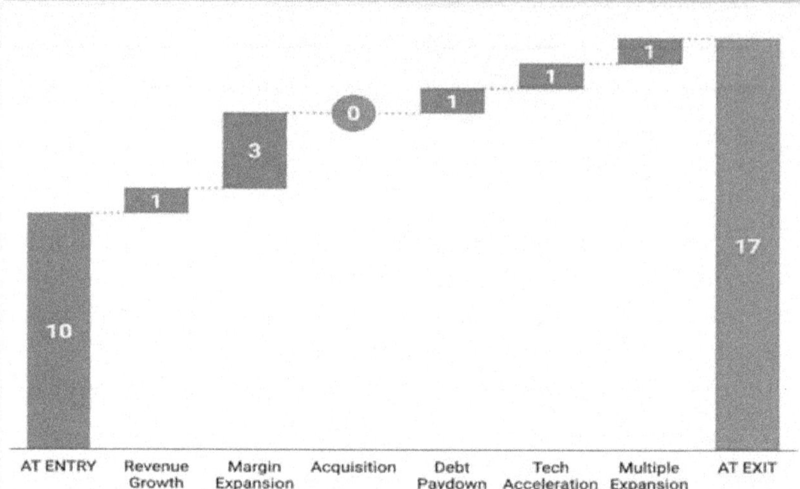

SCORE PANEL | **SCORE PANEL**

BENEFIT	COST	EASE	RISK	OVERALL
5	3	3	2	15/20
5/5	3/5	3/5	2/5	Value Score: 75/100 75/100

FIELD NOTES | **FIELD NOTES**

TRIGGERS

- No product or customer-level profitability data
- Revenue growing but margins compressing

PROOF ARTIFACTS

- Unit economics dashboard by product/customer
- Contribution margin improvement trend

DISQUALIFIERS

- Cost allocation too complex to be meaningful
- Single-product business with clear economics

Create visibility into unit-level economics and optimize contribution margins by product and customer.

Gambit 11

The Unit Economics Rewrite

Bridge Target: Operating Earnings Bridge (margin improvement through contribution margin clarity and optimization)

Time to Impact: Medium (six to twelve months for full visibility and optimization)

The Pattern

The Unit Economics Rewrite establishes contribution margin as the operating truth of the business. Most companies know their overall margins. Few know the contribution margin of each product, customer segment, channel, or transaction type. This gap prevents informed decision-making.

Contribution margin is revenue minus all variable costs directly attributable to that revenue: direct materials, direct labor, commissions, shipping, and transaction costs. It reveals how much each unit of business contributes to covering fixed costs and generating profit. Without this visibility, companies make pricing, mix, and investment decisions in the dark.

The Rewrite builds the visibility and then uses it to drive decisions. Some products or customers that appear profitable become questionable when true variable costs are allocated.

Others that seemed marginal become attractive. The rewrite changes behavior by changing information.

The Sacrifice

Analytical effort to build accurate contribution margin models. Organizational discomfort as sacred cows are revealed as unprofitable. Decision complexity as simple revenue metrics give way to nuanced margin analysis. Potential conflicts with teams whose performance looks worse under contribution margin measurement.

The Sequence

1. Define contribution margin structure. Establish clear definitions for what costs are included in contribution margin calculation. Distinguish between truly variable costs, semi-variable costs, and fixed costs.

2. Build the data infrastructure. Gather cost data at the required granularity. This often requires improving cost accounting systems, allocating costs that were previously unallocated, and creating new reporting structures.

3. Calculate contribution margins by segment. Compute contribution margin for each product line, customer segment, channel, and geography. Rank from highest to lowest margin.

4. Identify the profit pools. Determine which segments generate the majority of contribution. Often a small percentage of products or customers generate most of the profit.

5. Identify the profit drains. Find segments with negative or minimal contribution margin. Determine whether they can be fixed through pricing, cost reduction, or redesign, or whether they should be exited.

6. Embed contribution margin in decisions. Use contribution margin as a primary input for pricing decisions, product development priorities, customer targeting, and capacity allocation.

7. Align incentives to contribution. Incorporate contribution margin metrics into sales compensation, product management objectives, and operational performance measures.

8. Report contribution margin regularly. Build contribution margin into standard reporting. Review at leadership meetings. Make it as visible as revenue.

9. Refine continuously. As the business changes, update contribution margin calculations. Validate assumptions. Improve data quality. The model should become more accurate over time.

Preconditions

The Unit Economics Rewrite works when the organization lacks contribution margin visibility, when there is meaningful variation in profitability across segments, and when leadership will use the information to make difficult decisions. It struggles when cost allocation is too complex to be accurate, when all segments have similar margins, or when leadership is unwilling to act on unfavorable findings.

The Trap

The primary trap is false precision. Contribution margin calculations require assumptions and allocations that may not be accurate. Do not treat calculated margins as absolute truth. Use them as directional guidance while acknowledging their limitations.

The second trap is ignoring strategic considerations. Some low-margin business may be strategically important: entry points for expansion, competitive blocking, or relationship anchors. Contribution margin should inform decisions, not dictate them.

The Proof

Contribution margin visibility. Demonstration that contribution margin is now calculated and reported at granular levels.

Decisions influenced by contribution data. Examples of pricing, mix, or investment decisions that changed based on contribution margin analysis.

Overall margin improvement. Evidence that blended contribution margin improved as a result of informed decision-making.

Variants

Customer Profitability Analysis. Focus specifically on contribution margin by customer. Include cost-to-serve elements like support, customization, and payment terms.

Transaction-Level Economics. For businesses with high transaction volumes, calculate contribution margin at the transaction level. Identify transaction types that destroy value.

Lifetime Value Integration. Combine transaction contribution margin with customer lifetime value analysis. Some low-margin initial transactions may be justified by high-margin follow-on business.

DISQUALIFIERS: When This Gambit Is Wrong

- Cost allocation is too complex or arbitrary to produce reliable results
- All segments have similar contribution margins within five percentage points
- Leadership is unwilling to act on unfavorable findings about "sacred cow" products or customers
- Data systems cannot support the required granularity

If disqualified, consider: Gambit 2 (The Mix Elevator) using available segment data

GAMBITPLATE **#12**

THE THROUGHPUT UNLOCK

BRIDGE: Operating Earnings | **TIME:** 12 months

VALUE MECHANISM

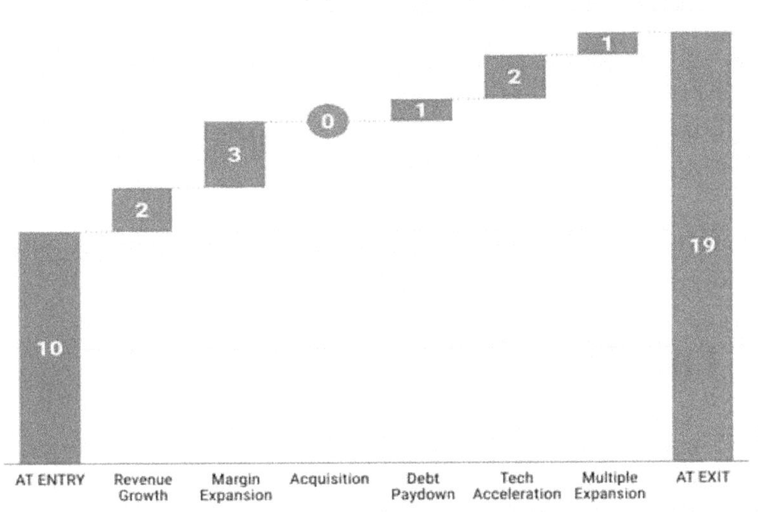

SCORE PANEL

BENEFIT	COST	EASE	RISK	OVERALL
4	3	3	2	14/20
4/5	3/5	3/5	2/5	Value Score: 70/100

FIELD NOTES

TRIGGERS

- Capacity utilization below 70%
- Bottlenecks limit output despite demand

PROOF ARTIFACTS

- Capacity utilization improvement documented
- Output per labor hour trending upward

DISQUALIFIERS

- Demand is the constraint, not capacity
- Capital investment required exceeds returns

Remove bottlenecks and improve cycle times to increase throughput with existing assets.

Gambit 12

The Throughput Unlock

Bridge Target: Operating Earnings Bridge (margin improvement through capacity utilization and cycle time reduction)

Time to Impact: Medium (six to eighteen months depending on operational complexity)

The Pattern

The Throughput Unlock increases output from existing capacity by improving utilization, reducing cycle time, and enhancing yield. Most operations have hidden capacity trapped by bottlenecks, variability, and inefficiency. Unlocking this capacity generates additional revenue without proportional cost increase.

Throughput improvement is particularly powerful because it creates operating leverage. The fixed cost base is already absorbed. Incremental output flows largely to margin. A facility running at seventy percent utilization has different economics than one running at eighty-five percent.

The Unlock combines three levers: increasing the time equipment or people are productively engaged, reducing the time required to complete each unit of work, and reducing waste and rework that consume capacity without producing output.

The Sacrifice

Investment in process improvement capability and tools. Operational disruption during improvement initiatives. Potential capital expenditure for debottlenecking. Management attention diverted from other priorities.

The Sequence

1. Measure current throughput. Establish baseline metrics for output, utilization, cycle time, and yield. Understand where the operation stands before attempting improvement.

2. Identify the constraint. Find the bottleneck that limits overall throughput. The constraint may be a machine, a process step, a skill, or a policy. Everything else is secondary until the constraint is addressed.

3. Analyze constraint utilization. Determine how much time the constraint is productively engaged versus waiting, changing over, or down. The gap represents immediate opportunity.

4. Maximize constraint availability. Reduce downtime through preventive maintenance, faster changeovers, and buffer management. Every minute of lost constraint time is lost throughput.

5. Reduce cycle time at the constraint. Find ways to complete work faster at the bottleneck: process improvement, automation, tooling, or method changes. Faster cycles mean more output per hour.

6. Improve yield. Reduce scrap, rework, and quality failures that consume constraint capacity without producing good output. Every defective unit wastes constraint time.

7. Subordinate non-constraints. Ensure that operations before and after the constraint support maximum constraint throughput. Non-constraints should neither starve nor flood the bottleneck.

8. Elevate if necessary. If the constraint cannot be sufficiently improved, consider investment to add capacity: additional equipment, additional shifts, or additional facilities.

9. Repeat the cycle. Once a constraint is improved, a new constraint emerges elsewhere. Continuous improvement means continuously finding and addressing the next bottleneck.

Preconditions

The Throughput Unlock works when current utilization is below practical capacity, when there is demand for additional output, and when operational capability exists to implement improvements. It struggles when the operation is already near maximum practical capacity, when demand is insufficient to absorb additional output, or when improvement capability is weak.

The Trap

The primary trap is improving non-constraints. Resources spent improving operations that are not the bottleneck do not increase overall throughput. Focus ruthlessly on the constraint.

The second trap is increasing throughput without corresponding demand. Additional capacity without customers to buy the output creates inventory, not profit. Align throughput improvement with commercial capability.

The Proof

Throughput increase. Measurement of output increase from the same asset base.

Utilization improvement. Tracking showing higher percentage of available time productively engaged.

Unit cost reduction. Demonstration that cost per unit declined as fixed costs spread over more output.

Variants

Service Throughput. Apply throughput thinking to service operations. The constraint may be skilled staff, appointment availability, or processing capacity.

Quick Changeover Focus. When changeover time is the primary constraint driver, apply single-minute exchange of die methodology to dramatically reduce setup time.

Yield Improvement Program. When quality issues consume significant capacity, focus specifically on reducing defects through root cause analysis and process control.

DISQUALIFIERS: When This Gambit Is Wrong

- Operations are already at or near maximum practical capacity
- Demand is insufficient to absorb additional output
- The constraint is external (customer orders, regulatory limits) not internal
- No operational improvement capability exists to implement changes

If disqualified, consider: Gambit 15 (The Footprint Rationalization) to right-size capacity to demand

GAMBITPLATE #13

THE SERVICE MODEL SURGERY

BRIDGE: Operating Earnings

TIME: 12 months

VALUE MECHANISM

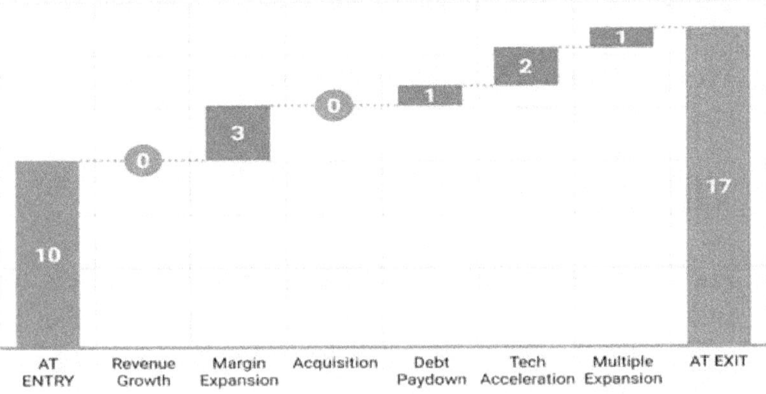

SCORE PANEL

BENEFIT	COST	EASE	RISK	OVERALL
4	3	3	3	13/20
4/5	3/5	3/5	3/5	65/100

FIELD NOTES

TRIGGERS

- Same service level for all customers regardless of value
- High-touch service for low-margin accounts

PROOF ARTIFACTS

- Cost-to-serve by segment documented
- Service cost ratio declining

DISQUALIFIERS

- Contractual service commitments prevent changes
- Service differentiation would damage brand

Align service levels to customer value, reducing cost-to-serve for low-value segments.

Gambit 13

The Service Model Surgery

Bridge Target: Operating Earnings Bridge (cost reduction through service level optimization by segment)

Time to Impact: Medium (six to twelve months for redesign and implementation)

The Pattern

The Service Model Surgery aligns service levels with customer profitability. Most companies provide the same service to all customers regardless of what they pay. High-value customers receive the same response time, customization, and attention as low-value customers. This is expensive and often unnecessary.

The Surgery creates differentiated service tiers matched to customer value. High-value customers receive premium service that reinforces their loyalty. Low-value customers receive efficient service that protects margin. Resources shift from over-serving unprofitable accounts to appropriately serving profitable ones.

This gambit requires courage. Reducing service to any customer feels risky. But undifferentiated service is often invisible to customers while being highly visible to cost structures. Thoughtful differentiation can improve profitability without damaging satisfaction.

The Sacrifice

Risk of customer dissatisfaction in segments receiving reduced service. Complexity of managing multiple service tiers. Internal resistance from service teams accustomed to uniform treatment. Potential for mistakes in customer tier classification.

The Sequence

1. Segment customers by profitability. Use contribution margin analysis to classify customers into profitability tiers. Include cost-to-serve in the calculation.

2. Document current service levels. Catalog all service elements: response time, delivery frequency, return policies, customization, support access, and dedicated resources. Understand what is currently provided.

3. Analyze cost-to-serve variation. Calculate the cost of providing each service element. Identify which elements drive significant cost and which are relatively inexpensive.

4. Design tiered service model. Create distinct service levels for different customer tiers. Define which elements are included at each level. Ensure premium tiers are genuinely valuable.

5. Model financial impact. Calculate the cost savings from reducing service to lower tiers and the cost of enhancing service to higher tiers. Ensure net impact is positive.

6. Test with pilot segments. Implement the new model with selected customer groups before broad rollout. Monitor satisfaction and retention closely.

7. Communicate changes appropriately. For customers whose service is enhanced, communicate the improvement. For customers whose service is reduced, manage the transition carefully or offer upgrade options.

8. Train service teams. Ensure service staff understand the new model, the rationale, and how to execute it. Provide tools to identify customer tiers quickly.

9. Monitor and adjust. Track satisfaction by tier, retention by tier, and cost-to-serve by tier. Adjust service definitions based on results.

Preconditions

The Service Model Surgery works when there is meaningful variation in customer profitability, when service cost is a significant expense, and when the organization can execute differentiated service consistently. It struggles when customers have similar profitability, when service is already minimal, or when systems cannot support tiered treatment.

The Trap

The primary trap is reducing service to customers who will then leave. Some customers are price-sensitive. Others are service-sensitive. Cutting service to service-sensitive customers triggers churn that exceeds the savings. Segment carefully.

The second trap is creating tiers so complex that service teams cannot execute consistently. Simplicity is essential. If frontline staff cannot quickly determine a customer's tier and applicable service level, the model breaks down.

The Proof

Cost-to-serve reduction. Measurement of service cost declining, particularly for lower-tier customers.

Retention maintenance. Evidence that customer retention did not degrade despite service changes.

High-tier satisfaction. Demonstration that premium customers are satisfied with enhanced service.

Variants

Self-Service Migration. Move lower-tier customers to self-service channels while maintaining high-touch for premium accounts.

Response Time Tiering. Differentiate primarily through response time: same-day for premium, next-day for standard, scheduled for basic.

Dedicated Resource Allocation. Assign dedicated account managers or support staff to top-tier customers while serving others through pooled resources.

DISQUALIFIERS: When This Gambit Is Wrong

- Customer profitability does not vary meaningfully across the base
- Service is already at minimum viable levels for all customers
- Systems cannot identify customer tiers or support differentiated treatment
- Contract terms require uniform service levels

If disqualified, consider: Gambit 11 (The Unit Economics Rewrite) to first establish profitability visibility

GAMBITPLATE #14

THE ORGANIZATIONAL FLATTENING

BRIDGE: Operating Earnings **TIME:** 6 months

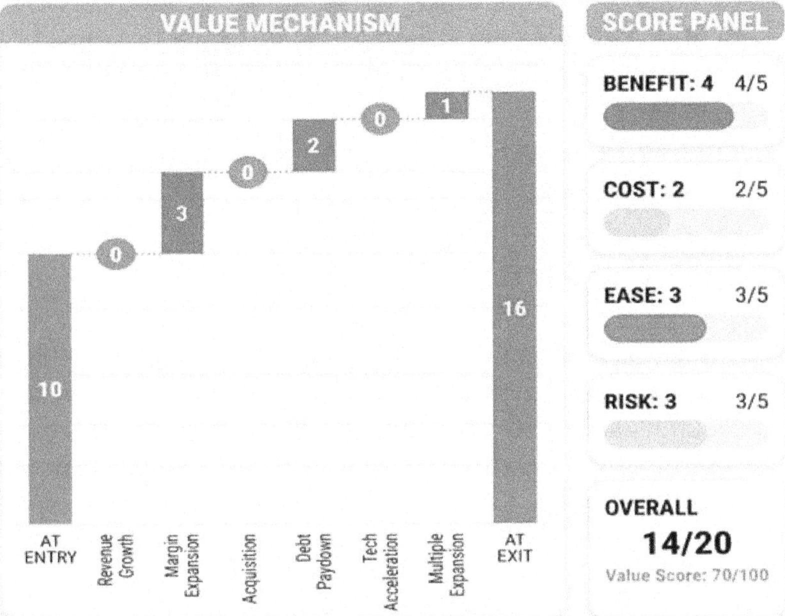

FIELD NOTES

TRIGGERS:
- More than seven layers from CEO to front line
- Span of control below five direct reports

PROOF ARTIFACTS:
- Layer count reduction documented
- Management headcount and cost reduction

DISQUALIFIERS:
- Organization already flat with wide spans
- Regulatory requirements mandate certain roles

Reduce management layers and increase spans of control for efficiency and speed.

Gambit 14

The Organizational Flattening

Bridge Target: Operating Earnings Bridge (overhead cost reduction and decision velocity improvement)

Time to Impact: Fast to Medium (three to nine months for implementation)

The Pattern

The Organizational Flattening removes management layers that add cost without adding value. Most organizations accumulate layers over time. Each layer adds salary cost, coordination overhead, and decision delay. Flattening increases spans of control, reduces cost, and speeds execution.

The typical organization has too many managers managing too few people. Spans of control of three or four are common when eight or ten are feasible. Each narrow span requires an additional layer to reach scale, multiplying the management overhead.

Flattening is not about eliminating management. It is about eliminating unnecessary management. The test is whether a layer adds value: does it improve decisions, develop people, or coordinate work that could not otherwise be coordinated? Layers that merely transmit information or review work that does not need review are candidates for elimination.

The Sacrifice

Workforce reduction with associated severance and morale impact. Increased burden on remaining managers. Loss of career progression paths that relied on upward movement through layers. Short-term disruption during reorganization.

The Sequence

1. Map current organizational structure. Document all reporting relationships. Calculate spans of control at each level. Identify the total number of layers from chief executive to frontline.

2. Benchmark against targets. Research appropriate spans of control for different functions. Set targets: typically six to ten for most functions, higher for standardized roles, lower for complex or developmental roles.

3. Identify layers that can be eliminated. Analyze each layer to determine what value it adds. Flag layers that primarily transmit information, review work without adding insight, or coordinate activities that could be coordinated differently.

4. Design target structure. Create the future organizational structure with appropriate spans and fewer layers. Ensure the structure can function effectively at the new configuration.

5. Identify affected positions. Determine which specific positions will be eliminated. Develop plans for each affected individual: redeployment to open positions, severance, or transition support.

6. Prepare remaining managers. Ensure managers who will have larger spans are ready for the increased responsibility. Provide training, tools, and support as needed.

7. Execute the reorganization. Announce and implement changes quickly once decisions are made. Prolonged uncertainty is more damaging than decisive action.

8. Redistribute work and authority. Ensure that work previously done by eliminated layers is either eliminated or clearly assigned to remaining roles. Push decision authority down where appropriate.

9. Monitor and stabilize. Watch for signs of overload or dysfunction in the new structure. Adjust as needed during the stabilization period.

Preconditions

The Organizational Flattening works when spans of control are narrow, when multiple layers exist between top and bottom of the organization, and when remaining managers have capacity for larger spans. It struggles when spans are already wide, when management layers perform essential coordination, or when talent depth is insufficient to handle increased responsibility.

The Trap

The primary trap is eliminating managers who performed essential coordination. Some management work is invisible but critical. Removing it causes operational problems that exceed the cost savings. Understand what managers actually do before eliminating positions.

The second trap is creating spans so wide that managers cannot perform effectively. There are practical limits to how many people one person can manage. Exceeding those limits degrades performance and burns out managers.

The Proof

Management cost reduction. Measurement of management headcount and cost declining.

Layer count reduction. Demonstration that the organization has fewer layers from top to bottom.

Decision velocity improvement. Evidence that decisions move faster through the flattened structure.

Variants

Function-Specific Flattening. Apply flattening to specific functions rather than organization-wide. Sales, operations, and finance are common starting points.

Title Compression. Reduce title proliferation that creates artificial layers. Consolidate multiple director levels into fewer. Eliminate titles that exist for status rather than function.

Player-Coach Model. Convert pure management roles into player-coach roles where managers carry individual contributor responsibilities alongside team leadership.

DISQUALIFIERS: When This Gambit Is Wrong

- Spans of control are already at eight or above across most functions
- Management layers perform essential coordination that cannot be eliminated
- Talent depth is insufficient for remaining managers to absorb larger spans
- Recent restructuring has exhausted organizational change capacity

If disqualified, consider: Gambit 9 (The Zero-Based Rebuild) for non-headcount overhead reduction

---

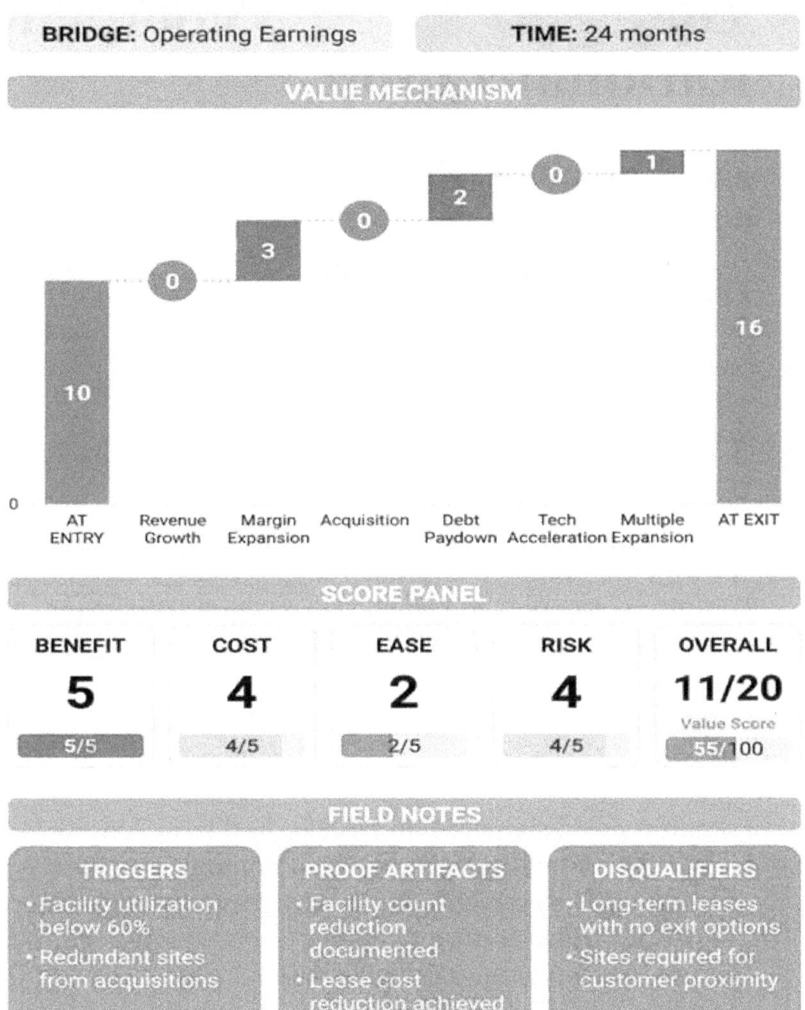

Consolidate facilities and exit underutilized sites to reduce fixed costs.

Gambit 15

The Footprint Rationalization

Bridge Target: Operating Earnings Bridge (fixed cost reduction through facilities and network optimization)

Time to Impact: Long (twelve to twenty-four months for full implementation due to lease terms and transition complexity)

The Pattern

The Footprint Rationalization optimizes the physical network of facilities, warehouses, branches, and offices. Footprints accumulate through acquisition, expansion, and historical circumstance. Rarely are they designed holistically. Rationalization applies network design principles to reduce cost while maintaining or improving service.

Footprint cost is largely fixed in the short term. Once a lease is signed or a facility built, the cost continues regardless of utilization. This creates inertia that prevents optimization. The Rationalization overcomes this inertia through systematic analysis and decisive action.

The opportunity often exceeds expectations. Companies that have grown through acquisition commonly have overlapping service territories, redundant facilities, and subscale locations that exist for historical reasons. Cleaning up this legacy releases significant cost.

The Sacrifice

One-time costs for facility closure, relocation, and lease termination. Workforce displacement in affected locations. Short-term service disruption during transition. Community and political impact from facility closures.

The Sequence

1. Inventory current footprint. Catalog all facilities: locations, sizes, functions, lease terms, and costs. Create a comprehensive view of the physical network.

2. Analyze utilization. Measure how effectively each facility is used. Identify underutilized space, redundant capabilities, and subscale operations.

3. Model service requirements. Understand what the network must deliver: customer proximity, delivery time, response capability. These requirements constrain network design.

4. Design optimal network. Using service requirements as constraints, design the minimum-cost network that meets needs. This is often dramatically different from the current network.

5. Calculate transition economics. Model the one-time costs of moving from current to optimal network: lease terminations, moving costs, severance, and capital investment. Compare to ongoing savings.

6. Sequence the transition. Determine the order of facility actions based on lease expiration, operational

dependency, and transition complexity. Create a multi-year roadmap.

7. Execute lease negotiations. For facilities to be closed or downsized, negotiate lease terminations, sublets, or early exits. Timing leverage varies; capture opportunities when they arise.

8. Manage workforce transitions. For affected employees, determine relocation options, severance packages, and transition support. Execute with respect and professionalism.

9. Monitor service levels. Track service quality during and after transition. Address issues quickly to prevent customer impact.

Preconditions

The Footprint Rationalization works when the current network is suboptimal due to acquisition history or organic growth, when service requirements can be met with fewer or different facilities, and when lease flexibility exists or can be negotiated. It struggles when the network is already optimized, when service requirements genuinely require current locations, or when lease obligations prevent action.

The Trap

The primary trap is underestimating service impact. Network changes that look efficient on paper may degrade customer experience. Test assumptions about service requirements before committing to closures.

The second trap is underestimating transition costs. Facility closures involve many hidden expenses: equipment moves, system transitions, customer notification, and productivity losses during transition. Model costs conservatively.

The Proof

Facility count and cost reduction. Measurement of facilities closed and associated cost savings.

Utilization improvement. Evidence that remaining facilities operate at higher utilization.

Service level maintenance. Demonstration that customer service metrics did not degrade during or after rationalization.

Variants

Hub and Spoke Conversion. Consolidate full-service facilities into central hubs with smaller satellite locations for customer access.

Remote Work Transition. For office-based functions, shift to remote work arrangements that reduce or eliminate office footprint.

Third-Party Network. Replace owned or leased facilities with third-party logistics, shared workspaces, or partner locations.

DISQUALIFIERS: When This Gambit Is Wrong

- The network is already optimized with no redundancy or underutilization
- Service requirements genuinely require current facility locations
- Lease obligations prevent action for the foreseeable future
- Workforce displacement costs and risks exceed potential savings

If disqualified, consider: Gambit 12 (The Throughput Unlock) to improve utilization within current footprint

GAMBITPLATE **#16**

THE VARIABLE COST DECOMPOSITION

BRIDGE: Operating Earnings **TIME:** 12 months

VALUE MECHANISM

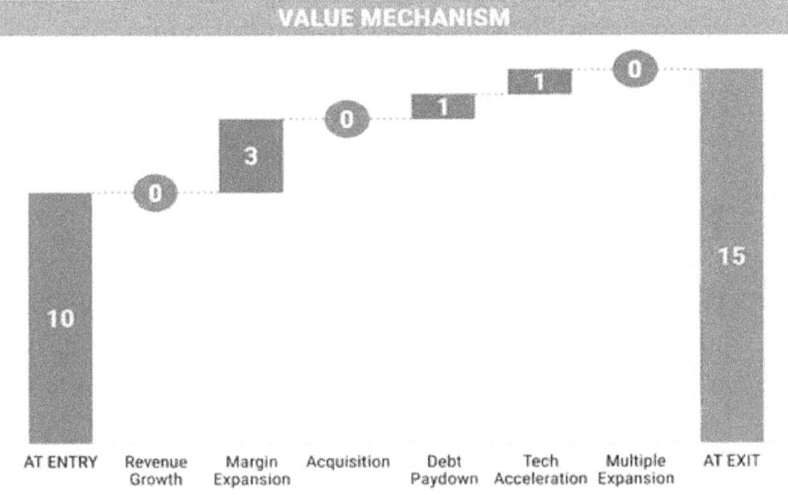

SCORE PANEL

BENEFIT	COST	EASE	RISK	OVERALL
4	2	3	2	15/20
4/5	2/5	3/5	2/5	Value Score: 75/100

FIELD NOTES

TRIGGERS
- Gross margin below industry benchmarks
- No visibility into COGS components

PROOF ARTIFACTS
- COGS decomposition dashboard
- Gross margin expansion documented

DISQUALIFIERS
- Already at best-in-class gross margins
- Commodity inputs with no control over pricing

Break down variable costs into components and optimize each element systematically.

Gambit 16

The Variable Cost Decomposition

Bridge Target: Operating Earnings Bridge (gross margin improvement through direct cost optimization)

Time to Impact: Medium (six to twelve months for systematic improvement)

The Pattern

The Variable Cost Decomposition breaks down direct costs into their component drivers and optimizes each systematically. Variable costs, including materials, direct labor, and production-related expenses, often represent the largest share of total cost. Small percentage improvements generate significant absolute savings.

Most companies manage variable costs at an aggregate level. They track total materials cost or total labor cost. The Decomposition drills deeper: material by component, labor by activity, scrap by source, yield by process step. This granularity reveals specific opportunities that aggregate analysis misses.

The Decomposition follows a simple logic: understand exactly where cost is incurred, identify why it is incurred at that level, and find ways to reduce it without affecting output. This requires data, analysis, and operational discipline. The reward is sustainable gross margin improvement.

The Sacrifice

Analytical effort to build detailed cost visibility. Operational focus on cost management that may distract from other priorities. Investment in measurement systems and process controls. Potential resistance from operations teams accustomed to current methods.

The Sequence

1. Build component-level cost visibility. Break down variable costs to the lowest practical level: individual materials, labor categories, process steps, and cost drivers. Create a detailed cost map.

2. Identify cost drivers. For each cost component, understand what drives the cost: input prices, consumption rates, efficiency levels, or waste rates. Trace costs to their root causes.

3. Benchmark against standards. For each cost component, establish what the cost should be based on engineering standards, historical best performance, or external benchmarks. Quantify the gap between actual and standard.

4. Prioritize improvement opportunities. Rank cost reduction opportunities by magnitude and feasibility. Focus on the largest gaps that can be closed with available capability.

5. Develop specific improvement plans. For each priority area, create an action plan with specific initiatives, owners, timelines, and targets. Convert analysis into action.

6. Implement material cost reductions. For material components, pursue specification optimization, supplier negotiation, waste reduction, and alternative sourcing.

7. Implement labor efficiency improvements. For labor components, pursue process improvement, training, automation, and scheduling optimization.

8. Reduce scrap and waste. Identify sources of scrap, rework, and yield loss. Implement controls and process improvements to reduce waste rates.

9. Install ongoing tracking. Build reporting that tracks variable cost performance against standards. Review variances regularly. Hold operations accountable for cost performance.

10. Establish continuous improvement rhythm. Make variable cost improvement an ongoing discipline, not a one-time project. Set annual improvement targets. Refresh standards as performance improves.

Preconditions

The Variable Cost Decomposition works when variable costs are significant, when cost data can be captured at the required granularity, and when operational capability exists to implement improvements. It struggles when variable costs are already optimized, when data systems cannot support detailed analysis, or when operations lack improvement capability.

The Trap

The primary trap is reducing cost at the expense of quality. Cost improvements that increase defects, reduce reliability, or damage customer experience destroy more value than they create. Monitor quality closely during cost reduction.

The second trap is analysis without action. Detailed cost decomposition is intellectually satisfying but worthless without execution. Ensure analytical work translates quickly into improvement initiatives.

The Proof

Gross margin improvement. Tracking showing gross margin percentage increasing through variable cost reduction.

Variance to standard reduction. Demonstration that actual costs are closer to standards over time.

Waste and scrap reduction. Measurement of scrap rates, rework rates, or yield improving.

Variants

Bill of Materials Optimization. Focus specifically on direct materials through specification review, standardization, and value engineering.

Labor Standards Program. Establish engineered labor standards for all major activities. Track performance to standard. Identify and address gaps.

Yield Improvement Initiative. Focus specifically on first-pass yield and total yield through quality at the source, process control, and root cause analysis.

DISQUALIFIERS: When This Gambit Is Wrong

- Variable costs are already at or near theoretical minimum
- Data systems cannot support the required cost granularity
- Operations lack the improvement capability to act on findings
- Quality is already at minimum acceptable levels and cannot absorb further pressure

If disqualified, consider: Gambit 10 (The Procurement Concentration) for supplier-side cost reduction

SECTION C

STRATEGIC ACQUISITION GAMBITS

Gambits 17 through 22

Acquisitions are the highest-leverage and highest-risk arena of value creation. The six gambits in this section address the primary sources of inorganic value: platform consolidation, category expansion, synergy capture, commercial integration, capability addition, and operational standardization.

Each gambit targets both the operating earnings bridge through synergy capture and the enterprise value bridge through scale, quality improvement, and multiple expansion. Acquisition gambits require exceptional execution discipline. The value is created in integration, not in deal-making. Select the gambits that match your acquisition thesis and invest heavily in integration capability.

GAMBITPLATE **#17**

THE PLATFORM ROLL-UP

BRIDGE: Enterprise Value **TIME:** 36 months

VALUE MECHANISM

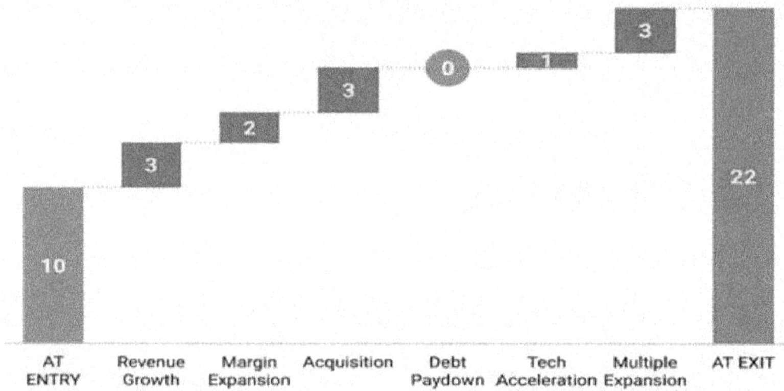

SCORE PANEL

BENEFIT	COST	EASE	RISK	OVERALL
5	5	2	4	10/20
5/5	5/5	2/5	4/5	Value Score: 50/100

FIELD NOTES

TRIGGERS

- Fragmented market with consolidation opportunity
- Platform has integration capability

PROOF ARTIFACTS

- Completed acquisitions with documented synergies
- Integration playbook with proven results

DISQUALIFIERS

- No integration capability or track record
- Market already consolidated

Acquire and integrate smaller competitors to build scale and capture synergies.

Gambit 17

The Platform Roll-Up

Bridge Target: Operating Earnings Bridge (scale economies and synergy capture) and Enterprise Value Bridge (multiple expansion through size and professionalization)

Time to Impact: Long (eighteen to thirty-six months for meaningful consolidation)

The Pattern

The Platform Roll-Up consolidates a fragmented industry by acquiring multiple smaller competitors and integrating them into a single, larger entity. Small companies in fragmented markets often trade at lower multiples than larger, more professional platforms. The roll-up captures this multiple arbitrage while building scale economies that smaller competitors cannot achieve.

Roll-ups work when the industry structure supports consolidation: many small players, limited differentiation, customers who value scale and reliability, and synergy potential from combining operations. The platform provides the management team, systems infrastructure, and integration capability to absorb acquisitions efficiently.

The value creation comes from three sources: operating synergies that improve margins, revenue synergies that accelerate growth, and multiple expansion as the combined entity becomes more attractive to buyers. Each acquisition should be accretive on at least one dimension, with the best acquisitions contributing on all three.

The Sacrifice

Management bandwidth consumed by acquisition and integration. Capital deployed for acquisitions rather than organic investment. Integration risk with each transaction. Execution complexity that increases with each additional acquisition. Cultural challenges combining multiple organizations.

The Sequence

1. Establish the platform. Ensure the initial platform company has strong management, scalable systems, and integration capability before pursuing acquisitions. The platform is the foundation for everything that follows.

2. Define acquisition criteria. Establish clear criteria for target selection: size range, geographic fit, customer overlap, cultural compatibility, and valuation parameters. Disciplined criteria prevent opportunistic acquisitions that do not fit.

3. Build the pipeline. Develop a systematic pipeline of acquisition targets. Cultivate relationships with owners before they are ready to sell. The best acquisitions often come from proprietary sourcing rather than competitive processes.

4. Execute disciplined diligence. Apply consistent diligence processes to each target. Validate synergy assumptions. Identify integration risks. Price

acquisitions to generate returns even if synergies underperform.

5. Develop standardized integration playbooks. Create repeatable integration processes for key functions: finance, operations, sales, and human resources. Each acquisition should follow the established playbook with targeted customization.

6. Capture synergies aggressively. Begin integration planning before close. Execute synergy capture in the first hundred days. Track synergy realization against the deal model. Do not let integration drift.

7. Maintain acquisition velocity. The roll-up benefits from momentum. Complete multiple acquisitions per year during the active consolidation phase. Build organizational muscle for continuous acquisition.

8. Professionalize the combined entity. As scale grows, invest in professional systems, reporting, and governance. Transform the combined entity from a collection of small businesses into an institutional platform.

9. Build the exit narrative. Document the transformation story: fragmented industry consolidated, synergies captured, professional platform built. The narrative justifies premium exit valuation.

Preconditions

The Platform Roll-Up works when the industry is genuinely fragmented with many potential targets, when consolidation creates real synergies, when the platform has strong integration capability, and when capital is available for acquisitions. It struggles when the industry has already consolidated, when synergies are theoretical rather than achievable, or when integration capability is weak.

The Trap

The primary trap is acquisition addiction. The pursuit of growth through acquisition can become a substitute for organic improvement. Some roll-ups keep acquiring to mask underlying performance problems. Each acquisition must stand on its own merits, not just add revenue.

The second trap is integration failure. Acquiring companies is easier than integrating them. Roll-ups that accumulate acquisitions without integrating them become holding companies, not platforms. They forfeit the synergies that justify consolidation and often trade at discounts rather than premiums.

The Proof

Synergy realization tracking. Documentation showing synergies captured as a percentage of synergies projected in deal models. Target Level 4 evidence with verified financial results.

Pro forma margin improvement. Evidence that acquired companies improved margins after integration.

Platform professionalization metrics. Demonstration of institutional capability: standardized systems, professional reporting, governance maturity.

Variants

Regional Consolidation. Focus roll-up on a specific geography to build regional density and market leadership before expanding.

Vertical Roll-Up. Combine horizontal consolidation with vertical integration, acquiring suppliers or customers to capture additional margin.

Founder Succession Strategy. Target companies with aging founders seeking succession solutions. These sellers often accept lower valuations for the right cultural fit and transition support.

DISQUALIFIERS: When This Gambit Is Wrong

- The industry has already consolidated with few remaining targets
- The platform lacks integration capability to absorb acquisitions
- Synergy projections are theoretical with no credible path to capture
- Capital availability or debt capacity is insufficient for acquisition program

If disqualified, consider: Gambit 4 (The Expansion Loop) for organic growth within existing base

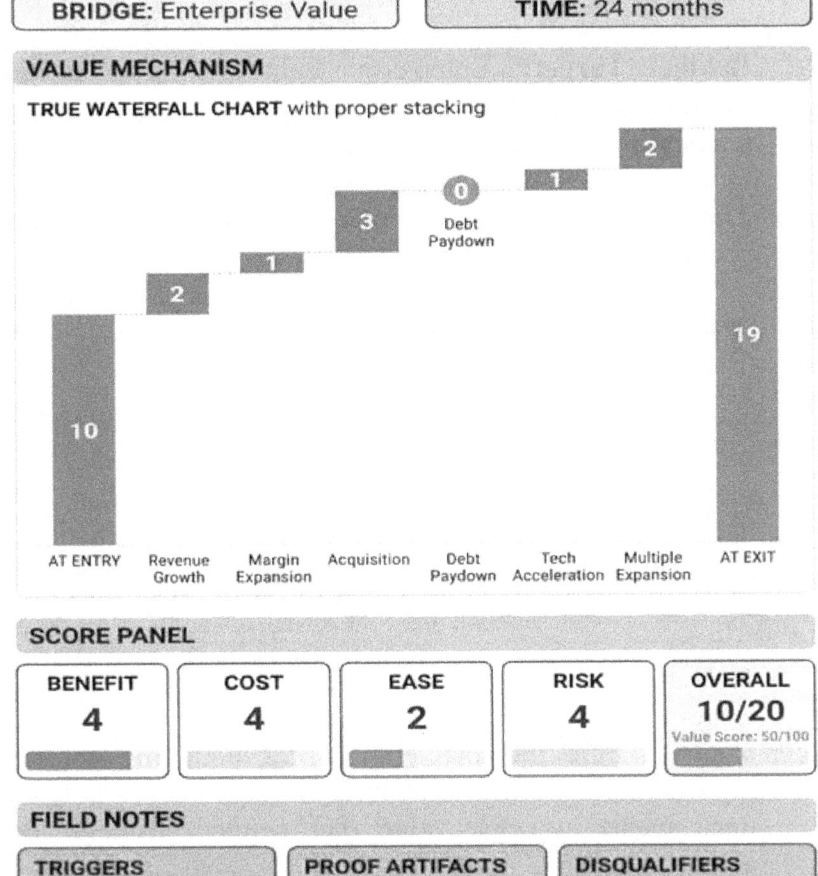
GAMBITPLATE
#18
THE ADJACENCY EXPANSION
BRIDGE: Enterprise Value
TIME: 24 months
VALUE MECHANISM
TRUE WATERFALL CHART with proper stacking
10
2
1
3
0
Debt Paydown
1
2
19
AT ENTRY
Revenue Growth
Margin Expansion
Acquisition
Debt Paydown
Tech Acceleration
Multiple Expansion
AT EXIT
SCORE PANEL
BENEFIT 4
COST 4
EASE 2
RISK 4
OVERALL 10/20
Value Score: 50/100
FIELD NOTES
TRIGGERS
• Core market growth slowing
• Customers requesting adjacent capabilities
PROOF ARTIFACTS
• Adjacent revenue as percent of total growing
• Cross-sell success between core and adjacent
DISQUALIFIERS
• No natural adjacency to current business
• Adjacent market requires different capabilities
Expand into adjacent categories through acquisition to reposition strategically

Gambit 18

The Adjacency Expansion

Bridge Target: Enterprise Value Bridge (category expansion and multiple improvement through strategic repositioning)

Time to Impact: Long (twelve to twenty-four months for acquisition and integration)

The Pattern

The Adjacency Expansion acquires into higher-multiple categories that are adjacent to the current business. Some industries trade at structurally higher multiples than others due to growth rates, recurring revenue characteristics, or strategic attractiveness. Acquiring into these categories can shift how the combined business is perceived and valued.

The adjacency must be genuine. The target should share customers, capabilities, or market position with the core business. Pure financial engineering, acquiring unrelated high-multiple businesses, rarely works. The combination must create strategic value that neither business could achieve alone.

Common adjacency patterns include: product companies acquiring services capabilities, hardware businesses acquiring software elements, and transactional businesses acquiring recurring revenue streams. Each pattern shifts the business toward characteristics that buyers value more highly.

The Sacrifice

Premium valuations for targets in attractive categories. Execution risk when entering new business models. Management stretch across diverse operations. Integration challenges when business models differ significantly.

The Sequence

1. Identify attractive adjacent categories. Analyze categories adjacent to the current business. Evaluate multiple differentials, growth rates, and strategic rationale for combination. Prioritize categories with the strongest value creation logic.

2. Define the strategic rationale. Articulate clearly why the adjacency creates value. What can the combined business do that neither could do alone? The rationale must be compelling enough to justify premium valuations.

3. Source appropriate targets. Identify companies in the target category that fit strategically and can be acquired at acceptable valuations. The best targets combine category attractiveness with reasonable entry price.

4. Validate the combination logic. Through diligence, test whether the strategic rationale holds. Will customers value the combination? Can operations be integrated? Will key talent stay?

5. Execute the acquisition. Complete the transaction with appropriate integration planning. Communicate

the strategic vision to employees, customers, and stakeholders.

6. Integrate to realize synergies. Capture the cross-business synergies that justify the combination. Create the integrated offering. Demonstrate to customers the value of the expanded capability.

7. Grow the adjacent business. After integration, invest in growing the adjacent capability. The adjacency should become a meaningful portion of the combined business, not just a minor addition.

8. Reposition the company narrative. Update how the company describes itself. Emphasize the characteristics of the higher-multiple category. Train investors and potential acquirers to see the business differently.

9. Build proof of the new model. Generate metrics demonstrating success in the adjacent category: growth rates, retention, and profitability. Build the evidence base for re-rating.

Preconditions

The Adjacency Expansion works when a genuine strategic connection exists between the current and target categories, when the target category trades at meaningfully higher multiples, and when the organization can operate successfully in the new category. It struggles when the adjacency is forced, when multiple differentials are too small to matter, or when the business lacks capability in the new area.

The Trap

The primary trap is paying too much for category entry. High-multiple categories attract premium valuations. Overpaying eliminates the value creation potential regardless of strategic fit. Maintain valuation discipline even when pursuing attractive categories.

The second trap is failing to grow the adjacency. Acquiring a small presence in an attractive category does not transform valuation. The adjacent business must become meaningful enough to shift how the overall company is perceived. Plan for post-acquisition growth, not just integration.

The Proof

Revenue mix shift. Tracking showing the higher-multiple category growing as a percentage of total revenue.

Cross-sell success. Evidence that the combination created revenue synergies through integrated offerings.

Comparable company positioning. Analysis showing the company is now comparable to higher-multiple peers rather than lower-multiple ones.

Variants

Services Wrap. For product companies, acquire services capabilities that create recurring revenue and customer stickiness around the product.

Software Layer. For traditional businesses, acquire software capabilities that add technology multiples to the valuation.

Subscription Conversion. Acquire companies that have already converted to subscription or recurring models, then apply their approaches to the legacy business.

DISQUALIFIERS: When This Gambit Is Wrong

- No genuine strategic connection exists between current and target categories
- Multiple differential is too small to justify acquisition premium and execution risk
- The organization lacks capability to operate in the adjacent category
- Available targets in the category are overpriced with no path to value creation

If disqualified, consider: Gambit 29 (The Revenue Quality Upgrade) to improve multiples organically

GAMBITPLATE #19

THE SYNERGY CAPTURE SYSTEM

BRIDGE: Operating Earnings | TIME: 12 months

VALUE MECHANISM

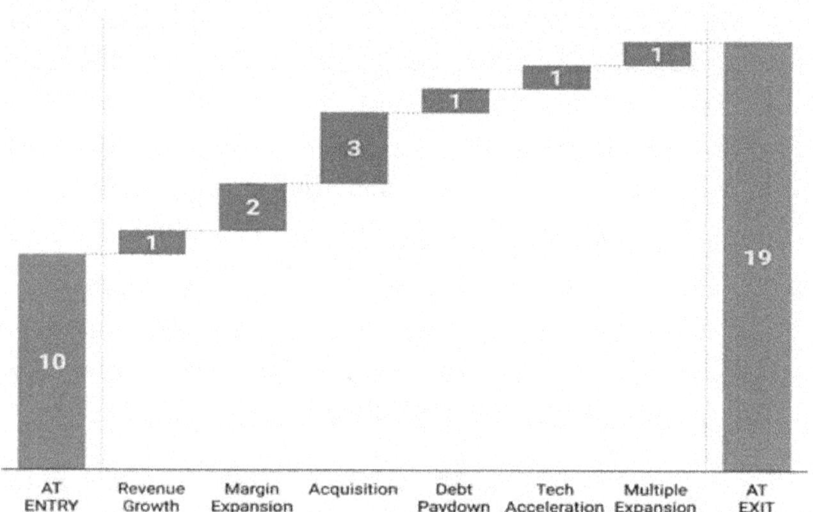

SCORE PANEL

BENEFIT	COST	EASE	RISK	OVERALL
5	3	3	3	14/20
5/5	3/5	3/5	3/5	Value Score: 70/100

FIELD NOTES

TRIGGERS
- Recent acquisition with projected synergies
- Integration underway without synergy tracking

PROOF ARTIFACTS
- Synergy tracking dashboard with actuals vs plan
- Cost synergies documented in P&L

DISQUALIFIERS
- No synergies were projected in deal model
- Integration so poor that synergies are unreachable

Install systematic tracking and accountability for deal synergy capture.

Gambit 19

The Synergy Capture System

Bridge Target: Operating Earnings Bridge (capturing the cost and revenue synergies projected in deal models)

Time to Impact: Fast to Medium (cost synergies in six to twelve months, revenue synergies in twelve to twenty-four months)

The Pattern

The Synergy Capture System is a disciplined methodology for realizing the synergies projected during acquisition diligence. Most acquisitions underperform synergy projections because integration drifts, accountability is unclear, and management moves on to the next priority. The System prevents this by treating synergy capture as a project with the same rigor applied to any critical initiative.

The System distinguishes between cost synergies, which are largely within management control and should be captured quickly, and revenue synergies, which depend on customer response and take longer to materialize. Different approaches apply to each type.

The core insight is that synergies do not capture themselves. They require active management, resource allocation, and accountability. The System provides the structure to make synergy capture happen rather than hoping it happens.

The Sacrifice

Management bandwidth dedicated to integration rather than operations. Investment in integration management office and tracking systems. Organizational disruption during synergy capture. Political capital spent forcing difficult integration decisions.

The Sequence

1. Document synergy assumptions. Before close, catalog every synergy assumed in the deal model. Specify the source, amount, timing, and owner for each synergy. Create the baseline against which capture will be measured.
2. Establish an integration management office. Create a dedicated team responsible for driving integration. Staff with strong project managers who have authority to escalate issues and remove obstacles.
3. Assign synergy owners. For each synergy line item, assign a specific executive owner who is accountable for capture. Synergies without owners do not get captured.
4. Develop detailed capture plans. For each synergy, create an action plan with specific milestones, resource requirements, and dependencies. Convert synergy targets into executable projects.
5. Execute cost synergies immediately. Begin cost synergy capture on day one. Headcount synergies should be realized within ninety days. Procurement synergies should be negotiated within the first six months. Do not let cost synergy capture drift.
6. Build revenue synergy foundation. For revenue synergies, begin foundation work immediately: cross-training sales teams, developing integrated

offerings, and identifying target customers. Execution takes longer, but preparation should start early.

7. Track and report weekly. During active integration, review synergy capture progress weekly. Track actuals against plan. Identify issues early and address them immediately.
8. Escalate aggressively. When synergy capture falls behind plan, escalate immediately. Do not wait for problems to resolve themselves. Integration momentum is difficult to recover once lost.
9. Validate and document capture. Verify that captured synergies appear in financial results. Document the capture for investor communication and exit preparation.

Preconditions

The Synergy Capture System works when synergies are real and achievable, when management is committed to integration, and when resources are available for capture activities. It struggles when synergy projections were unrealistic, when management is distracted by other priorities, or when integration resources are insufficient.

The Trap

The primary trap is confusing activity with results. Integration teams can be very busy without actually capturing synergies. The test is whether synergies appear in the financial statements, not whether meetings are held and reports are produced.

The second trap is claiming synergies that are not real. Some companies report synergy capture that does not show up in verified financial results. This works until diligence for the next transaction or exit, when the gap is discovered. Track and validate rigorously.

The Proof

Synergy realization rate. Percentage of projected synergies actually captured, verified against financial statements. Target Level 4 on the Evidence Standard Ladder.

Synergy capture timeline. Demonstration that synergies were captured on or ahead of schedule.

Margin improvement attribution. Bridge analysis showing the contribution of acquisition synergies to overall margin improvement.

Variants

Clean Team Approach. For larger or complex acquisitions, use clean teams to plan integration before close, accelerating synergy capture after close.

Synergy-Funded Investment. Allocate a portion of captured synergies to fund growth investments, reinvesting part of the savings rather than letting it all flow to the bottom line.

Rolling Integration. For serial acquirers, maintain a permanent integration capability that applies the same system to each acquisition, building organizational muscle over time.

DISQUALIFIERS: When This Gambit Is Wrong

- Synergy projections in the deal model were unrealistic or aspirational
- The acquisition was strategic (capability, market access) with minimal synergy expectation
- Management bandwidth is consumed by urgent operational issues at either company
- Integration resources are not available or cannot be funded

If disqualified, consider: Gambit 21 (The Capability Tuck-In) for strategic acquisitions without major synergy expectations

GAMBITPLATE #20

THE CROSS-SELL FUSE

BRIDGE: Operating Earnings

TIME: 18 months

VALUE MECHANISM

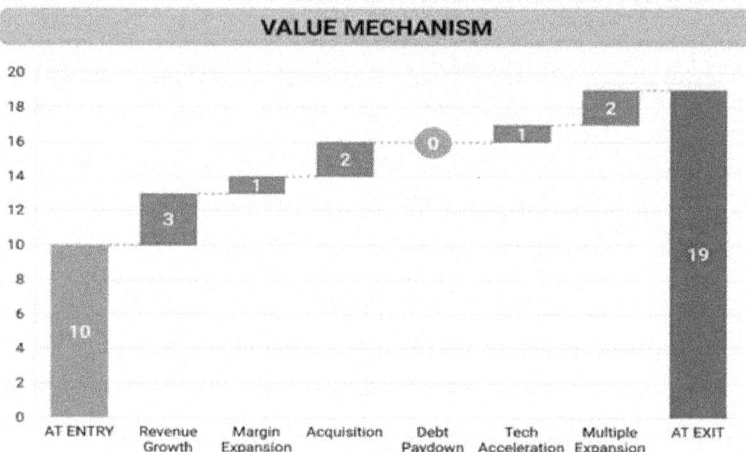

SCORE PANEL

BENEFIT	COST	EASE	RISK	OVERALL
4	2	3	3	14/20
4/5	2/5	3/5	3/5	Value Score: 70/100

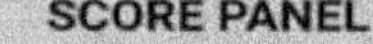

FIELD NOTES

TRIGGERS
- Acquisition brought complementary customer base
- Cross-sell potential identified but not pursued

PROOF ARTIFACTS
- Cross-sell revenue tracked separately
- Customer penetration increasing post-merger

DISQUALIFIERS
- No customer overlap between entities
- Products do not complement each other

Systematically sell acquired products to existing customers and vice versa.

Gambit 20

The Cross-Sell Fuse

Bridge Target: Operating Earnings Bridge (revenue synergies through combined customer relationships)

Time to Impact: Medium to Long (twelve to twenty-four months for meaningful revenue synergies)

The Pattern

The Cross-Sell Fuse activates revenue synergies by selling each company's products to the other company's customers. Most acquisitions project significant revenue synergies from cross-selling, but few achieve them. The Fuse creates the structure, incentives, and accountability to make cross-sell actually happen.

Revenue synergies are harder than cost synergies because they depend on customer response. Customers must see value in the combined offering. Sales teams must learn new products. Pricing and packaging must work across the portfolio. The Fuse addresses each of these challenges systematically.

The power of cross-sell comes from leveraging existing customer relationships. Acquiring a new customer is expensive. Selling additional products to existing customers is far more efficient. The Fuse captures this efficiency by connecting complementary products to established relationships.

The Sacrifice

Investment in sales training and enablement. Compensation redesign to motivate cross-sell. Potential channel conflict when territories or accounts overlap. Risk of damaging customer relationships through poorly executed outreach.

The Sequence

1. Map customer overlaps. Identify customers who buy from one company but could buy from the other. Quantify the addressable cross-sell opportunity.
2. Identify natural bundles. Determine which products or services naturally fit together. Create integrated offerings that provide customer value beyond purchasing separately.
3. Develop cross-sell pricing. Create pricing that makes bundles attractive without cannibalizing existing revenue. The customer should save money while the company increases wallet share.
4. Train the sales organization. Equip both sales teams to sell the combined portfolio. This requires product training, objection handling, and comfort with unfamiliar offerings.
5. Align incentives for cross-sell. Create compensation structures that reward cross-selling. Include cross-sell targets in quota. Pay full commission on cross-sell revenue.
6. Develop targeted customer lists. Prioritize customers with the highest cross-sell potential. Create account plans for priority targets. Avoid scattering effort across too many accounts.

7. Execute coordinated outreach. Approach target customers with the combined value proposition. Use existing relationship owners as entry points. Position as expanded capability, not aggressive upselling.
8. Track cross-sell pipeline. Manage cross-sell opportunities as a distinct pipeline. Monitor activity, conversion, and revenue. Hold sales teams accountable for cross-sell targets.
9. Refine based on results. Analyze what works and what does not. Adjust targeting, messaging, and offerings based on customer feedback. Iterate toward higher conversion.

Preconditions

The Cross-Sell Fuse works when products are genuinely complementary, when customer overlap exists, and when sales teams can be motivated to sell unfamiliar products. It struggles when products do not naturally fit together, when customer bases do not overlap, or when sales teams resist selling outside their comfort zone.

The Trap

The primary trap is damaging existing relationships through aggressive cross-sell. Customers who feel pushed to buy products they do not need may reconsider the entire relationship. Cross-sell must be consultative, not pushy.

The second trap is projecting revenue synergies that never materialize. Many deals assume significant cross-sell that proves elusive in practice. Be realistic about what is achievable and track actual results against projections.

The Proof

Cross-sell revenue tracking. Measurement of revenue from selling acquired company products to legacy customers and vice versa.

Multi-product customer growth. Tracking showing the percentage of customers buying multiple products increasing over time.

Wallet share improvement. Evidence that the company is capturing a larger share of customer spending in relevant categories.

Variants

Lead Sharing Model. Rather than training all salespeople on all products, create a lead-sharing system where specialists handle their products but share leads across teams.

Bundled Pricing Only. Create bundles that are only available as combinations, forcing customers to buy across the portfolio to access the best value.

Customer Success Driven. Route cross-sell through customer success rather than sales. Position as helping customers get more value rather than selling more products.

____
____
____

DISQUALIFIERS: When This Gambit Is Wrong

____
____
____

- Products are not complementary and do not create natural bundles
- Customer bases do not overlap (different industries, geographies, or buyer types)
- Sales teams actively resist selling unfamiliar products despite incentives
- Existing customer relationships are fragile and cannot tolerate additional commercial pressure

If disqualified, consider: Gambit 19 (The Synergy Capture System) focused on cost synergies instead

____
____
____

GAMBITPLATE **#21**

THE CAPABILITY TUCK-IN

BRIDGE: Enterprise Value | **TIME:** 12 months

VALUE MECHANISM

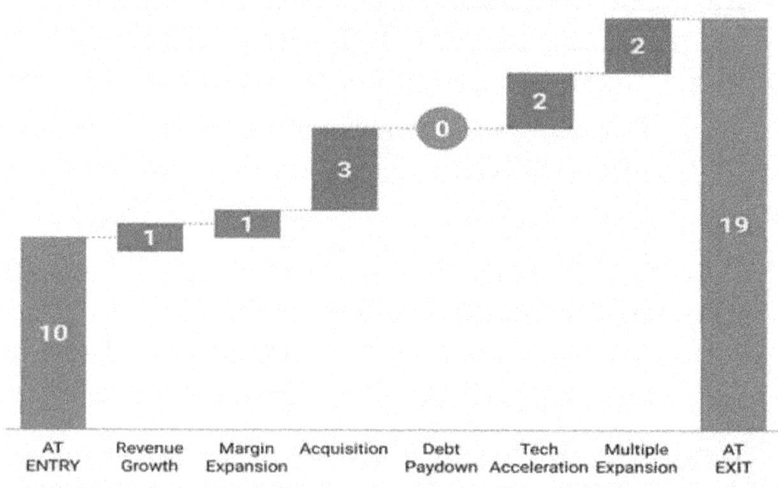

SCORE PANEL

BENEFIT	COST	EASE	RISK	OVERALL 11/20
4	4	2	3	Value Score: 55/100

FIELD NOTES

TRIGGERS
- Strategic capability gap limiting growth
- Build vs buy analysis favors acquisition

PROOF ARTIFACTS
- Capability deployed in core business
- Revenue enabled by acquired capability

DISQUALIFIERS
- Capability can be built faster than acquired
- Key talent unlikely to stay post-acquisition

Acquire small targets to gain specific capabilities faster than organic build.

Gambit 21

The Capability Tuck-In

Bridge Target: Enterprise Value Bridge (capability acquisition to enable growth or improve competitive position)

Time to Impact: Medium (six to eighteen months for capability integration and deployment)

The Pattern

The Capability Tuck-In acquires a specific capability rather than a business. The target may have limited revenue but possesses technology, talent, or expertise that would take years to build organically. The acquisition buys time and reduces execution risk.

Unlike traditional acquisitions valued on earnings or revenue, capability tuck-ins are valued on strategic impact. What would it cost to build this capability internally? How long would it take? What competitive risk exists if we do not acquire it? These questions drive valuation rather than financial multiples.

The Tuck-In succeeds when the acquired capability is rapidly deployed across the larger platform. The capability becomes an accelerant for the core business rather than a standalone entity. Integration means absorption, not operation as a separate unit.

The Sacrifice

Premium valuations relative to current financial performance. Risk that key talent departs after acquisition. Integration complexity when absorbing different technical or operational approaches. Opportunity cost of capital deployed for capability rather than earnings.

The Sequence

1. Define capability gaps. Identify specific capabilities that limit growth, competitive position, or operational effectiveness. Quantify the impact of closing these gaps.
2. Evaluate build versus buy. For each capability gap, assess whether internal development or acquisition is more effective. Consider time to capability, risk, and total cost.
3. Identify acquisition targets. Source companies that possess the required capability. Look for targets where the capability is proven but scale is limited, creating opportunity for platform leverage.
4. Assess talent retention risk. Understand which individuals are critical to the capability. Develop retention plans before acquisition. Losing key people defeats the purpose.
5. Structure for retention. Design deal structure and integration approach that motivates key talent to stay and perform. This may include earnouts, retention packages, or meaningful roles in the combined organization.
6. Execute rapid integration. Move quickly to integrate the capability into the core platform. Extended standalone operation allows the acquired team to drift and reduces leverage potential.
7. Deploy capability across the platform. Apply the acquired capability to the broader business. If you

acquired pricing technology, deploy it across all product lines. If you acquired engineering talent, apply them to core product challenges.

8. Measure capability impact. Track how the acquired capability affects business performance. Quantify the value created by closing the capability gap.
9. Institutionalize the capability. Transfer knowledge from acquired individuals to the broader organization. The capability should become organizational rather than dependent on specific people.

Preconditions

The Capability Tuck-In works when the capability gap is real and significant, when acquisition provides material advantage over building, and when the acquired capability can be successfully integrated. It struggles when the capability gap is unclear, when building internally would be faster or cheaper, or when integration risks are high.

The Trap

The primary trap is losing the talent that makes the capability valuable. Many capability acquisitions fail because key people leave shortly after close. Retention planning must begin during diligence and continue through integration.

The second trap is acquiring capability that does not transfer. Some capabilities are context-specific and do not work when transplanted. Validate that the capability can be applied to your environment before acquiring.

The Proof

Talent retention. Tracking showing key individuals remained through the critical integration period.

Capability deployment. Evidence that the acquired capability is now operating across the broader platform.

Business impact metrics. Measurement of how the capability improved business outcomes: faster development, better products, improved operations.

Variants

Acqui-Hire. Focus specifically on acquiring talented teams rather than technology or products. The company may be dissolved but the people join the platform.

Technology Acquisition. Focus specifically on acquiring proprietary technology that would be difficult to replicate. The value is in the intellectual property rather than the team.

Process Acquisition. Acquire a company specifically because it has developed operational processes that could be applied across the platform.

____
____
____

DISQUALIFIERS: When This Gambit Is Wrong

____
____
____

- The capability gap is not clearly defined or its business impact is speculative
- Internal development would be faster, cheaper, or lower risk than acquisition
- Key talent has already indicated they will not remain post-acquisition
- The acquired capability is context-specific and unlikely to transfer to your environment

If disqualified, consider: Internal capability building with targeted external hires

____
____
____

GAMBITPLATE #22

THE STANDARDIZATION PROGRAM

BRIDGE: Operating Earnings | **TIME:** 36 months

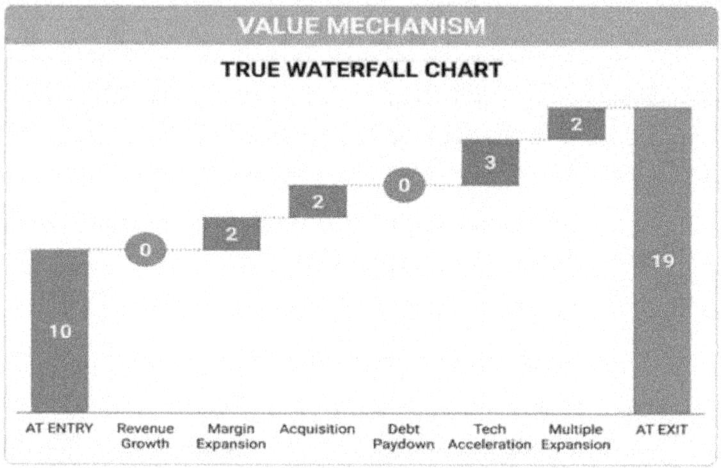

SCORE PANEL

BENEFIT	COST	EASE	RISK	OVERALL
4	4	2	3	11/20
4/5	4/5	2/5	3/5	Value Score: 55/100

FIELD NOTES

TRIGGERS

- Multiple acquisitions running different systems
- Synergy capture limited by system fragmentation

PROOF ARTIFACTS

- System count reduction documented
- Operating efficiency improvement from standards

DISQUALIFIERS

- Single-system environment already exists
- Business units require unique capabilities

Harmonize systems and processes across acquired entities for efficiency and scalability.

Gambit 22

The Standardization Program

Bridge Target: Operating Earnings Bridge (efficiency and synergy capture through system and process harmonization) and Enterprise Value Bridge (professionalization and scalability)

Time to Impact: Long (twelve to thirty-six months for full standardization across multiple acquisitions)

The Pattern

The Standardization Program harmonizes systems, processes, and operating approaches across multiple acquired companies. Without standardization, a platform becomes a holding company: a collection of independent businesses sharing only ownership. With standardization, it becomes an integrated enterprise capable of scale economies and operational leverage.

Standardization creates value in several ways. It reduces complexity and the cost of managing disparate systems. It enables best practice sharing across business units. It creates common data that supports enterprise-wide analysis. It demonstrates operational maturity that buyers value at exit.

The Program is particularly important for serial acquirers. Each acquisition adds complexity. Without active standardization, complexity compounds until the organization becomes unmanageable. The Program controls complexity by continuously converging toward common approaches.

The Sacrifice

Investment in systems and process redesign. Organizational resistance to change from acquired companies. Short-term productivity loss during transitions. Loss of local flexibility as standard approaches are imposed.

The Sequence

1. Define the platform standard. Establish the target operating model: which systems, processes, and approaches will be standard across the platform. This becomes the template for integration.
2. Assess current state variation. Document the systems, processes, and approaches currently in use across all entities. Quantify the gap between current state and the platform standard.
3. Prioritize standardization domains. Not everything can be standardized at once. Prioritize based on value creation potential and implementation feasibility. Finance systems, customer relationship management, and core operations are common priorities.
4. Build the platform systems. Invest in systems capable of supporting standardization across the enterprise. This may require upgrading existing systems or implementing new ones.
5. Develop standardization playbooks. Create detailed implementation guides for each standardization domain. Include timelines, resource requirements, and success criteria.

6. Execute in waves. Standardize entities in planned waves rather than all at once. Learn from early implementations. Refine approaches before scaling.
7. Manage change actively. Standardization requires behavior change. Invest in change management: communication, training, and support. Address resistance directly.
8. Integrate new acquisitions immediately. For new acquisitions, apply the platform standard from day one. Do not allow new entities to operate on legacy approaches.
9. Monitor compliance and value realization. Track standardization progress and the value created. Enforce compliance. Calculate the synergy value from standardization.

Preconditions

The Standardization Program works when the platform has clear standards to impose, when there are multiple entities requiring harmonization, and when leadership commits to enforcement. It struggles when the platform standard is unclear, when acquired businesses have genuinely different requirements, or when leadership allows exceptions that undermine standardization.

The Trap

The primary trap is standardizing on the wrong approach. If the platform standard is itself suboptimal, imposing it across the enterprise locks in mediocrity. Validate that the platform standard represents best practice before mandating it.

The second trap is allowing exceptions that accumulate. Each exception to the standard creates complexity.

Exceptions should be rare and require senior approval. Without discipline, the platform reverts to a collection of independent entities.

The Proof

Standardization completion rate. Tracking showing the percentage of entities operating on platform standard systems and processes.

System consolidation metrics. Reduction in the number of distinct systems and platforms across the enterprise.

Efficiency gains. Cost savings and productivity improvements attributable to standardization.

Variants

Finance First. Prioritize standardizing finance and reporting systems to create enterprise-wide visibility and control. Other functions follow once financial integration is complete.

Customer-Facing First. Prioritize standardizing customer-facing systems to enable cross-sell and unified customer experience. Back-office follows.

Best Practice Adoption. Rather than imposing the platform approach, evaluate each acquisition for best practices that should be adopted platform-wide. Standardization becomes continuous improvement.

DISQUALIFIERS: When This Gambit Is Wrong

- The platform lacks clear standards worth imposing
- Acquired businesses have genuinely different requirements that cannot be standardized
- Leadership routinely grants exceptions that undermine standardization efforts
- The investment required exceeds the value of the synergies captured

If disqualified, consider: Operating as a holding company with shared services rather than full standardization

SECTION D

CASH AND DEBT GAMBITS

Gambits 23 through 28

Cash is the bridge between operating performance and equity value. The six gambits in this section address the primary levers for converting earnings into debt reduction: working capital optimization, cash conversion acceleration, capital discipline, debt paydown strategy, cash visibility, and covenant management.

Each gambit targets the equity value bridge directly through debt reduction. Every dollar of debt paid down increases equity value by exactly one dollar. These gambits also provide defensive value: cash discipline creates resilience against downturns and reduces financial risk. Select the gambits that match your cash flow profile and debt structure.

GAMBITPLATE **#23**

THE WORKING CAPITAL SPRINT

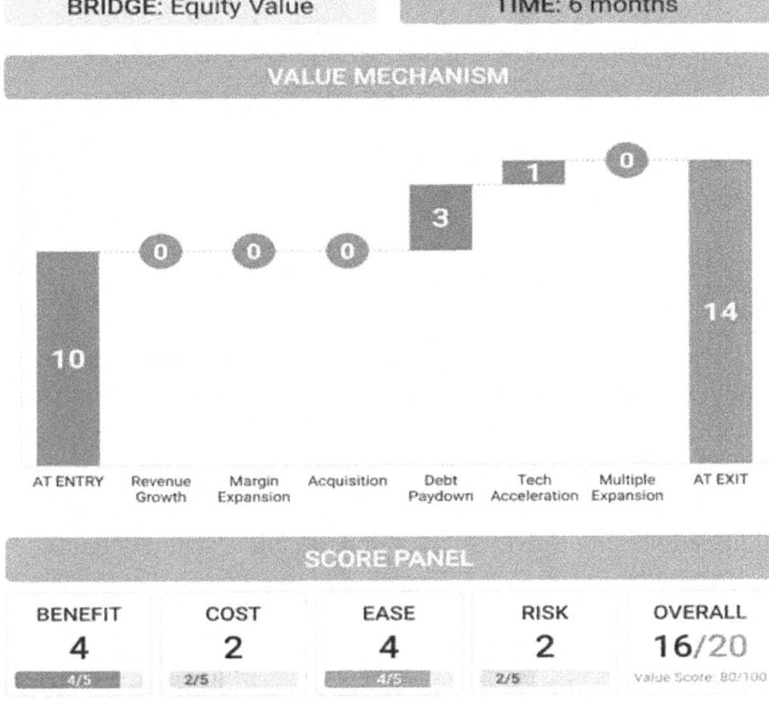

FIELD NOTES

TRIGGERS

- DSO or DIO exceeds industry benchmarks
- Cash conversion cycle longer than peers

PROOF ARTIFACTS

- DSO/DIO/DPO improvement documented
- Cash released quantified

DISQUALIFIERS

- Already at best-in-class working capital
- Customer terms contractually fixed

Reduce receivables, inventory, and payables timing to release trapped cash.

Gambit 23

The Working Capital Sprint

Bridge Target: Equity Value Bridge (one-time cash release through working capital reduction)

Time to Impact: Fast (three to six months for meaningful cash release)

The Pattern

The Working Capital Sprint releases cash trapped in receivables, inventory, and payables through intensive short-term focus. Working capital is often neglected because it does not appear directly on the income statement. But it consumes cash that could otherwise reduce debt or fund growth. The Sprint makes working capital visible and actionable.

Most companies have more cash tied up in working capital than necessary. Receivables age beyond terms because collection is not prioritized. Inventory accumulates because forecasting is imprecise or safety stock targets are excessive. Payables are paid early because discount capture is uncoordinated. Each represents trapped cash.

The Sprint addresses all three components simultaneously through intensive focus. It is designed as a time-limited initiative with clear targets and accountability. The intensity creates momentum and demonstrates what is possible. After the Sprint, ongoing management prevents working capital from creeping back.

The Sacrifice

Management attention diverted from other priorities during the Sprint. Potential customer friction from aggressive collection. Potential supplier friction from extended payment terms. Risk of inventory stockouts if reductions are too aggressive.

The Sequence

1. Establish working capital baseline. Calculate current days sales outstanding, days inventory outstanding, and days payable outstanding. Compute the cash conversion cycle. Quantify the cash tied up in working capital.
2. Benchmark against targets. Research industry benchmarks and best-in-class performance for each working capital component. Set aggressive but achievable targets for the Sprint.
3. Age receivables and prioritize collection. Generate detailed receivables aging. Identify the largest and oldest balances. Assign collection responsibility to specific individuals with specific targets.
4. Execute aggressive collection. Contact overdue customers directly. Escalate as needed. Resolve disputes quickly. Consider offering discounts for immediate payment on severely aged receivables.
5. Analyze inventory by category. Segment inventory by turnover rate, value, and risk of obsolescence. Identify slow-moving and excess inventory that can be liquidated or written down.
6. Reduce inventory levels. Liquidate excess inventory through promotions, secondary channels, or scrap. Reduce reorder points and safety stock targets. Tighten purchasing controls.

7. Optimize payables timing. Review payment terms with major suppliers. Extend terms where possible without damaging relationships. Ensure payments are made on the due date, not before.
8. Track progress weekly. During the Sprint, review working capital metrics weekly. Celebrate progress. Address obstacles immediately. Maintain intensity throughout the Sprint period.
9. Lock in gains with ongoing management. After the Sprint, establish monthly working capital reviews. Set permanent targets. Prevent the released cash from being reabsorbed.

Preconditions

The Working Capital Sprint works when working capital is currently above benchmark levels, when management can dedicate focus to the initiative, and when there is genuine excess in receivables, inventory, or payables timing. It struggles when working capital is already optimized, when customer or supplier relationships cannot tolerate pressure, or when inventory reductions would cause stockouts.

The Trap

The primary trap is damaging customer or supplier relationships through excessive pressure. Aggressive collection that alienates customers or extended terms that anger suppliers may release cash short-term but damage the business long-term. Balance intensity with relationship preservation.

The second trap is one-time release without ongoing discipline. Working capital tends to grow back if not actively managed. The Sprint must be followed by permanent process changes that prevent working capital from returning to pre-Sprint levels.

The Proof

Cash released. Quantification of cash generated through working capital reduction.

Days improvement by component. Tracking showing days sales outstanding, days inventory outstanding, and days payable outstanding movement.

Sustainability over time. Evidence that working capital improvements were maintained after the Sprint ended.

Variants

Receivables Focus. Concentrate the Sprint specifically on receivables collection if that is the primary opportunity.

Inventory Blitz. Focus specifically on inventory reduction for businesses with excess stock.

Terms Renegotiation. Focus specifically on extending supplier payment terms without damaging relationships.

DISQUALIFIERS: When This Gambit Is Wrong

- Working capital is already at or below industry benchmarks
- Customer relationships are fragile and cannot tolerate collection pressure
- Inventory reductions would cause stockouts affecting revenue
- Payment term extensions would damage critical supplier relationships

If disqualified, consider: Gambit 24 (The Cash Conversion Engine) for ongoing improvement rather than intensive sprint

GAMBITPLATE **#24**

THE CASH CONVERSION ENGINE

BRIDGE: Equity Value **TIME:** 12 months

VALUE MECHANISM

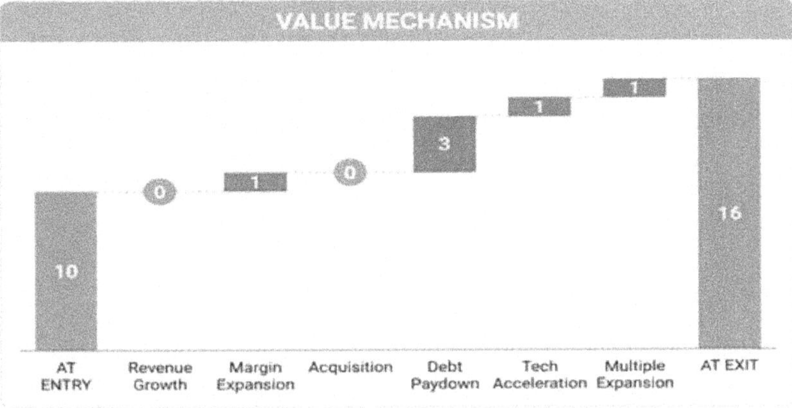

SCORE PANEL

BENEFIT	COST	EASE	RISK	OVERALL
5	2	3	2	16/20
5/5	2/5	3/5	2/5	Value Score: 80/100

FIELD NOTES

TRIGGERS

- Cash conversion ratio below 80%
- Earnings not translating to cash

PROOF ARTIFACTS

- Cash conversion ratio trend improving
- Free cash flow as % EBITDA tracked

DISQUALIFIERS

- Business model requires heavy reinvestment
- Already at 90%+ conversion

Improve the ongoing ratio of operating cash flow to reported earnings.

Gambit 24

The Cash Conversion Engine

Bridge Target: Equity Value Bridge (improving the ongoing ratio of operating cash flow to operating earnings)

Time to Impact: Medium (six to twelve months to establish sustainable conversion improvement)

The Pattern

The Cash Conversion Engine transforms the ongoing relationship between earnings and cash flow. While the Working Capital Sprint releases trapped cash once, the Engine improves conversion permanently. It ensures that each dollar of operating earnings produces the maximum possible cash for debt reduction.

Cash conversion suffers when working capital grows with revenue, when capital expenditures exceed depreciation, or when other items consume cash without appearing in operating earnings. The Engine addresses each leakage point systematically.

The goal is a cash conversion ratio approaching or exceeding one hundred percent: every dollar of operating earnings converts to a dollar of operating cash flow. High conversion means the business funds its own growth and generates surplus for debt reduction. Low conversion means the business consumes cash even when profitable.

The Sacrifice

Constraints on growth investments that consume cash. Discipline required to maintain working capital ratios during growth. Potential limitation on capital expenditure that would improve operations. Ongoing management attention to cash conversion.

The Sequence

1. Calculate current conversion ratio. Determine the ratio of operating cash flow to operating earnings over the past several years. Understand the baseline and its variability.
2. Decompose the conversion gap. Identify what causes operating earnings to differ from operating cash flow: working capital changes, capital expenditure, and other items. Quantify each source of leakage.
3. Set working capital intensity targets. Establish target working capital as a percentage of revenue. Require that working capital grow no faster than revenue. Ideally, working capital intensity should decline over time.
4. Implement capital expenditure discipline. Establish investment criteria for capital expenditure. Require returns analysis for all significant investments. Track actual returns against projections.
5. Address one-time items. Identify and minimize cash items that do not flow through operating earnings: restructuring costs, legal settlements, and other unusual items. Plan for these in cash forecasting.
6. Build cash forecasting capability. Develop accurate thirteen-week cash forecasts. Track actual versus forecast weekly. Understand what drives cash flow variation.

7. Align incentives to cash. Include cash conversion metrics in management compensation. Make operating leaders accountable for working capital in their areas. Connect bonus outcomes to cash performance.
8. Report cash conversion monthly. Track and report conversion ratio alongside traditional financial metrics. Discuss at leadership meetings. Make cash as visible as earnings.
9. Investigate and correct deviations. When conversion falls below target, investigate root causes immediately. Address issues before they become patterns.

Preconditions

The Cash Conversion Engine works when there is a meaningful gap between earnings and cash flow, when the organization has the discipline to maintain cash focus, and when the business model can support high conversion. It struggles when the business inherently requires high working capital or capital expenditure, or when leadership prioritizes growth over cash.

The Trap

The primary trap is underinvesting in the business to maximize short-term cash. Some capital expenditure is essential for maintaining competitive position. Some working capital supports growth. Cutting these to inflate conversion damages long-term value.

The second trap is managing to the ratio rather than the business. Cash conversion is a diagnostic metric, not an end in itself. The goal is building a cash-generative business, not manipulating a ratio.

The Proof

Conversion ratio improvement. Tracking showing operating cash flow as a percentage of operating earnings increasing over time.

Working capital intensity decline. Evidence that working capital as a percentage of revenue is stable or declining.

Capital efficiency metrics. Demonstration that capital expenditure is disciplined and generating expected returns.

Variants

Asset-Light Model. Restructure the business model to reduce capital intensity: outsourcing, leasing, or third-party logistics.

Negative Working Capital Target. For businesses with favorable terms, target negative working capital where customers pay before suppliers must be paid.

Growth-Adjusted Conversion. Accept lower conversion during high-growth periods when working capital naturally expands, but require conversion to normalize as growth moderates.

DISQUALIFIERS: When This Gambit Is Wrong

- Cash conversion is already near one hundred percent with limited improvement potential
- The business model inherently requires high working capital or capital expenditure
- Leadership prioritizes growth investment over cash conversion
- The finance function lacks capability to track and forecast cash accurately

If disqualified, consider: Gambit 25 (The Capital Discipline Framework) for investment governance

GAMBITPLATE **#25**

THE CAPITAL DISCIPLINE FRAMEWORK

BRIDGE: Equity Value | **TIME:** 12 months

VALUE MECHANISM

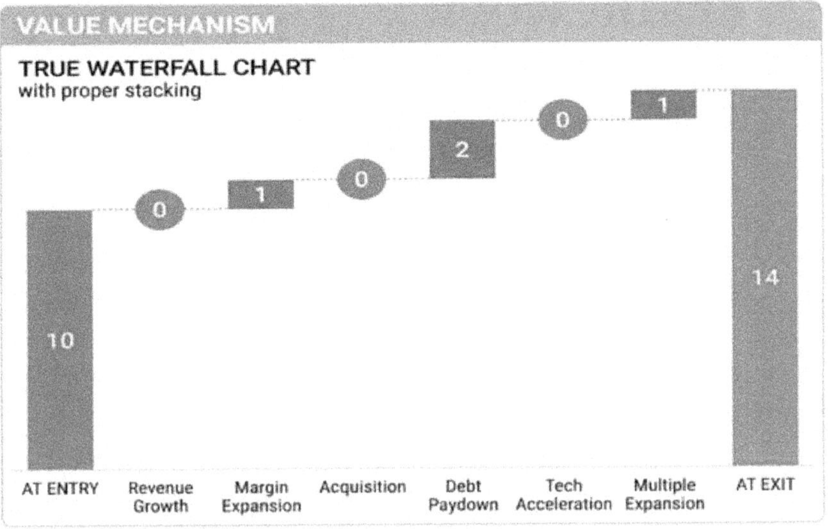

SCORE PANEL

BENEFIT	COST	EASE	RISK	OVERALL
4	2	3	2	15/20
4/5	2/5	3/5	2/5	Value Score 75/100

FIELD NOTES

TRIGGERS
- Capex decisions made without ROI analysis
- Projects approved without post-investment review

PROOF ARTIFACTS
- Investment criteria documented and used
- Capex as % revenue controlled

DISQUALIFIERS
- Capex already minimal and disciplined
- Regulatory mandates drive capital spend

Install governance to ensure capital investments generate acceptable returns.

Gambit 25

The Capital Discipline Framework

Bridge Target: Equity Value Bridge (maximizing cash available for debt reduction through rigorous investment governance)

Time to Impact: Medium (six to twelve months to implement framework and change investment behavior)

The Pattern

The Capital Discipline Framework establishes rigorous governance over all significant cash investments: capital expenditure, acquisitions, and growth initiatives. Without discipline, capital flows to projects that consume cash without adequate returns. With discipline, every investment competes for scarce capital and must justify itself.

The Framework treats capital as precious. In a leveraged environment, cash used for investment is cash not used for debt reduction. Every investment must generate returns that exceed the cost of keeping the debt. This is a higher bar than most organizations apply.

The Framework does not prevent investment. It ensures that investments are intentional, justified, and tracked. Good investments should be made. Bad investments should be stopped before they consume cash. The Framework distinguishes between the two.

The Sacrifice

Administrative burden of investment review process. Potential delay in executing investments that require approval. Frustration from managers whose projects are rejected. Risk of underinvestment if the process is too restrictive.

The Sequence

1. Define investment categories. Categorize investments by type: maintenance capital, growth capital, technology, and acquisitions. Different categories may have different approval processes and return requirements.
2. Establish hurdle rates. Set minimum return thresholds for each investment category. Returns should exceed the weighted average cost of capital with a margin for execution risk. Be explicit about how returns are calculated.
3. Create approval thresholds. Define who can approve investments at different sizes. Small investments may be approved locally. Large investments require executive or board approval. No investment should be unreviewed.
4. Develop standard investment templates. Create templates that require consistent analysis: investment amount, expected returns, payback period, risks, and alternatives. Standardization enables comparison across projects.
5. Implement portfolio review process. Review the full investment portfolio quarterly. Compare proposed investments. Prioritize based on returns and strategic fit. Some worthy projects may be deferred if better alternatives exist.

6. Track actual versus projected returns. After investment, measure actual performance against projections. Hold sponsors accountable for delivered results. Use historical accuracy to calibrate future projections.
7. Separate maintenance from growth. Ensure maintenance capital is funded to preserve existing capability. Growth capital should compete on returns. Do not starve maintenance to fund growth.
8. Review and kill underperforming investments. Monitor investments in progress. If performance falls materially below projections, consider stopping rather than continuing to invest. Sunk cost should not justify additional investment.
9. Report investment performance regularly. Include investment performance in standard reporting. Show returns delivered by past investments. Build organizational memory about what works.

Preconditions

The Capital Discipline Framework works when capital investment is significant and discretionary, when leadership commits to enforcing the process, and when the organization has the analytical capability to evaluate investments properly. It struggles when investment decisions are highly decentralized, when leadership exempts favored projects from review, or when analytical capability is weak.

The Trap

The primary trap is bureaucracy that prevents timely investment. If the approval process takes months, the organization loses competitive responsiveness. The Framework should be rigorous but not slow.

The second trap is optimistic projections that game the system. If sponsors know that high projected returns win approval, they will project high returns regardless of reality. Hold sponsors accountable for delivered results to maintain projection integrity.

The Proof

Investment return tracking. Documentation showing actual returns from completed investments relative to projections.

Portfolio optimization evidence. Examples of investments that were rejected, deferred, or killed based on Framework analysis.

Capital intensity improvement. Tracking showing capital expenditure as a percentage of revenue stable or declining.

Variants

Zero-Based Capital Budgeting. Require all capital requests to justify themselves from zero each year rather than building on historical budgets.

Sponsored Investment Model. Require each investment to have an executive sponsor whose compensation is tied to delivered returns.

Investment Committee Governance. Establish a dedicated investment committee that reviews all significant investments and maintains portfolio perspective.

DISQUALIFIERS: When This Gambit Is Wrong

- Capital investment is minimal and does not warrant formal governance
- Leadership routinely exempts favored projects from review requirements
- The organization lacks analytical capability to evaluate investment returns
- Speed of investment decisions is critical to competitive positioning

If disqualified, consider: Simplified investment guidelines with post-facto tracking

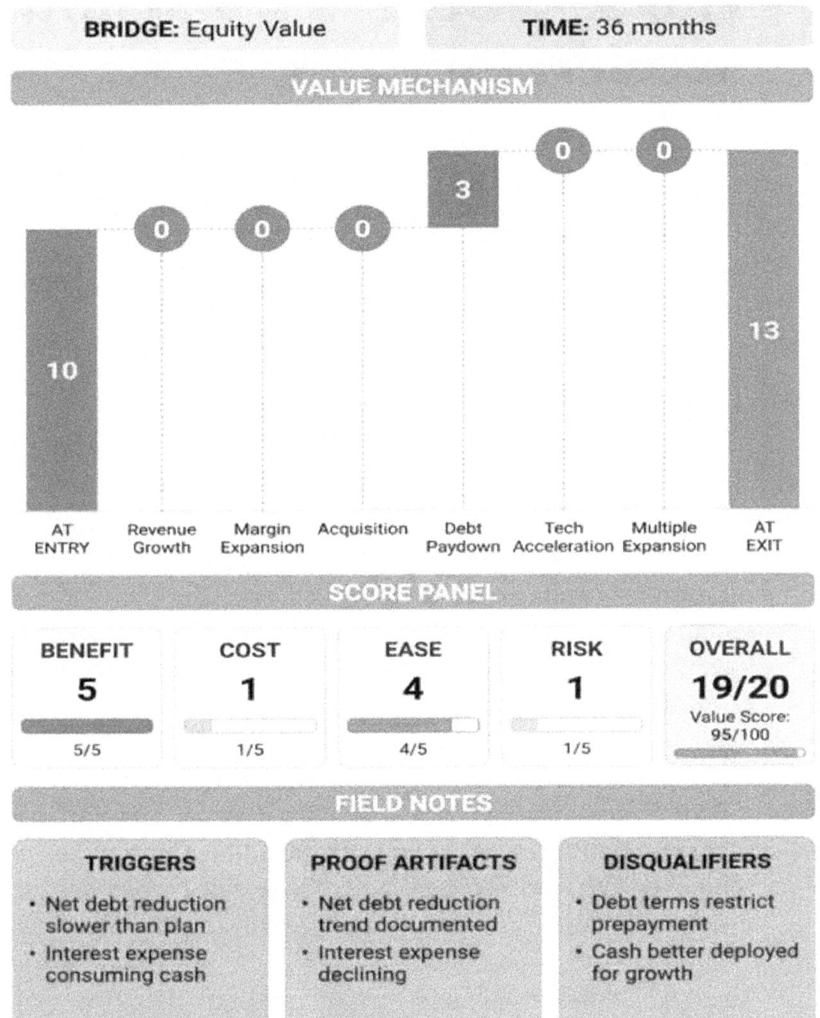
GAMBITPLATE
#26
THE DEBT PAYDOWN ACCELERATOR
BRIDGE: Equity Value
TIME: 36 months
VALUE MECHANISM
10
0
0
0
3
0
0
13
AT ENTRY
Revenue Growth
Margin Expansion
Acquisition
Debt Paydown
Tech Acceleration
Multiple Expansion
AT EXIT
SCORE PANEL
BENEFIT
5
5/5
COST
1
1/5
EASE
4
4/5
RISK
1
1/5
OVERALL
19/20
Value Score: 95/100
FIELD NOTES
TRIGGERS
• Net debt reduction slower than plan
• Interest expense consuming cash
PROOF ARTIFACTS
• Net debt reduction trend documented
• Interest expense declining
DISQUALIFIERS
• Debt terms restrict prepayment
• Cash better deployed for growth
Systematically convert operating cash to debt reduction for equity value.

Gambit 26

The Debt Paydown Accelerator

Bridge Target: Equity Value Bridge (accelerating debt reduction to maximize equity value creation)

Time to Impact: Ongoing (continuous acceleration throughout the hold period)

The Pattern

The Debt Paydown Accelerator treats debt reduction as a primary objective, not a residual outcome. Most companies pay down debt passively: whatever cash remains after operations and investment goes to the lender. The Accelerator makes debt reduction proactive, targeting specific paydown amounts and treating them as commitments.

Debt paydown has a one-to-one relationship with equity value. Every dollar paid reduces net debt by one dollar and increases equity value by exactly one dollar. This makes debt paydown the most direct path from operations to value creation. The math is simple and certain.

The Accelerator creates organizational focus on cash generation and debt reduction. It establishes targets, tracks progress, and celebrates achievement. Debt paydown becomes a shared objective that connects all parts of the organization to value creation.

The Sacrifice

Cash committed to debt reduction is unavailable for other uses. Growth investment may be constrained. Financial flexibility is reduced during the paydown period. Management may feel pressure from aggressive paydown targets.

The Sequence

1. Establish baseline debt level. Document current total debt including all facilities, notes, and other obligations. This is the starting point for paydown tracking.
2. Set paydown targets. Establish annual and quarterly debt paydown targets. Make targets aggressive but achievable. Connect targets to cash flow forecasts.
3. Create paydown waterfall priority. Determine the order for paying down different tranches. Typically, highest-interest debt first, but prepayment penalties and covenant considerations may affect priority.
4. Build paydown into cash management. Structure cash management to prioritize debt paydown. Maintain minimum operating cash. Sweep excess to debt reduction regularly.
5. Connect management incentives to paydown. Include debt paydown targets in management bonus calculations. Make paydown a shared objective across the leadership team.
6. Track and report paydown monthly. Monitor actual paydown against targets. Report progress to leadership and board. Investigate shortfalls immediately.
7. Celebrate paydown milestones. Mark significant paydown achievements. Connect paydown to value

creation. Help the organization understand how their efforts translate to results.

8. Consider opportunistic paydown. When excess cash materializes from asset sales, working capital release, or outperformance, direct it to debt paydown rather than other uses.
9. Refinance when advantageous. As debt is paid down and performance improves, consider refinancing to reduce interest cost or extend maturity. Improved credit profile enables better terms.

Preconditions

The Debt Paydown Accelerator works when the business generates free cash flow, when debt levels are significant relative to equity value, and when leadership commits to paydown discipline. It struggles when the business does not generate consistent cash, when debt is already low, or when leadership prioritizes other uses of cash.

The Trap

The primary trap is starving the business to accelerate paydown. If debt paydown prevents necessary investment in growth, maintenance, or talent, it destroys more value than it creates. Balance paydown against business needs.

The second trap is ignoring prepayment penalties. Some debt structures penalize early repayment. Factor these costs into paydown decisions. Sometimes holding debt is cheaper than paying it off early.

The Proof

Debt reduction tracking. Documentation showing debt declining over time against targets.

Leverage ratio improvement. Tracking showing debt-to-operating-earnings ratio declining.

Interest expense reduction. Evidence that lower debt is reducing interest expense and improving cash available for further paydown.

Variants

Excess Cash Sweep. Implement automatic sweep of cash above a minimum threshold to debt repayment.

Asset Sale Paydown. Identify non-core assets that can be sold with proceeds directed to debt reduction.

Dividend Recapitalization Alternative. As leverage declines, consider refinancing to return capital to equity holders while maintaining reasonable leverage.

____

____

____

DISQUALIFIERS: When This Gambit Is Wrong

____

____

____

- The business does not generate consistent free cash flow
- Debt levels are already low relative to equity value
- Prepayment penalties exceed the value of accelerated paydown
- The business requires significant reinvestment that paydown would prevent

If disqualified, consider: Gambit 24 (The Cash Conversion Engine) to improve cash generation first

____

____

____

GAMBITPLATE #27

THE CASH VISIBILITY SYSTEM

BRIDGE: Equity Value **TIME:** 3 months

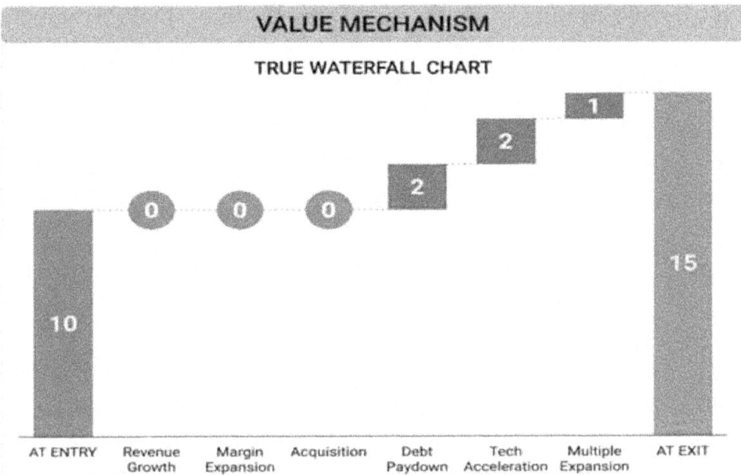

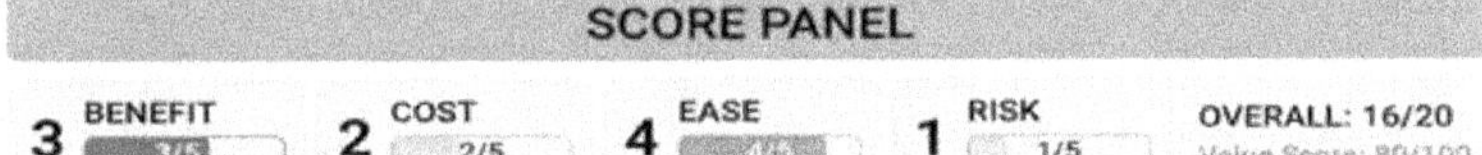

FIELD NOTES

TRIGGERS
- No 13-week cash forecast in place
- Cash surprises occurring regularly

PROOF ARTIFACTS
- 13-week forecast with variance tracking
- Forecast accuracy improving

DISQUALIFIERS
- Robust cash forecasting already exists
- Business too simple to need elaborate system

Install cash forecasting and tracking infrastructure for management visibility.

Gambit 27

The Cash Visibility System

Bridge Target: Equity Value Bridge (enabling cash management through forecasting and tracking infrastructure)

Time to Impact: Fast (one to three months to establish basic system, six months to mature)

The Pattern

The Cash Visibility System provides the forecasting and tracking infrastructure that makes cash management possible. Most companies know their cash position but cannot accurately predict their cash position in six or thirteen weeks. This blindness prevents proactive management.

The System combines rolling cash forecasts with actual tracking and variance analysis. It reveals where cash comes from, where it goes, and what drives variation from expectations. This visibility enables the discipline required for working capital management, debt paydown, and capital allocation.

The thirteen-week cash forecast is the centerpiece. Thirteen weeks provides enough visibility to anticipate problems and enough granularity to be actionable. The forecast is updated weekly and compared to actuals, creating a continuous improvement cycle for cash prediction.

The Sacrifice

Finance team time devoted to forecasting and analysis. Investment in systems and tools. Organizational discipline to maintain the forecasting rhythm. Discomfort when forecasts prove inaccurate, exposing prediction limitations.

The Sequence

1. Establish cash position baseline. Determine current cash position across all accounts and entities. Ensure complete visibility including any trapped or restricted cash.
2. Map cash flows. Identify all major cash inflows and outflows. Categorize by type: customer receipts, supplier payments, payroll, debt service, capital expenditure, and other. Understand timing patterns.
3. Build the thirteen-week forecast model. Create a rolling forecast that projects cash position weekly for thirteen weeks. Include all significant inflows and outflows. Start simple and add complexity as capability develops.
4. Establish forecast update rhythm. Update the forecast weekly. Roll forward one week. Refresh assumptions based on new information. Make forecasting a permanent process, not a periodic project.
5. Track actual versus forecast. Each week, compare actual cash flows to forecast. Identify significant variances. Understand what drove the difference.
6. Improve forecast accuracy over time. Use variance analysis to improve future forecasts. Address systematic biases. Refine assumptions. Build organizational learning about cash behavior.
7. Report cash position and forecast to leadership. Include cash reporting in standard management

packages. Review at leadership meetings. Make cash as visible as revenue and earnings.

8. Use forecast for decision-making. Base cash-related decisions on forecast data: timing of major payments, debt paydown scheduling, and investment timing. The forecast should inform action, not just report status.
9. Extend horizon as capability matures. As forecast accuracy improves, extend the horizon beyond thirteen weeks for longer-term planning purposes while maintaining weekly detail near-term.

Preconditions

The Cash Visibility System works when the organization lacks cash forecasting capability, when cash flow is significant and variable, and when finance has the capability to build and maintain the system. It struggles when cash flows are already well understood, when the business has minimal cash flow complexity, or when finance lacks the resources for ongoing maintenance.

The Trap

The primary trap is building a forecast that is too complex to maintain. Elaborate models that require extensive effort to update will be abandoned. Start simple. Add complexity only where it improves accuracy meaningfully.

The second trap is treating the forecast as a reporting exercise rather than a management tool. Forecasts that are produced but not used for decisions add no value. Connect the forecast to action.

The Proof

Forecast accuracy metrics. Tracking showing forecast variance declining over time.

Decision examples. Documentation of cash decisions that were informed by forecast data.

Issue anticipation. Evidence that the forecast identified potential cash issues before they became problems.

Variants

Daily Cash Tracking. For businesses with high cash flow volatility, implement daily tracking and short-term daily forecasting.

Scenario-Based Forecasting. Develop multiple forecast scenarios to understand cash implications of different business outcomes.

Automated Cash Pooling. Implement automated concentration of cash across entities to maximize visibility and minimize trapped cash.

____

____

____

DISQUALIFIERS: When This Gambit Is Wrong

____

____

____

- The organization already has mature cash forecasting capability
- Cash flows are simple and predictable without formal forecasting
- Finance lacks the resources to build and maintain the system
- Cash position is not a material concern given liquidity levels

If disqualified, consider: Enhancing existing cash management processes rather than building new infrastructure

____

____

____

GAMBITPLATE **#28**

THE COVENANT MANAGEMENT PROGRAM

BRIDGE: Equity Value **TIME:** 3 months

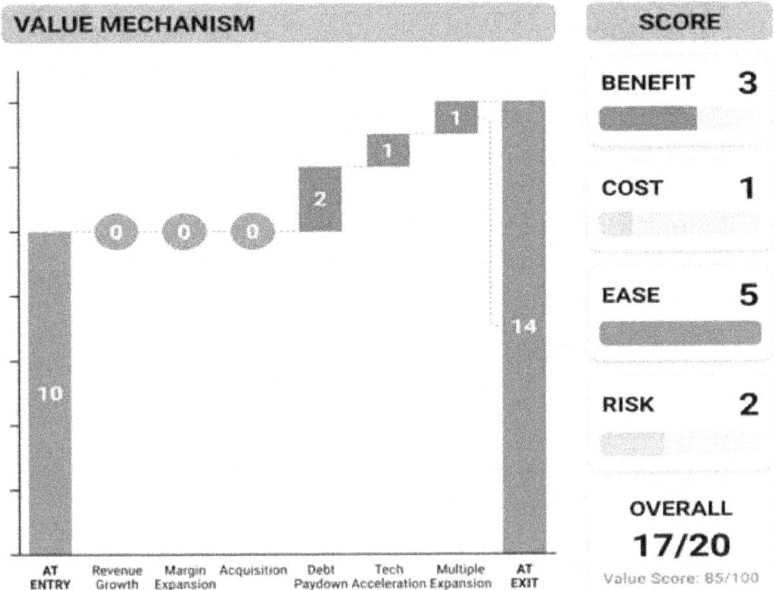

FIELD NOTES

TRIGGERS

- Operating near covenant thresholds
- No systematic covenant monitoring

PROOF ARTIFACTS

- Covenant tracking dashboard operational
- Buffer to breach documented monthly

DISQUALIFIERS

- No financial covenants in debt agreements
- Covenant headroom consistently large

Install systematic monitoring and management of financial covenant compliance.

Gambit 28

The Covenant Management Program

Bridge Target: Equity Value Bridge (protecting value through financial compliance management)

Time to Impact: Fast (one to two months to establish monitoring, ongoing thereafter)

The Pattern

The Covenant Management Program prevents value destruction through proactive monitoring and management of debt covenant compliance. Covenant breaches trigger default provisions that can result in accelerated repayment, increased interest rates, or loss of control. Prevention is far better than cure.

Most covenant issues are predictable before they occur. The Program establishes monitoring systems that identify potential breaches with enough lead time to take corrective action. This may mean operational adjustments, proactive lender communication, or amendment requests before technical default.

The Program also ensures the organization understands covenant implications of business decisions. Some initiatives that seem attractive operationally may threaten covenant compliance. Leaders should understand these implications before committing.

The Sacrifice

Finance team time devoted to covenant monitoring. Constraints on business decisions that might affect covenant compliance. Cost of amendments if covenant relief is needed. Relationship management with lenders.

The Sequence

1. Document all covenant requirements. Compile a complete list of financial covenants from all debt agreements. Specify exact definitions, measurement periods, and thresholds. Create a single reference document.
2. Establish current compliance status. Calculate current performance against each covenant. Determine headroom: the margin between current performance and covenant thresholds.
3. Build covenant forecasting model. Create a model that projects covenant performance based on business forecasts. Link to the operating plan and cash forecast. Understand how business performance translates to covenant metrics.
4. Define early warning thresholds. Establish internal triggers that indicate potential compliance issues. These should fire well before actual breach. Typical triggers are when headroom falls below a defined threshold.
5. Monitor monthly or quarterly. Track covenant performance each period. Update forecasts. Identify any trends toward breach. Report to leadership.

6. Screen business decisions for covenant impact. Before committing to significant initiatives, assess covenant implications. Acquisitions, restructuring, and major investments all affect covenant metrics.
7. Develop breach response playbook. Create response plans for potential breach scenarios. Identify corrective actions, communication strategies, and amendment approaches. Preparation enables faster response.
8. Maintain lender relationships. Communicate proactively with lenders about business performance. Address issues before they become surprises. Lenders respond better to transparent borrowers.
9. Request amendments proactively if needed. If forecasts indicate likely breach, approach lenders before the breach occurs. Request amendments with supporting rationale. Proactive requests are more likely to succeed than reactive ones.

Preconditions

The Covenant Management Program works when the company has meaningful covenant requirements, when finance has the capability to monitor and forecast, and when leadership takes covenant compliance seriously. It struggles when covenants have excessive headroom, when forecasting is unreliable, or when leadership ignores compliance risks.

The Trap

The primary trap is optimistic forecasting that masks emerging problems. Forecasts that systematically overestimate performance can create false comfort. Use conservative assumptions and stress test against downside scenarios.

The second trap is surprising lenders with bad news. Lenders who learn about problems from management respond better than lenders who discover problems from financial statements. Maintain communication and transparency.

The Proof

Continuous compliance. Documentation showing the company maintained covenant compliance throughout the period.

Forecast accuracy. Evidence that covenant forecasts were accurate enough to provide useful early warning.

Proactive management examples. Documentation of instances where the Program enabled proactive response to emerging issues.

Variants

Covenant Dashboard. Build a real-time or near-real-time dashboard showing covenant status and headroom.

Stress Testing Protocol. Regularly stress test covenant compliance against adverse scenarios: revenue decline, margin compression, working capital spike.

Covenant-Adjusted Planning. Integrate covenant constraints into the annual planning process so that plans are covenant-compliant by design.

____
____
____

DISQUALIFIERS: When This Gambit Is Wrong

____
____
____

- Covenants have excessive headroom with no realistic risk of breach
- The business has no debt or no meaningful covenant requirements
- Finance lacks capability to monitor and forecast covenant metrics accurately
- Leadership routinely ignores covenant risks and will not respond to warnings

If disqualified, consider: Basic covenant tracking without formal program infrastructure

____
____
____

SECTION E

MULTIPLE EXPANSION GAMBITS

Gambits 29 through 34

The multiple is where perception meets reality. The six gambits in this section address the primary drivers of how buyers value a business: revenue quality transformation, customer concentration reduction, management depth building, recurring revenue conversion, risk mitigation, and exit narrative construction.

Each gambit targets the enterprise value bridge by improving the characteristics that drive premium valuations. Unlike operational improvements that affect earnings directly, multiple expansion gambits change how the market perceives and values those earnings. The same dollar of operating profit is worth more when it comes from a business with the right characteristics. Select the gambits that address your business's valuation constraints.

GAMBITPLATE **#29**

THE REVENUE QUALITY UPGRADE

BRIDGE: Enterprise Value | **TIME:** 24 months

VALUE MECHANISM

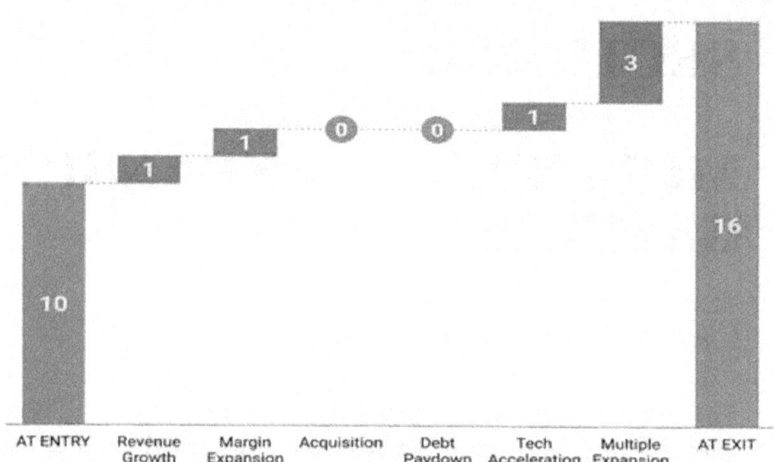

SCORE PANEL

BENEFIT	COST	EASE	RISK	OVERALL
5	3	2	3	13/20
5/5	3/5	2/5	3/5	Value Score: 65/100

FIELD NOTES

TRIGGERS:
- Revenue primarily transactional or project-based
- Low recurring revenue percentage

PROOF ARTIFACTS:
- Recurring revenue percentage increasing
- Revenue retention metrics documented

DISQUALIFIERS:
- Business model cannot support recurring revenue
- Customers unwilling to commit to contracts

Transform revenue characteristics to justify higher valuation multiples.

Gambit 29

The Revenue Quality Upgrade

Bridge Target: Enterprise Value Bridge (multiple expansion through improved revenue characteristics)

Time to Impact: Long (twelve to twenty-four months for meaningful quality shift)

The Pattern

The Revenue Quality Upgrade transforms the characteristics of revenue from those that buyers discount to those that buyers value. Not all revenue is equal. Buyers pay premium multiples for revenue that is recurring, predictable, diversified, and growing. They discount revenue that is transactional, volatile, concentrated, or declining.

The Upgrade systematically shifts the revenue mix toward higher-quality characteristics. This may mean converting transactional customers to contracts, building recurring service revenue around product sales, or deliberately growing high-quality segments faster than low-quality ones. The goal is a revenue base that commands premium valuation.

Revenue quality affects multiple through risk perception. Recurring revenue is less risky than transactional. Diversified revenue is less risky than concentrated. Predictable revenue is less risky than volatile. Buyers pay more for the same dollar of profit when they believe it will persist.

The Sacrifice

Short-term revenue growth may slow during the transition. Investment required to build new revenue streams. Operational complexity during the transition period. Risk that new revenue models do not achieve expected adoption.

The Sequence

1. Assess current revenue quality. Analyze revenue across quality dimensions: recurring versus transactional, contracted versus at-will, diversified versus concentrated, predictable versus volatile. Quantify the mix.
2. Identify quality improvement opportunities. Determine which quality dimensions can be improved and how. Some businesses can add contracts to existing relationships. Others can layer services onto products. Identify the feasible paths.
3. Define target revenue composition. Establish specific targets for revenue mix: percentage recurring, percentage contracted, concentration limits, retention targets. These become the objectives for the Upgrade.
4. Develop conversion strategies. For each quality improvement, create a strategy to convert existing revenue or acquire new high-quality revenue. Define value propositions, pricing, and go-to-market approaches.
5. Execute conversion programs. Implement the strategies to shift revenue quality. Convert transactional customers to contracts. Launch

recurring revenue offerings. Grow high-quality segments deliberately.

6. Track quality metrics alongside revenue. Monitor revenue quality metrics as rigorously as revenue growth. Report recurring percentage, retention rates, and concentration metrics. Make quality as visible as quantity.
7. Build proof of quality improvement. Generate data showing quality metrics improving over time. Create cohort analyses demonstrating retention. Document the quality transformation.
8. Align organization around quality. Ensure compensation, goals, and priorities reinforce revenue quality. Do not reward revenue growth that degrades quality.
9. Communicate the transformation. As quality improves, ensure the narrative reflects the change. Update investor communications, sales messaging, and exit materials to emphasize revenue quality.

Preconditions

The Revenue Quality Upgrade works when there is a genuine path to improving revenue characteristics, when customers will accept different commercial models, and when the organization can execute the transition. It struggles when the business model inherently produces low-quality revenue, when customers resist changes, or when execution capability is limited.

The Trap

The primary trap is sacrificing revenue growth for quality. While quality matters, buyers also value growth. An upgrade that improves quality but stalls growth may not improve valuation. Balance quality improvement with continued growth.

The second trap is superficial quality claims. Labeling transactional revenue as recurring does not make it recurring. Buyers conduct diligence. False quality claims will be exposed and damage credibility. Quality must be genuine.

The Proof

Recurring revenue percentage. Tracking showing the percentage of recurring or contracted revenue increasing over time. Target Level 4 evidence with sustained trend.

Retention metrics. Evidence of gross and net revenue retention improving.

Revenue predictability. Demonstration that revenue forecasting accuracy has improved as quality increased.

Variants

Contract Conversion. Focus specifically on converting at-will customer relationships to multi-year contracts with committed revenue.

Services Layer. For product businesses, add recurring service revenue that creates ongoing customer relationships.

Subscription Transformation. Convert perpetual license or one-time purchase models to subscription or recurring payment structures.

DISQUALIFIERS: When This Gambit Is Wrong

- The business model inherently produces transactional, project-based revenue
- Customers strongly resist contract commitments or recurring payment models
- Revenue growth would stall significantly during the quality transition
- The organization lacks capability to execute commercial model changes

If disqualified, consider: Gambit 30 (The Concentration Reduction) if concentration is the primary multiple constraint

GAMBITPLATE **#30**

THE CONCENTRATION REDUCTION

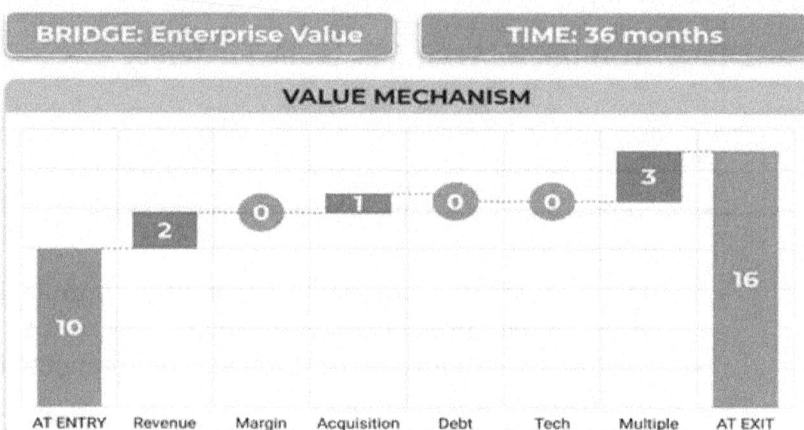

SCORE PANEL

BENEFIT: 4 — 4/5

COST: 3 — 3/5

EASE: 2 — 2/5

RISK: 3 — 3/5

OVERALL: 12/20

Value Score: 60/100

FIELD NOTES

TRIGGERS:

- Top customer exceeds 15% of revenue
- Top 5 customers exceed 40% of revenue

PROOF ARTIFACTS:

- Top customer percentage declining
- New customer revenue contribution growing

DISQUALIFIERS:

- Concentration is structural to the market
- Large customers are also most profitable

Reduce customer concentration risk to improve buyer confidence and multiple.

Gambit 30

The Concentration Reduction

Bridge Target: Enterprise Value Bridge (multiple expansion through reduced customer concentration risk)

Time to Impact: Long (twelve to thirty-six months for meaningful diversification)

The Pattern

The Concentration Reduction systematically diversifies the customer base to reduce single-customer dependency. Customer concentration is one of the most common valuation discounts. When a significant percentage of revenue depends on one or a few customers, buyers perceive the business as risky. That risk perception compresses multiples.

The discount thresholds are well understood. A customer representing more than fifteen percent of revenue triggers concern. A customer representing more than twenty-five percent triggers significant discount. Multiple customers above these thresholds compound the concern. The Reduction works to bring concentration below these thresholds.

Reducing concentration does not mean shrinking large customer relationships. It means growing other customers faster. The goal is to dilute concentration through diversified growth rather than to abandon valuable customers. The best outcome is when the concentrated customer stays flat or grows modestly while other customers grow faster.

The Sacrifice

Sales and marketing investment to acquire new customers. Potential underinvestment in the concentrated customer relationship. Time required for new customer revenue to scale. Risk that new customers are less profitable than the concentrated one.

The Sequence

1. Quantify current concentration. Calculate revenue concentration by customer. Identify customers above fifteen percent. Understand trends: is concentration increasing or decreasing over time?
2. Set concentration reduction targets. Establish target concentration levels and timelines. Be realistic: meaningful diversification takes years, not months. Plan accordingly.
3. Secure the concentrated relationship. Before focusing elsewhere, ensure the concentrated customer relationship is stable. Long-term contracts, strong relationships, and high satisfaction reduce the risk that diversification efforts are undermined by concentrated customer loss.
4. Identify diversification opportunities. Determine where new customer growth will come from: new market segments, new geographies, new products, or more aggressive penetration of existing markets.
5. Reallocate sales and marketing investment. Shift resources toward diversification targets. This may mean reducing investment in the concentrated

customer, which is often over-served relative to its potential.

6. Execute diversification programs. Acquire new customers aggressively. Build new market presence. Grow second-tier customers into larger relationships. Pursue multiple diversification paths simultaneously.
7. Track concentration monthly. Monitor concentration metrics alongside revenue growth. Celebrate diversification progress. Identify when concentration is rising and take corrective action.
8. Build the diversification narrative. As concentration declines, document the transformation. Show the trend. Explain the strategy. Build buyer confidence that concentration risk is being actively managed.
9. Maintain vigilance against new concentration. As some customers shrink as a percentage, others may grow. Continuously monitor and prevent new concentration from emerging.

Preconditions

The Concentration Reduction works when there are viable opportunities to acquire new customers, when the concentrated relationship can be secured during diversification, and when the organization has the capability to execute growth outside its traditional base. It struggles when the business model inherently requires few large customers, when the concentrated customer is at risk of leaving, or when new customer acquisition is prohibitively expensive.

The Trap

The primary trap is neglecting the concentrated customer in pursuit of diversification. If the concentrated customer leaves while diversification is underway, the result is catastrophic. Protect the base while building alternatives.

The second trap is diversifying into unprofitable customers. If new customers are acquired at unfavorable economics, diversification destroys value even as it reduces concentration. Maintain economic discipline in customer acquisition.

The Proof

Concentration decline trend. Tracking showing top customer percentage declining over multiple periods.

New customer growth. Evidence that diversification came from new customer acquisition, not concentrated customer decline.

Concentrated customer stability. Documentation that the concentrated relationship remained strong during diversification.

Variants

Segment Diversification. Focus diversification on entering new market segments where the concentrated customer does not operate.

Geographic Expansion. Reduce concentration by expanding into new geographies with different customer bases.

Product Line Diversification. Launch new products that attract different customers than the concentrated relationship.

DISQUALIFIERS: When This Gambit Is Wrong

- The business model inherently requires serving a small number of large customers
- The concentrated customer is at risk of leaving during diversification efforts
- New customer acquisition cost is prohibitively high relative to lifetime value
- Timeline to exit does not allow meaningful concentration reduction

If disqualified, consider: Securing the concentrated relationship through long-term contracts to mitigate discount

GAMBITPLATE #31

THE MANAGEMENT DEPTH BUILD

BRIDGE: Enterprise Value | **TIME: 18 months**

VALUE MECHANISM

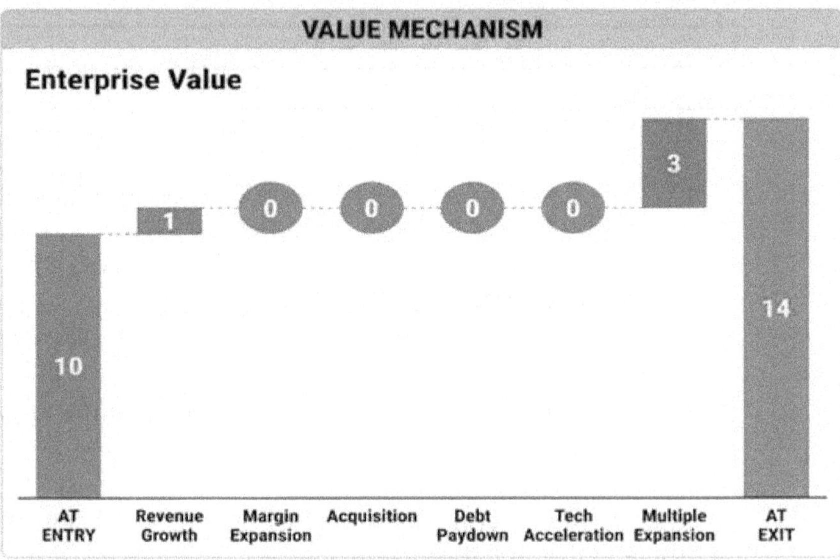

SCORE PANEL

BENEFIT	COST	EASE	RISK	OVERALL
4	3	3	2	14/20
4/5	3/5	3/5	2/5	Value Score: 70/100

FIELD NOTES

TRIGGERS
- Key-person dependency on CEO or founder
- No succession plan for critical roles

PROOF ARTIFACTS
- Org chart with succession plans
- Decision-making distributed across team

DISQUALIFIERS
- Management team already deep and stable
- Budget cannot support additional hires

Build management depth to reduce key-person risk and improve scalability.

Gambit 31

The Management Depth Build

Bridge Target: Enterprise Value Bridge (multiple expansion through reduced key-person dependency and improved scalability)

Time to Impact: Medium to Long (twelve to twenty-four months to build meaningful depth)

The Pattern

The Management Depth Build creates a professional leadership team that reduces dependency on any single individual. Key-person risk is a common valuation discount. When business success depends heavily on the founder, the chief executive, or a small group of critical individuals, buyers perceive risk. That risk compresses multiples.

The Build addresses key-person risk by developing capable leaders in all critical roles, creating succession depth at multiple levels, and institutionalizing knowledge that currently resides in individuals. The goal is a business that can thrive regardless of any single departure.

Management depth also signals operational maturity. A business with deep management is more scalable, more acquirable, and more valuable. Buyers see a platform they can build on rather than a fragile operation they must worry about.

The Sacrifice

Investment in recruiting and developing leadership talent. Increased compensation expense from building a senior team. Founder or chief executive willingness to delegate and develop others. Time required for new leaders to become effective.

The Sequence

1. Assess current key-person risk. Identify individuals whose departure would materially harm the business. Evaluate the depth below them. Understand where concentration of knowledge and capability exists.
2. Define target organizational structure. Design the leadership team the business needs for its current scale and planned growth. Identify gaps between current state and target.
3. Prioritize critical role gaps. Not all gaps are equally important. Prioritize roles where key-person risk is highest, where capability gaps limit growth, or where succession depth is thinnest.
4. Recruit to fill gaps. For priority roles, conduct professional searches to find qualified candidates. Invest in recruiting capability. Do not settle for underqualified candidates who perpetuate gaps.
5. Develop internal succession candidates. Identify high-potential individuals who could grow into leadership roles. Invest in their development through stretch assignments, mentoring, and training.
6. Institutionalize key knowledge. Transfer knowledge from key individuals to the organization. Document

processes. Create playbooks. Build systems that capture institutional knowledge.

7. Transition responsibilities deliberately. As new leaders join and internal candidates develop, transfer responsibilities from key individuals. Create genuine delegation, not just titles.
8. Demonstrate depth to buyers. During exit preparation, showcase the management team. Have leaders other than the chief executive present their functions. Show that the business does not depend on one person.
9. Maintain depth as an ongoing priority. Leadership depth requires continuous attention. Plan for succession at all levels. Make talent development a permanent organizational priority.

Preconditions

The Management Depth Build works when key-person risk exists and is recognized, when the business can afford to invest in leadership talent, and when key individuals are willing to delegate and develop others. It struggles when founders resist delegation, when the business cannot afford professional leadership compensation, or when the talent market is too competitive to attract qualified candidates.

The Trap

The primary trap is hiring senior talent without delegating authority. If new leaders have titles but the founder continues to make all decisions, key-person risk remains. Real delegation is required, not cosmetic hiring.

The second trap is overpaying for underperformers. In the rush to build depth, some companies hire candidates who look good but do not perform. Maintain performance standards. Address underperformance quickly rather than tolerating it because the role needs filling.

The Proof

Leadership team completeness. Documentation showing all critical leadership roles filled with qualified individuals.

Succession depth. Evidence of identified successors for key roles and development plans in place.

Delegation evidence. Demonstration that key individuals have genuinely delegated responsibility and the business operates effectively without their daily involvement.

Variants

Chief Executive Transition. For founder-led businesses, hire a professional chief executive while the founder transitions to a different role.

Functional Professionalization. Focus on professionalizing specific functions with the highest key-person risk: sales, operations, or technology.

Board Strengthening. Add independent board members who bring credibility and can demonstrate governance maturity to buyers.

DISQUALIFIERS: When This Gambit Is Wrong

- The founder or key individuals refuse to delegate meaningful authority
- The business cannot afford professional leadership compensation
- The talent market is too competitive to attract qualified candidates at available compensation
- Timeline to exit is too short to demonstrate depth to buyers

If disqualified, consider: Retention agreements and earnout structures to mitigate key-person risk at exit

GAMBITPLATE **#32**

THE RECURRING REVENUE CONVERSION

BRIDGE: Enterprise Value | **TIME:** 36 months

VALUE MECHANISM

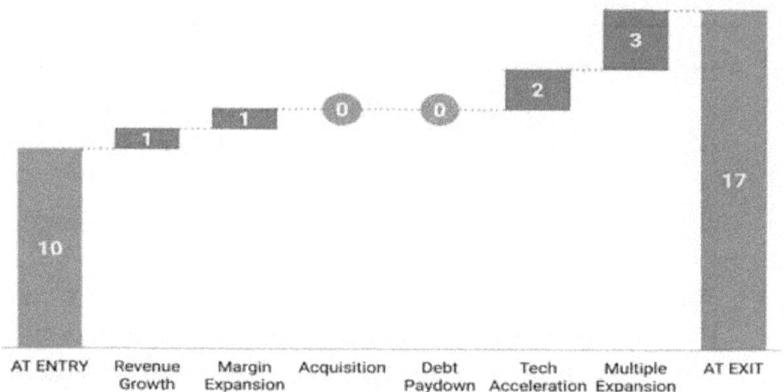

SCORE PANEL

BENEFIT	COST	EASE	RISK	OVERALL
5	4	2	4	11/20
5/5	4/5	2/5	4/5	Value Score: 55/100

FIELD NOTES

TRIGGERS

- Project or perpetual revenue model
- Peers trading at higher multiples with recurring model

PROOF ARTIFACTS

- Recurring revenue as percentage of total growing
- Customer adoption of subscription model

DISQUALIFIERS

- Customers strongly prefer current model
- Conversion would significantly reduce near-term revenue

Transform business model from transactional to recurring revenue.

Gambit 32

The Recurring Revenue Conversion

Bridge Target: Enterprise Value Bridge (multiple expansion through business model transformation)

Time to Impact: Long (eighteen to thirty-six months for meaningful model shift)

The Pattern

The Recurring Revenue Conversion transforms the fundamental revenue model from transactional to recurring. Recurring revenue businesses trade at significantly higher multiples than transactional businesses. The multiple differential can be two to three turns or more. This makes business model transformation one of the most powerful value creation levers.

Recurring revenue is valued higher because it is more predictable. Once customers subscribe, they tend to remain. Revenue next year is largely visible based on customers retained this year. This predictability reduces risk and enables premium valuation.

The Conversion requires rethinking how customers buy and how the business delivers value. Some transitions are natural: product companies adding maintenance contracts, perpetual licenses converting to subscriptions, or transactional services moving to retainer models. Others require more fundamental redesign.

The Sacrifice

Short-term revenue decline as large one-time transactions convert to smaller recurring payments. Investment in infrastructure to support recurring model. Customer resistance to model changes. Organizational change to support different sales and service approaches.

The Sequence

1. Assess conversion opportunity. Evaluate whether the business can support a recurring model. Some businesses have natural recurring elements to emphasize. Others require more fundamental transformation. Determine feasibility.
2. Design the recurring model. Define what the recurring offering will include: product access, service level, support, updates, or consumables. Determine pricing that is attractive to customers while economically sound for the business.
3. Model the transition economics. Understand the financial impact of conversion. Revenue may decline short-term as large transactions spread over time. Model cash flow implications carefully.
4. Build supporting infrastructure. Recurring models require different systems: subscription billing, usage tracking, renewal management, and customer success. Build or acquire necessary capabilities.
5. Launch with new customers first. Introduce the recurring model to new customers before converting existing ones. Work out operational issues with a fresh customer base.
6. Convert existing customers gradually. Develop migration strategies for existing customers. Offer

incentives to convert. Allow time for adoption. Do not force conversion that triggers churn.

7. Track recurring metrics. Monitor the metrics that matter for recurring businesses: monthly or annual recurring revenue, net revenue retention, customer lifetime value, and customer acquisition cost. Report these prominently.
8. Retrain the organization. Sales, finance, and operations must adapt to recurring model requirements. Train teams on new metrics, processes, and success criteria.
9. Build recurring revenue proof points. Generate multiple quarters of recurring revenue performance. Demonstrate retention. Show the predictability that justifies premium valuation.

Preconditions

The Recurring Revenue Conversion works when the business has ongoing customer relationships that can support recurring revenue, when customers will accept recurring models, and when the organization can build necessary capabilities. It struggles when customer relationships are inherently transactional, when customers strongly prefer one-time purchases, or when the investment required exceeds available resources.

The Trap

The primary trap is forcing conversion that triggers churn. If existing customers reject the recurring model and leave, the business is worse off. Conversion must be attractive enough that customers choose it willingly.

The second trap is underestimating the transition investment. Recurring models require different systems, skills, and processes. Companies that underinvest in infrastructure struggle to deliver the customer experience that recurring models require.

The Proof

Recurring revenue percentage. Tracking showing the percentage of total revenue that is recurring increasing over time.

Net revenue retention. Evidence that recurring customers expand over time, with net retention above one hundred percent.

Cohort performance. Cohort analysis showing strong retention and expansion patterns in the recurring customer base.

Variants

Subscription Transformation. Convert perpetual license or one-time purchase models to subscription pricing.

Maintenance and Support Model. For product businesses, build recurring maintenance and support contracts around one-time product sales.

Consumables Model. Design products that require recurring consumable purchases, creating predictable repeat revenue.

DISQUALIFIERS: When This Gambit Is Wrong

- Customer relationships are inherently transactional with no ongoing need
- Customers strongly resist recurring payment models and will churn if forced
- The business lacks resources to invest in recurring model infrastructure
- Short-term revenue decline from conversion would breach covenants or threaten operations

If disqualified, consider: Gambit 29 (The Revenue Quality Upgrade) for incremental quality improvements

GAMBITPLATE #33

THE RISK MITIGATION PACKAGE

BRIDGE: Enterprise Value | **TIME:** 12 months

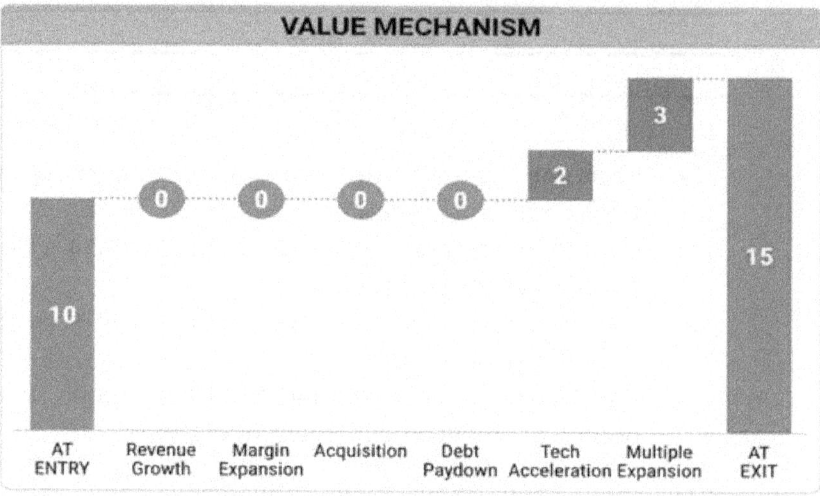

SCORE PANEL

BENEFIT	COST	EASE	RISK	OVERALL
4	3	3	2	14/20
4/5	3/5	3/5	2/5	Value Score: 70/100

FIELD NOTES

TRIGGERS

- Identified risks that buyers will discount for
- Regulatory, legal, or compliance concerns

PROOF ARTIFACTS

- Risk register with mitigation status
- Compliance certifications obtained

DISQUALIFIERS

- Risks are already well-managed
- Mitigation cost exceeds value impact

Systematically reduce specific risks that would compress exit multiple.

Gambit 33

The Risk Mitigation Package

Bridge Target: Enterprise Value Bridge (multiple expansion through systematic risk reduction)

Time to Impact: Medium (six to eighteen months depending on risk types addressed)

The Pattern

The Risk Mitigation Package systematically identifies and addresses the risks that cause buyers to discount valuation. Buyers conduct diligence specifically to find risks. Each risk discovered becomes leverage for price reduction or deal structure adjustment. The Package addresses risks proactively before buyers discover them.

Common risks that compress multiples include: earnings quality issues where reported earnings overstate sustainable performance, deferred maintenance where underinvestment creates future obligations, compliance exposure where regulatory or legal issues create liability, technology debt where outdated systems threaten operations, and contract risks where unfavorable terms create vulnerability.

The Package works like pre-flight inspection. Issues found and fixed before diligence do not become negotiating points. Issues discovered during diligence become deductions from value. The same investment in risk remediation yields better results when made proactively.

The Sacrifice

Investment required to remediate identified risks. Management attention diverted to risk issues. Potential earnings impact from addressing deferred expenses. Short-term disruption from compliance or system remediation.

The Sequence

1. Conduct sell-side risk assessment. Examine the business through a buyer's eyes. Identify issues that would concern an acquirer during diligence. Be thorough and honest.
2. Categorize risks by impact and remediability. Assess each risk for potential valuation impact and difficulty of remediation. Prioritize risks that significantly impact value and can be addressed.
3. Address earnings quality issues. Review revenue recognition, expense timing, and non-recurring items. Ensure reported earnings reflect sustainable performance. Clean up accounting that might raise questions.
4. Remediate deferred maintenance. Invest in deferred capital expenditure, technology upgrades, and facility improvements. Address maintenance that has been postponed.
5. Resolve compliance exposure. Address regulatory issues, licensing gaps, or legal vulnerabilities. Ensure the business is fully compliant with applicable requirements.
6. Clean up contracts. Review and renegotiate unfavorable contracts. Address customer contracts with problematic terms. Resolve supplier arrangements that create risk.

7. Document remediation. For each risk addressed, create documentation showing the issue, the remediation taken, and the current status. Build the evidence base for clean diligence.
8. Prepare disclosure for remaining risks. For risks that cannot be fully remediated, prepare clear disclosure and mitigation explanations. Transparency about known issues is better than discovery during diligence.
9. Conduct mock diligence. Before going to market, conduct a mock diligence process to identify any remaining issues. Address anything that surfaces.

Preconditions

The Risk Mitigation Package works when there are identifiable risks that can be addressed, when resources are available for remediation, and when timing allows for completion before exit. It struggles when risks are too fundamental to remediate, when remediation costs exceed value protection, or when exit timing does not allow adequate remediation.

The Trap

The primary trap is hiding rather than fixing risks. Concealing issues does not eliminate them. Sophisticated buyers will discover hidden problems, and the discovery damages credibility as well as value. Fix or disclose rather than hide.

The second trap is overspending on immaterial risks. Not every risk materially affects valuation. Focus remediation resources on risks that buyers would actually discount. Do not invest heavily in issues buyers would ignore.

The Proof

Risk remediation documentation. Records showing identified risks and completed remediation actions.

Clean diligence results. Evidence from sell-side diligence or mock diligence showing limited findings.

Earnings quality confirmation. Third-party earnings quality report with minimal adjustments.

Variants

Sell-Side Earnings Quality. Commission a third-party earnings quality report before going to market. Address any issues found.

Technology Due Diligence. For technology-dependent businesses, conduct technical diligence to identify and address technology risks.

Legal Cleanup. Engage legal counsel to identify and resolve contract, intellectual property, and compliance issues before sale.

____

____

____

DISQUALIFIERS: When This Gambit Is Wrong

____

____

____

- Risks are too fundamental to remediate within available time and resources
- Remediation costs would exceed the value protected
- Exit timeline does not allow adequate time for remediation
- The business has minimal diligence-sensitive risks

If disqualified, consider: Negotiated risk allocation through representations, warranties, and escrow structures

____

____

____

GAMBITPLATE #34

THE EXIT NARRATIVE CONSTRUCTION

BRIDGE: Enterprise Value | **TIME:** 6 months

VALUE MECHANISM

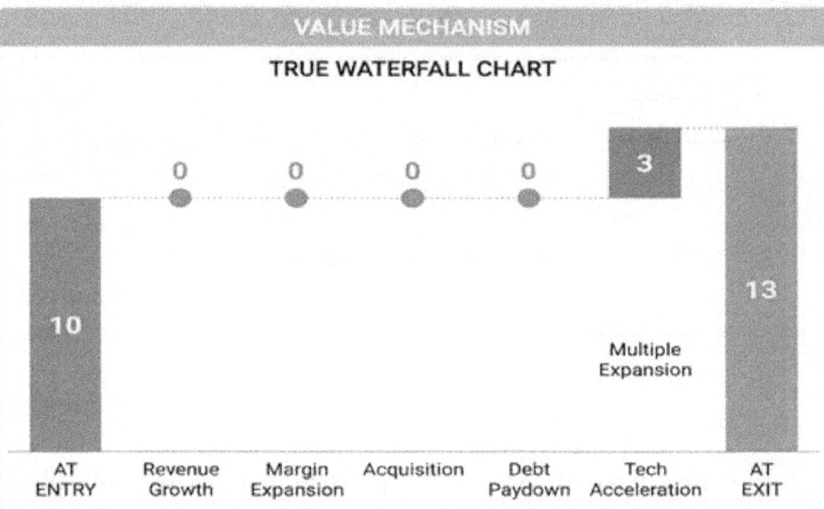

SCORE PANEL

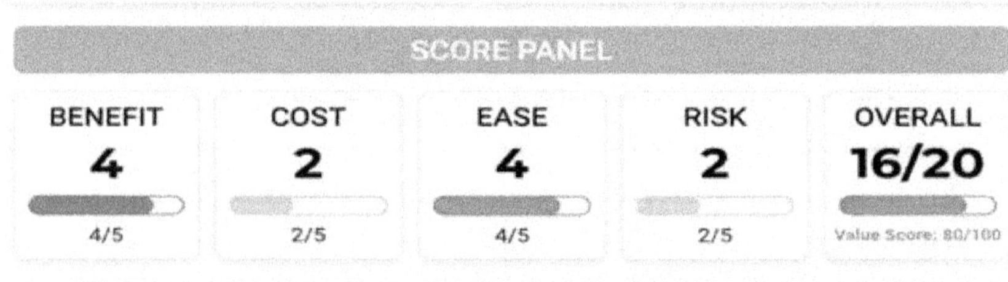

FIELD NOTES

TRIGGERS
- Exit process approaching within 12 months
- No clear articulation of value creation story

PROOF ARTIFACTS
- Management presentation with clear thesis
- Proof points documented for each theme

DISQUALIFIERS
- Exit timeline uncertain or distant
- No meaningful value creation to narrate

Construct compelling buyer communication that articulates value creation.

Gambit 34

The Exit Narrative Construction

Bridge Target: Enterprise Value Bridge (multiple expansion through compelling buyer communication)

Time to Impact: Fast to Medium (three to nine months to develop and validate narrative)

The Pattern

The Exit Narrative Construction builds the story that helps buyers understand and value the business. Buyers do not just buy financials. They buy a vision of what the business is and can become. The narrative shapes how they interpret the numbers and what multiple they are willing to pay.

The narrative must be grounded in truth but framed for impact. It explains the transformation during the hold period, the competitive advantages that drive success, the market opportunity ahead, and the proof points that validate the story. A compelling narrative helps buyers see value that raw numbers might not convey.

The Construction is not about spin or exaggeration. It is about organizing genuine achievements and opportunities into a coherent story that resonates with buyer priorities. Different buyers may respond to different narratives, and the best sellers adapt their story to each audience.

The Sacrifice

Management time to develop and refine the narrative. Investment in presentation materials and data rooms. Discipline to maintain consistency between narrative and reality. Vulnerability from exposing the business to buyer scrutiny.

The Sequence

1. Define the core value proposition. Articulate clearly what makes this business valuable. What does it do? Who does it serve? Why is it better than alternatives? What is defensible?
2. Document the transformation story. Describe what changed during the hold period. What was the business at entry? What is it now? What drove the improvement? This demonstrates value creation capability.
3. Articulate the market opportunity. Explain the market size, growth dynamics, and trends that favor the business. Show that the opportunity ahead is large enough to justify premium valuation.
4. Identify competitive advantages. Explain what makes the business difficult to replicate or displace. Customer relationships, technology, scale economies, or talent depth all contribute to defensibility.
5. Build the proof package. Assemble the data that validates the narrative: financial performance, customer metrics, operational achievements, and market position evidence. The narrative must be provable.
6. Develop tailored buyer narratives. Understand what different buyer types value. Strategic buyers may

care about synergies. Financial buyers may care about growth potential. Adapt the narrative to resonate with each.

7. Create compelling presentation materials. Develop a confidential information memorandum, management presentation, and supporting materials that communicate the narrative effectively.
8. Train the management team. Ensure all presenters can articulate the narrative consistently and compellingly. Practice management presentations. Prepare for challenging questions.
9. Test and refine. Test the narrative with advisors or friendly audiences. Refine based on feedback. Iterate until the story resonates.

Preconditions

The Exit Narrative Construction works when there is a genuine story to tell, when proof points exist to validate the narrative, and when management can present it credibly. It struggles when the business lacks distinguishing characteristics, when performance does not support the narrative, or when management cannot articulate the story effectively.

The Trap

The primary trap is a narrative that does not survive diligence. If buyers discover that the story is exaggerated or unsupported, credibility collapses. The resulting distrust affects every aspect of the transaction. The narrative must be honest.

The second trap is a generic narrative that does not differentiate. Every business claims to have great people, strong customer relationships, and market opportunity. Effective narratives are specific and distinctive. They explain why this business, not just any business.

The Proof

Buyer engagement. Evidence that the narrative generates buyer interest and advances conversations.

Narrative consistency. Demonstration that the narrative remains consistent and credible through diligence.

Valuation support. Evidence that buyers cite narrative elements in justifying their valuations.

Variants

Platform Story. Position the business as a platform for future acquisitions. Emphasize the infrastructure and capability to execute a consolidation strategy.

Synergy Story. For strategic buyers, emphasize the synergies that the acquisition would create. Help buyers see value they can uniquely capture.

Growth Story. For growth-focused buyers, emphasize the untapped potential and the investments that would accelerate growth.

DISQUALIFIERS: When This Gambit Is Wrong

- The business lacks distinguishing characteristics worth highlighting
- Financial performance does not support claims of transformation or quality
- Management cannot articulate the narrative credibly under buyer scrutiny
- The business is being sold in distress where narrative has limited impact

If disqualified, consider: Focus on operational improvement before exit rather than narrative construction

SECTION F

TECHNOLOGY AND AUTOMATION GAMBITS

Gambits 35 through 40

Technology is an accelerant, not an arena. The six gambits in this section address how technology amplifies value creation across all other arenas: process automation, data infrastructure, artificial intelligence deployment, technology debt remediation, digital product enhancement, and technology-enabled service delivery.

Each gambit targets the operating earnings bridge through efficiency and capability improvement, or the enterprise value bridge through competitive differentiation and scalability. Technology gambits rarely stand alone. They amplify the impact of revenue, margin, and other gambits. Select technology gambits that support your broader value creation strategy rather than pursuing technology for its own sake.

GAMBITPLATE #35

THE PROCESS AUTOMATION WAVE

BRIDGE: Operating Earnings | **TIME:** 12 months

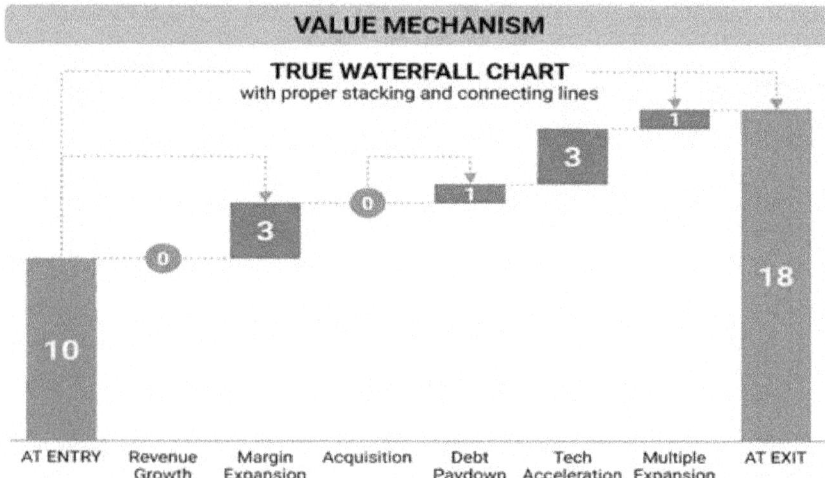

SCORE PANEL

BENEFIT	COST	EASE	RISK	OVERALL
4	3	3	2	14/20
				Value Score: 70/100

FIELD NOTES

TRIGGERS

- High labor cost in repetitive processes
- Error rates in manual workflows

PROOF ARTIFACTS

- FTE reduction or reallocation documented
- ROI on automation investments tracked

DISQUALIFIERS

- Processes too variable for automation
- Volume too low to justify investment

Systematically automate repetitive manual processes in successive waves.

Gambit 35

The Process Automation Wave

Bridge Target: Operating Earnings Bridge (margin improvement through labor efficiency and error reduction)

Time to Impact: Medium (six to twelve months for meaningful automation deployment)

The Pattern

The Process Automation Wave systematically identifies and automates repetitive manual processes across the organization. Most businesses carry substantial hidden labor cost in tasks that are rule-based, repetitive, and automatable. The Wave converts this labor into technology, reducing cost while improving speed and accuracy.

Automation targets processes that follow consistent rules, involve structured data, require high volume of repetitive actions, and are prone to human error. Finance, operations, customer service, and administrative functions typically contain significant automation opportunity.

The Wave approach deploys automation in successive waves, starting with high-impact, lower-complexity processes. Each wave builds organizational capability and confidence. Early successes fund and motivate subsequent waves. The goal is a systematic transformation of how work gets done.

The Sacrifice

Investment in automation technology and implementation. Workforce disruption as roles change or are eliminated. Risk of automation failures disrupting operations. Ongoing maintenance requirements for automated processes.

The Sequence

1. Map current processes. Document the major processes across the organization. Understand inputs, steps, outputs, and labor involved. Create visibility into where work happens.
2. Assess automation potential. Evaluate each process for automation suitability: rule-based logic, structured data, high volume, error-prone. Score and rank processes by automation potential.
3. Quantify automation value. For high-potential processes, calculate the labor cost, error cost, and speed improvement from automation. Build business cases that justify investment.
4. Prioritize the first wave. Select three to five processes for the initial automation wave. Choose processes with high value, clear requirements, and manageable complexity. Early success builds momentum.
5. Select automation technology. Choose appropriate technology for the target processes. Robotic process automation handles repetitive tasks. Workflow automation handles approvals and routing. Integration platforms connect systems.
6. Implement with discipline. Deploy automation with proper testing, exception handling, and monitoring. Ensure automated processes are reliable before scaling.

7. Capture the labor savings. As automation deploys, realize the labor savings through role elimination, redeployment, or avoiding hiring. Savings that are not captured are not real.
8. Launch subsequent waves. After the first wave succeeds, launch subsequent waves targeting additional processes. Build organizational capability for continuous automation.
9. Establish automation as ongoing discipline. Create permanent capability to identify and automate new processes. Automation should be continuous, not a one-time project.

Preconditions

The Process Automation Wave works when significant manual process labor exists, when processes are sufficiently standardized to automate, and when the organization has capability to implement automation technology. It struggles when processes are highly variable, when systems are too fragmented to integrate, or when workforce resistance prevents adoption.

The Trap

The primary trap is automating broken processes. Automation amplifies whatever process it touches. If the underlying process is flawed, automation makes it faster at being wrong. Fix processes before automating them.

The second trap is underestimating maintenance requirements. Automated processes require ongoing monitoring, exception handling, and updates when underlying systems change. Factor maintenance into the business case.

The Proof

Labor cost reduction. Tracking showing headcount or labor cost reduction attributable to automation.

Process throughput improvement. Evidence that automated processes handle higher volume at faster speed.

Error rate reduction. Documentation showing error rates declined in automated processes.

Variants

Finance Automation Focus. Concentrate on automating finance processes: accounts payable, accounts receivable, reconciliations, and reporting.

Customer Service Automation. Focus on automating customer service processes: inquiry routing, response generation, and case management.

Operations Automation. Target operational processes: order processing, inventory management, and logistics coordination.

____
____
____

DISQUALIFIERS: When This Gambit Is Wrong

____
____
____

- Processes are highly variable and lack standardization required for automation
- Systems are too fragmented to support automation integration
- Workforce resistance is strong and leadership lacks will to enforce adoption
- Manual labor costs are low relative to automation investment required

If disqualified, consider: Process standardization and simplification before attempting automation

____
____
____

GAMBITPLATE **#36**

THE DATA INFRASTRUCTURE BUILD

BRIDGE: Enterprise Value | **TIME:** 18 months

VALUE MECHANISM

TRUE WATERFALL CHART

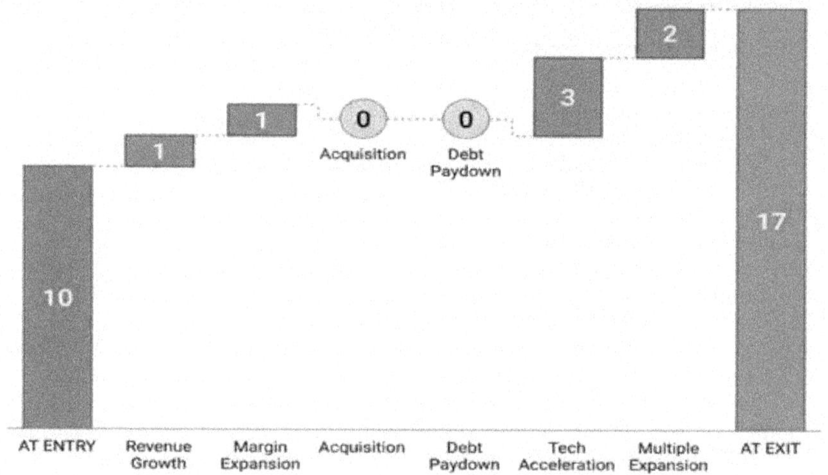

SCORE PANEL

BENEFIT 4 — 4/5

COST 4 — 4/5

EASE 2 — 2/5

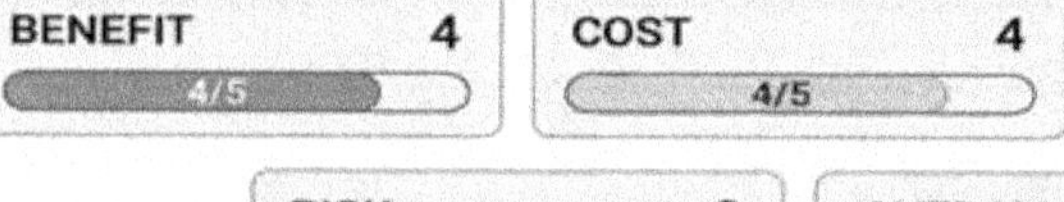

RISK 3 — 3/5

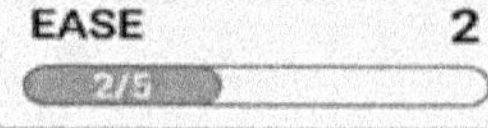

OVERALL
11/20, Value Score: 55/100

FIELD NOTES

TRIGGERS
- Data scattered across disconnected systems
- No single source of truth for key metrics

PROOF ARTIFACTS
- Data platform operational
- Analytics use cases deployed

DISQUALIFIERS
- Data infrastructure already mature
- Business too simple to need sophisticated data

Build foundation for data-driven decisions through consolidated data platform.

Gambit 36

The Data Infrastructure Build

Bridge Target: Operating Earnings Bridge (decision quality improvement) and Enterprise Value Bridge (enabling advanced analytics and machine-supported analysis)

Time to Impact: Medium to Long (nine to eighteen months for meaningful data capability)

The Pattern

The Data Infrastructure Build creates the foundation that makes data-driven decision making possible. Most companies have data scattered across systems, inconsistent in format, and difficult to access. The Build consolidates, standardizes, and makes data accessible for analysis and action.

Data infrastructure is prerequisite for advanced analytics, machine-supported analysis, and operational optimization. Without clean, accessible data, these capabilities remain theoretical. The Build creates the platform on which analytics and intelligence are built.

The value comes not from the infrastructure itself but from what it enables. Better data leads to better decisions. Better decisions lead to better outcomes. The infrastructure investment pays off through improved performance across the business.

The Sacrifice

Significant investment in technology and implementation. Time required before value materializes. Organizational change to adopt data-driven approaches. Ongoing investment in data quality and maintenance.

The Sequence

1. Assess current data state. Inventory existing data sources, systems, and quality. Understand what data exists, where it lives, and how accessible it is.
2. Define priority use cases. Identify the highest-value decisions and analyses that better data would enable. Focus infrastructure on supporting these use cases first.
3. Design target architecture. Define the target state for data infrastructure: where data will be consolidated, how it will be organized, and how users will access it.
4. Build data integration. Create the pipelines that move data from source systems into consolidated infrastructure. Ensure data flows reliably and timely.
5. Establish data quality processes. Implement processes to validate, clean, and maintain data quality. Poor quality data undermines everything built on top of it.
6. Create analytics and reporting layer. Build the tools and interfaces that make data accessible to decision-makers. Dashboards, reports, and self-service analytics enable consumption.
7. Deploy priority use cases. Implement the high-value use cases that justified the investment. Demonstrate tangible value from improved data capability.

8. Expand and scale. After initial success, expand the infrastructure to support additional use cases. Build toward comprehensive data capability.
9. Build data culture. Train the organization to use data in decision-making. Create accountability for data-driven performance. Make data central to how the business operates.

Preconditions

The Data Infrastructure Build works when data exists across the organization, when high-value use cases can be identified, and when the organization will adopt data-driven approaches. It struggles when data is fundamentally unavailable, when the investment cannot be justified by use cases, or when the organization resists change.

The Trap

The primary trap is building infrastructure without use cases. Data platforms that do not connect to business decisions become expensive technology projects without returns. Start with use cases, not infrastructure.

The second trap is underestimating data quality challenges. If source data is flawed, the infrastructure amplifies the problems. Invest heavily in data quality from the start.

The Proof

Use case deployment. Documentation of specific use cases enabled by the infrastructure and their business impact. Target Level 3 or higher on the Evidence Standard Ladder.

Data accessibility metrics. Evidence that decision-makers can access the data they need when they need it.

Decision quality improvement. Examples of better decisions enabled by improved data capability.

Variants

Customer Data Platform. Focus specifically on consolidating and activating customer data for marketing, sales, and service.

Operational Data Hub. Focus on operational data to enable real-time visibility and optimization.

Financial Data Consolidation. Prioritize financial and performance data to enable better reporting and analysis.

DISQUALIFIERS: When This Gambit Is Wrong

- Data fundamentally does not exist or cannot be captured in the business
- High-value use cases cannot be identified to justify the investment
- The organization will not adopt data-driven approaches regardless of infrastructure
- Available investment is insufficient for minimum viable infrastructure

If disqualified, consider: Targeted analytics for specific decisions rather than enterprise infrastructure

GAMBITPLATE #37

MACHINE-SUPPORTED ANALYSIS PROGRAM

BRIDGE: Operating Earnings | **TIME:** 12 months

VALUE MECHANISM

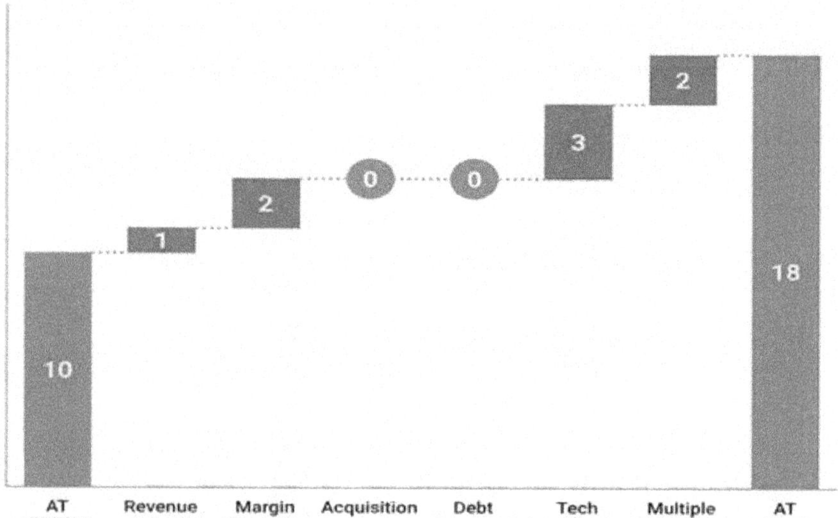

SCORE PANEL

BENEFIT	COST	EASE	RISK	OVERALL
4	3	3	3	13/20
4/5	3/5	3/5	3/5	Value Score: 65/100

FIELD NOTES

TRIGGERS
- Repetitive analytical tasks consuming skilled labor
- Competitors deploying machine learning

PROOF ARTIFACTS
- Use cases deployed with measured productivity gains
- ROI on machine learning investments

DISQUALIFIERS
- Data quality insufficient for machine learning
- Organization lacks capability to maintain

Deploy machine learning for productivity and decision quality improvement.

Gambit 37

The Machine-Supported Analysis Program

Bridge Target: Operating Earnings Bridge (productivity and capability improvement) and Enterprise Value Bridge (competitive differentiation)

Time to Impact: Fast to Medium (three to twelve months depending on application complexity)

The Pattern

The Machine-Supported Analysis Program systematically identifies and implements applications that use machine learning and language models to improve business performance. These technologies have moved from theoretical to practical. Effective deployment can meaningfully improve productivity, decision quality, and customer experience.

The Program focuses on practical applications with measurable returns rather than technology experimentation. Successful deployment typically starts with focused use cases that address specific business problems. These early wins build capability and confidence for broader deployment.

Machine-supported analysis creates value by augmenting human capability: helping people work faster, make better decisions, and deliver better service. The most successful deployments focus on human-machine collaboration rather than full automation. People remain in the loop while technology amplifies their effectiveness.

The Sacrifice

Investment in technology and implementation. Learning curve for the organization to adopt new tools. Risk that applications do not deliver expected value. Ongoing costs for services and maintenance.

The Sequence

1. Identify opportunity areas. Survey the business for tasks that involve pattern recognition, content generation, prediction, or recommendation. These are natural application areas.
2. Prioritize by value and feasibility. Evaluate each opportunity for business impact and implementation difficulty. Prioritize high-value, lower-complexity applications for early deployment.
3. Select initial use cases. Choose two to four initial use cases that can demonstrate value quickly. Common starting points include content generation, customer service assistance, document processing, and decision support.
4. Choose appropriate technology. Select tools appropriate for the use cases. This may include large language models for content and analysis, machine learning for prediction, or specialized models for specific domains.
5. Implement with user involvement. Involve end users in implementation. Design workflows that integrate technology naturally into existing work. Train users to work effectively with new tools.

6. Measure impact rigorously. Track productivity gains, quality improvements, and cost savings from each deployment. Build the evidence base for value created.
7. Scale successful applications. After proving value in initial deployments, expand to additional users and use cases. Build on what works.
8. Build governance. Establish policies for use: data privacy, output review, and appropriate applications. Ensure responsible deployment.
9. Develop internal capability. Build internal expertise to identify, implement, and manage applications. Create organizational capability for ongoing adoption.

Preconditions

The Machine-Supported Analysis Program works when practical use cases exist, when the organization is open to new ways of working, and when basic data infrastructure supports applications. It struggles when use cases are unclear, when the workforce resists adoption, or when data is insufficient to support applications.

The Trap

The primary trap is deploying technology without clear business cases. Technology for its own sake does not create value. Every deployment should connect to measurable business improvement.

The second trap is over-relying on automated outputs without human oversight. These systems make mistakes. Applications that do not include human review for critical outputs risk significant errors. Keep humans in the loop.

The Proof

Productivity improvement. Measurement of time savings and output increases from deployment.

Quality metrics. Evidence that technology-assisted work meets or exceeds quality standards.

Adoption metrics. Tracking showing active use of tools by target users.

Variants

Content and Communication Focus. Focus on tools for writing, communication, and content creation across the organization.

Customer Service Focus. Deploy technology to assist customer service teams with inquiry handling, response generation, and case resolution.

Decision Support Focus. Implement tools for analysis, forecasting, and recommendation to support management decisions.

DISQUALIFIERS: When This Gambit Is Wrong

- Practical use cases with measurable business impact cannot be identified
- The workforce actively resists adoption of new technology tools
- Data infrastructure is insufficient to support applications
- Regulatory or compliance constraints prohibit use of these technologies

If disqualified, consider: Gambit 36 (The Data Infrastructure Build) to establish prerequisites first

---

GAMBITPLATE #38

THE TECHNOLOGY DEBT REMEDIATION

BRIDGE: Enterprise Value **TIME:** 24 months

VALUE MECHANISM

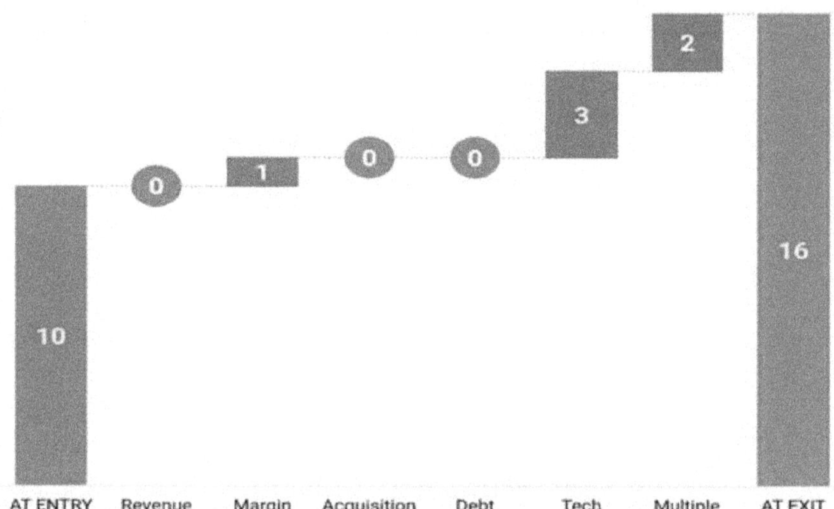

SCORE PANEL

BENEFIT	COST	EASE	RISK	OVERALL
4	4	2	3	11/20
4/5	4/5	2/5	3/5	Value Score: 55/100

FIELD NOTES

TRIGGERS
- Legacy systems constraining growth
- Security vulnerabilities in technology stack

PROOF ARTIFACTS
- Technology debt inventory with progress tracking
- Maintenance cost reduction achieved

DISQUALIFIERS
- Technology stack already modern
- Business model changing makes remediation moot

Systematically address accumulated technical debt and security issues.

Gambit 38

The Technology Debt Remediation

Bridge Target: Operating Earnings Bridge (reduced maintenance cost and improved reliability) and Enterprise Value Bridge (reduced risk and improved scalability)

Time to Impact: Medium to Long (twelve to twenty-four months for significant debt reduction)

The Pattern

The Technology Debt Remediation systematically addresses accumulated technical debt that creates risk and constrains capability. Technology debt is the accumulated cost of quick fixes, deferred maintenance, and outdated systems. Like financial debt, it accumulates interest: ongoing cost to work around limitations and growing risk of failure.

Common technology debt includes: legacy systems that are difficult to maintain or integrate, outdated infrastructure that limits performance, security vulnerabilities from unpatched systems, and code quality issues that slow development. Each creates ongoing cost and risk.

The Remediation prioritizes debt by impact and remediates systematically. Not all debt requires immediate attention. The most damaging debt, systems that create risk or prevent capability, receives priority. Lower-impact debt may be tolerated or addressed over longer timeframes.

The Sacrifice

Investment in technology modernization. Engineering resources diverted from new features to remediation. Disruption during system transitions. Risk during migration from old to new systems.

The Sequence

1. Inventory technology debt. Catalog existing technical debt across systems, infrastructure, and code. Understand the scope of the problem.
2. Assess impact and risk. For each debt item, evaluate the ongoing cost, risk of failure, and constraint on capability. Understand what the debt is costing.
3. Prioritize remediation. Rank debt items by impact and remediability. Focus on high-impact items that can be addressed. Some debt may be accepted rather than remediated.
4. Develop remediation roadmap. Create a phased plan for addressing priority debt. Balance remediation with ongoing operations and new development.
5. Address security vulnerabilities first. Prioritize debt that creates security risk. Unpatched systems, known vulnerabilities, and access control issues require immediate attention.
6. Modernize critical systems. Replace or upgrade legacy systems that constrain capability. Migrate to modern platforms that support future needs.
7. Improve infrastructure. Upgrade infrastructure components that limit performance, reliability, or

scalability. Move to modern cloud or hybrid architectures where appropriate.

8. Refactor problematic code. Address code quality issues that slow development or create bugs. Improve test coverage and documentation.
9. Establish debt prevention practices. Implement practices that prevent new debt accumulation: code standards, architecture review, and maintenance discipline.

Preconditions

The Technology Debt Remediation works when significant debt exists and creates meaningful cost or risk, when resources can be allocated to remediation, and when the organization commits to the long-term effort. It struggles when debt is minimal, when resources cannot be spared from other priorities, or when the scope of debt is overwhelming.

The Trap

The primary trap is pursuing perfection over progress. Complete debt elimination is rarely practical or necessary. Focus on high-impact debt. Accept that some debt will remain.

The second trap is big-bang replacement. Large system replacements carry high risk. Prefer incremental modernization that reduces risk and delivers value progressively.

The Proof

System reliability improvement. Tracking showing reduced outages, incidents, and maintenance issues.

Security posture improvement. Evidence that vulnerabilities have been addressed and security improved.

Development velocity improvement. Demonstration that teams can deliver faster after debt remediation.

Variants

Security-Focused Remediation. Prioritize security-related debt: patching, access controls, and vulnerability remediation.

Cloud Migration. Address infrastructure debt by migrating to modern cloud platforms.

Application Modernization. Focus on replacing or upgrading specific legacy applications that create the most constraint.

DISQUALIFIERS: When This Gambit Is Wrong

- Technology debt is minimal and does not create meaningful cost or risk
- Resources cannot be spared from other priorities without damaging operations
- The scope of debt is so overwhelming that remediation is not practical
- Exit timeline is too short to realize value from remediation investment

If disqualified, consider: Gambit 33 (The Risk Mitigation Package) to disclose and mitigate technology risk at exit

GAMBITPLATE **#39**

THE DIGITAL PRODUCT ENHANCEMENT

BRIDGE: Operating Earnings **TIME:** 12 months

VALUE MECHANISM

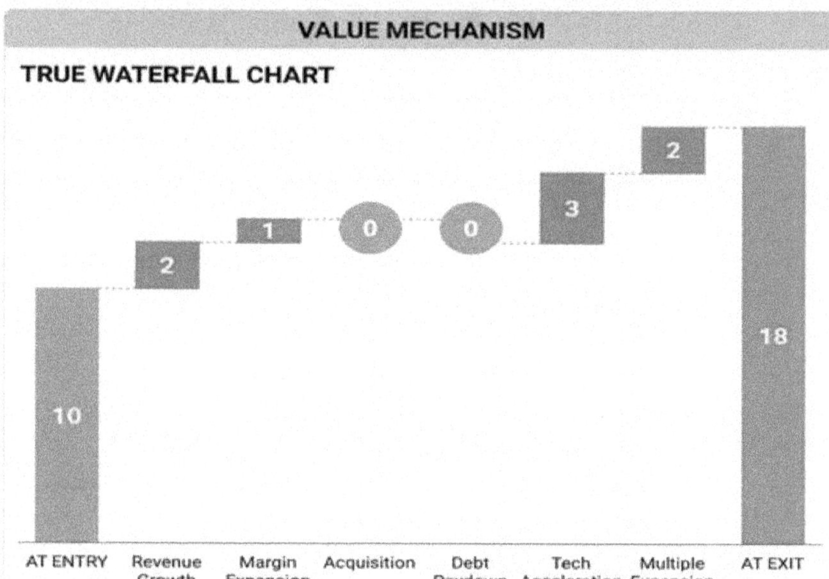

SCORE PANEL

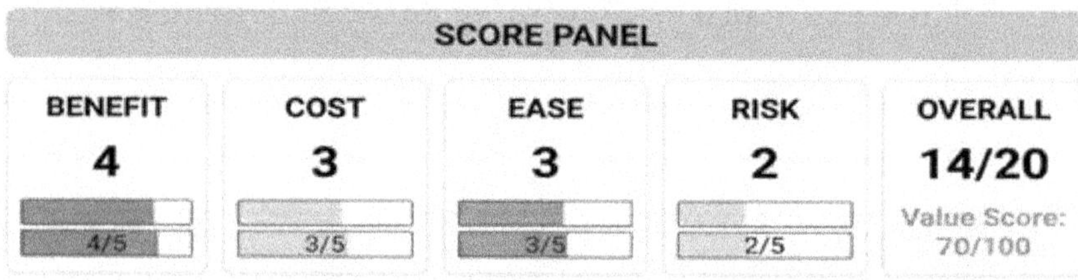

FIELD NOTES

TRIGGERS
- Digital product experience lagging competitors
- Customer feedback citing usability issues

PROOF ARTIFACTS
- User experience metrics improving
- Retention improvement correlated to changes

DISQUALIFIERS
- Digital product not core to value proposition
- Resources insufficient for meaningful improvement

Improve digital products that drive customer value and differentiation.

Gambit 39

The Digital Product Enhancement

Bridge Target: Operating Earnings Bridge (revenue growth and retention improvement) and Enterprise Value Bridge (product differentiation and customer value)

Time to Impact: Medium (six to twelve months for meaningful product improvement)

The Pattern

The Digital Product Enhancement improves the digital products and experiences that drive customer value. For businesses with software, applications, or digital interfaces, product quality directly affects revenue, retention, and competitive position. Better products win more customers and keep them longer.

The Enhancement focuses on improvements that matter to customers: usability, performance, functionality, and reliability. Customer feedback and usage data guide prioritization. The goal is measurable improvement in customer value and business outcomes.

Digital product quality affects multiple value drivers. Better products support price increases. Higher quality reduces churn. Competitive differentiation improves win rates. The Enhancement addresses all these outcomes through focused product investment.

The Sacrifice

Investment in product development resources. Time for improvements to reach customers and affect metrics. Risk that enhancements do not achieve expected impact. Ongoing investment required to maintain product quality.

The Sequence

1. Assess current product state. Evaluate current product quality across dimensions that matter to customers: usability, performance, features, and reliability. Understand strengths and weaknesses.
2. Gather customer feedback. Collect systematic feedback from customers on product strengths, weaknesses, and desired improvements. Understand what customers actually value.
3. Analyze usage data. Review product analytics to understand how customers use the product. Identify friction points, unused features, and engagement patterns.
4. Prioritize improvements. Based on customer feedback and data, identify the improvements that will have the greatest impact on customer value and business outcomes.
5. Invest in development capacity. Ensure adequate resources for product improvement. This may mean adding developers, designers, or product managers.
6. Execute improvement roadmap. Implement prioritized improvements in a structured roadmap. Deliver improvements regularly to demonstrate momentum.
7. Measure impact. Track the effect of improvements on customer metrics: satisfaction scores, usage,

retention, and expansion. Connect product investment to business outcomes.

8. Communicate improvements to customers. Inform customers about enhancements. Reinforce the value they receive. Use improvements to support retention and expansion conversations.
9. Establish continuous improvement rhythm. Make product improvement an ongoing discipline, not a one-time project. Continuously gather feedback, prioritize, and deliver.

Preconditions

The Digital Product Enhancement works when digital products are central to customer value, when there are meaningful opportunities for improvement, and when the organization has product development capability. It struggles when products are not strategic, when products are already excellent, or when development capability is insufficient.

The Trap

The primary trap is building features customers do not want. Without rigorous customer input, product teams build what they think is valuable rather than what customers actually need. Root all improvements in customer feedback and data.

The second trap is infinite enhancement without measurement. Continuous improvement is valuable only if it creates results. Measure the impact of enhancements. Stop investing in areas that do not move customer metrics.

The Proof

Customer satisfaction improvement. Tracking showing satisfaction scores increasing over time.

Usage and engagement metrics. Evidence that customers are using the product more and deriving more value.

Retention impact. Demonstration that product improvements contributed to improved retention.

Variants

User Experience Overhaul. Focus specifically on improving usability and user experience design.

Performance Optimization. Concentrate on improving product speed, reliability, and responsiveness.

Feature Expansion. Add new capabilities that address customer needs and expand product value.

DISQUALIFIERS: When This Gambit Is Wrong

- Digital products are not central to customer value or competitive position
- Products are already excellent with limited improvement opportunity
- Development capability is insufficient and cannot be built or acquired
- Customer churn is driven by factors unrelated to product quality

If disqualified, consider: Gambit 5 (The Retention Firewall) if retention issues are service-related rather than product-related

GAMBITPLATE **#40**

TECHNOLOGY-ENABLED SERVICE MODEL

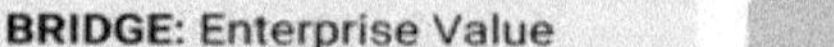

BRIDGE: Enterprise Value | **TIME:** 18 months

VALUE MECHANISM

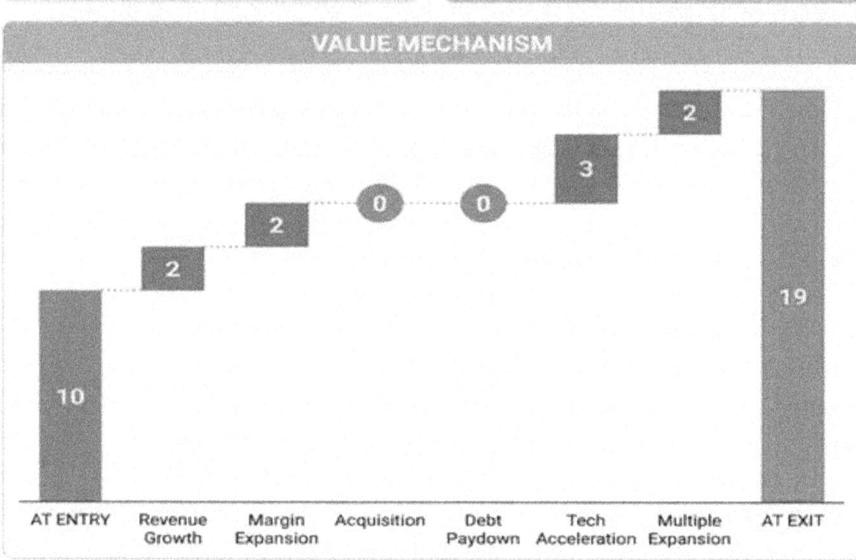

SCORE PANEL

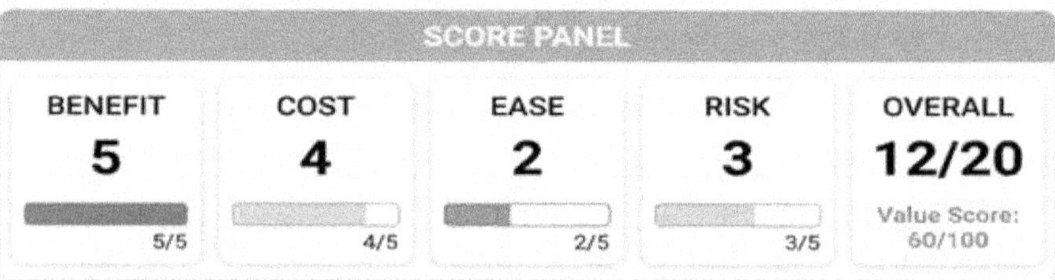

FIELD NOTES

TRIGGERS

- Service margins below potential
- Service delivery dependent on heroic effort

PROOF ARTIFACTS

- Service margin improvement documented
- Technology enabling faster delivery

DISQUALIFIERS

- Service model cannot be technology-enabled
- Investment exceeds margin improvement potential

Transform service delivery by embedding technology to improve margins and scale.

Gambit 40

The Technology-Enabled Service Model

Bridge Target: Operating Earnings Bridge (service margin improvement) and Enterprise Value Bridge (scalability and competitive differentiation)

Time to Impact: Medium to Long (twelve to eighteen months for meaningful service transformation)

The Pattern

The Technology-Enabled Service Model transforms how services are delivered by embedding technology into service processes. Traditional services are labor-intensive and difficult to scale. Technology-enabled services use tools, automation, and data to deliver better outcomes at lower cost and higher consistency.

The Model does not replace people with technology. It amplifies human capability. Technology handles routine tasks, provides decision support, and ensures consistency. People focus on high-value activities that require judgment, creativity, and relationship.

Technology-enabled services command premium pricing because they deliver better outcomes. They also scale more efficiently because technology leverage reduces the labor required per customer. This combination of premium pricing and efficient delivery creates margin expansion as the model scales.

The Sacrifice

Investment in technology development and integration. Workforce transition as roles change. Risk of service disruption during transformation. Ongoing technology investment to maintain capability.

The Sequence

1. Map current service delivery. Document how services are delivered today: processes, tasks, tools, and labor. Understand where time is spent and value is created.
2. Identify technology leverage points. Determine where technology could improve service delivery: automation of routine tasks, decision support tools, customer-facing interfaces, and quality assurance.
3. Design the enabled model. Define how technology will transform service delivery. Specify which tasks will be automated, which will be technology-assisted, and which remain human-dependent.
4. Build or acquire enabling technology. Develop or purchase the technology required for the enabled model. This may include workflow platforms, automation tools, analytics systems, and customer interfaces.
5. Pilot with select services or customers. Test the enabled model with a subset of services or customers. Validate that technology improves outcomes and efficiency before scaling.
6. Train the workforce on new model. Prepare service teams to work in the enabled model. Roles shift from execution to oversight, judgment, and relationship. This requires new skills.

7. Scale across the service portfolio. After proving the model, extend to additional services and customers. Build toward comprehensive transformation.
8. Adjust pricing to reflect value. As the enabled model delivers better outcomes, adjust pricing to capture the value created. Technology-enabled services should command premium positioning.
9. Continuously enhance the model. Treat the enabled model as a platform for ongoing improvement. Add new technology capabilities. Refine based on experience. Build competitive advantage.

Preconditions

The Technology-Enabled Service Model works when services are labor-intensive and scalable through technology, when technology can meaningfully improve outcomes, and when customers will value enhanced delivery. It struggles when services require primarily human judgment, when technology cannot add value, or when customers prefer traditional delivery.

The Trap

The primary trap is degrading service quality through excessive automation. If technology reduces quality or customer experience, the model fails. Technology should enhance, not replace, the elements that customers value.

The second trap is underinvesting in the human elements. Even technology-enabled services require skilled people. Cutting too deeply into workforce capability undermines the model. Balance technology and human investment.

The Proof

Service margin improvement. Tracking showing service margins increasing as technology leverage grows.

Customer outcome metrics. Evidence that technology-enabled services deliver better outcomes than traditional delivery.

Scalability evidence. Demonstration that the model can grow revenue faster than headcount.

Variants

Platform Service Model. Build a technology platform that customers access directly, with human support available as needed.

Hybrid Delivery Model. Combine technology-enabled delivery with premium human-intensive options for customers who prefer high-touch service.

Outcome-Based Pricing. Transition from time-and-materials to outcome-based pricing that captures value from technology-enabled improvement.

DISQUALIFIERS: When This Gambit Is Wrong

- Services require primarily human judgment that technology cannot replicate
- Technology cannot meaningfully improve outcomes in the service domain
- Customers strongly prefer traditional human-delivered service
- The investment required exceeds available resources and return potential

If disqualified, consider: Gambit 13 (The Service Model Surgery) for service optimization without technology transformation

PART FOUR

GAME DAY

From Gambits to Value

Chapter 11

Stacking the Gambits

Individual gambits create value. Stacked gambits multiply it.

The forty gambits in this book are not meant to be selected one at a time like items from a menu. The greatest value creation comes from combinations, where the impact of one gambit amplifies another. Pricing discipline combined with mix improvement compounds margin gains. Working capital efficiency combined with debt paydown acceleration compounds equity value growth. Revenue quality improvement combined with exit narrative construction compounds multiple expansion.

This chapter addresses how to select and sequence gambits for maximum impact. The goal is not to deploy all forty, which would overwhelm any organization, but to identify the five to ten that matter most for your specific situation and execute them in the right order.

Stacking Rules: How Patterns Combine

Four dimensions that determine safe combination

Rules Dashboard

Prerequisites

What must be true first

Dependency

What must happen before what

Conflicts

What competes for the same resources

Sequencing logic

Order that compounds vs order that creates friction

WHAT THIS ENABLES

- Faster impact
- Fewer reversals
- Cleaner attribution
- Stronger buyer confidence

WHERE IT BREAKS

- Overloading teams
- Mixed signals
- Competing metrics
- Benefit not captured

The Stacking Principle

Gambits stack in three ways: sequential, parallel, and reinforcing.

Sequential stacking means one gambit creates the conditions for another. Data infrastructure enables machine-supported analysis deployment. Process automation enables organizational flattening. Working capital sprint creates cash for debt paydown acceleration. The first gambit must complete before the second can begin.

Parallel stacking means multiple gambits execute simultaneously without dependency. Revenue gambits can run alongside margin gambits. Technology initiatives can proceed while acquisition integration happens. Parallel execution compresses time-to-value.

Reinforcing stacking means gambits amplify each other's impact. Pricing ratchet improves revenue while mix elevator improves margin, and together they compound operating earnings. Revenue quality upgrade improves retention while exit narrative construction communicates the improvement, and together they multiply the multiple impact.

The best value creation plans use all three types of stacking. They sequence gambits that build on each other, execute independent gambits in parallel, and select gambits that reinforce each other's effects.

Stack Recipe Template

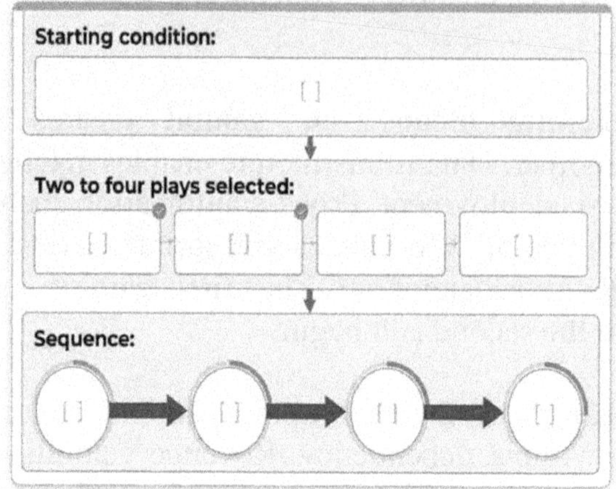

Proof artifacts to capture

- [Artifact 1]
- [Artifact 2]
- [Artifact 3]
- [Artifact 4]
- [Artifact 5]

Selecting the Right Gambits

Gambit selection starts with diagnosis. What are the binding constraints on value creation? Where is the business underperforming its potential? Which bridges offer the greatest opportunity?

Start with the bridge analysis from Part One. Look at operating earnings: is the opportunity in revenue growth, margin expansion, or both? Look at enterprise value: is the opportunity in earnings improvement or multiple expansion? Look at equity value: is the opportunity in operational improvement or debt reduction?

Then consider the arena analysis from Part Two. Which arenas contain the greatest opportunity? A business with obvious pricing power and underdeveloped price realization will find more value in revenue gambits. A business with bloated cost structure will find more value in margin gambits. A business in a fragmented industry will find more value in acquisition gambits.

Finally, consider preconditions. Each gambit has requirements that must be met for success. The pricing ratchet requires pricing power. The platform roll-up requires acquisition capability. Machine-supported analysis deployment requires data infrastructure. Select gambits whose preconditions you can satisfy.

Common Gambit Combinations

Certain gambit combinations appear repeatedly in successful value creation plans. These patterns work because the gambits reinforce each other.

The Margin Multiplier Stack: Pricing Ratchet plus Mix Elevator plus Zero-Based Rebuild. This combination attacks margin from three directions simultaneously: better price realization, higher-margin revenue mix, and lower overhead costs. The effects compound. A business that improves pricing by three points, mix contribution by two points, and overhead by two points captures seven margin points, not through a single initiative but through coordinated action.

The Cash Acceleration Stack: Working Capital Sprint plus Cash Conversion Engine plus Debt Paydown Accelerator. This combination releases trapped cash, improves ongoing conversion, and directs cash to debt reduction. The sprint provides immediate cash. The engine ensures operating improvements convert to cash. The accelerator ensures cash reaches the balance sheet. Together, they compress debt reduction timeline significantly.

The Multiple Expansion Stack: Revenue Quality Upgrade plus Concentration Reduction plus Exit Narrative Construction. This combination addresses the primary sources of multiple discount and builds the story to communicate improvement. Quality upgrade addresses revenue risk. Concentration reduction addresses customer dependency. Narrative construction packages the transformation for buyers. Together, they can shift a business from discount to premium valuation.

The Acquisition Value Stack: Platform Roll-Up plus Synergy Capture System plus Standardization Program. This combination executes consolidation strategy with the discipline to realize value. Roll-up provides the acquisition strategy. Synergy capture ensures projected synergies materialize. Standardization builds the integrated platform that justifies premium valuation.

The Technology Leverage Stack: Data Infrastructure Build plus Machine-Supported Analysis Program plus Process Automation Wave. This combination creates the foundation for technology-enabled efficiency. Data infrastructure provides the platform. Machine-supported analysis amplifies human capability. Process automation eliminates manual work. Together, they create operating leverage that improves margins and scalability.

Sequencing for Impact

The order of gambit execution matters. Some gambits create quick wins that build momentum and fund further investment. Others require longer development but create larger impact. Some must precede others due to dependencies.

A typical sequencing approach follows three phases.

Phase One: Foundation and Quick Wins. In the first six months, execute fast-impact gambits that generate early value while building foundation for larger initiatives. Cash Visibility System, Pricing Ratchet, and Working Capital Sprint are common Phase One gambits. They create momentum, demonstrate capability, and generate cash for reinvestment.

Phase Two: Core Value Creation. From months six through eighteen, execute the gambits that drive the majority of value creation. These are typically medium-impact gambits that require more time but create substantial value. Zero-Based Rebuild, Conversion Rebuild, and Synergy Capture System are common Phase Two gambits. They require more investment but deliver material bridge impact.

Phase Three: Multiple and Exit Preparation. From months eighteen through exit, focus shifts to gambits that affect how the business is valued. Revenue Quality Upgrade, Management Depth Build, and Exit Narrative Construction are common Phase Three gambits. They ensure that operating improvements translate into maximum exit valuation.

Avoiding Overload

The most common mistake in value creation planning is overcommitting. Ambition exceeds execution capacity. Too many gambits launch simultaneously. None receive adequate attention. Results disappoint.

A realistic limit is five to seven active gambits at any time. This assumes the operating business continues to run, which consumes most of management attention. Major gambits require dedicated leadership, change management effort, and organizational bandwidth. Spreading too thin ensures poor execution across all initiatives.

When forced to prioritize, select gambits with the highest impact-to-effort ratio. A medium-impact gambit that can be executed well beats a high-impact gambit that will be executed poorly. Execution quality determines actual results, not theoretical potential.

Also consider interdependencies. Some gambits share resources, leadership attention, or organizational change capacity. Running two major change initiatives in the same function simultaneously usually means neither succeeds. Sequence competing initiatives rather than running them in parallel.

Tracking Gambit Performance

Each gambit should have clear success metrics tied to bridge impact. Execution tracking is necessary but insufficient. The question is not whether actions were taken but whether value was created.

Create a gambit scorecard that tracks three dimensions for each active gambit. First, execution status: are the sequence steps being completed on schedule? Second, leading indicators: are the early signs of impact materializing? Third, bridge impact: is the gambit moving the targeted bridge metric?

Review the scorecard monthly with the leadership team. Celebrate progress. Address obstacles. Make course corrections. Kill gambits that are not working rather than continuing to invest in failure.

The discipline of regular tracking ensures gambits do not drift. It creates accountability for results. It provides early warning when execution is lagging. Most importantly, it maintains focus on value creation rather than activity.

Chapter 12

Building Your Bridge

The bridge is not something you analyze. It is something you build.

This book has provided the concepts, the arenas, and the gambits. But concepts do not create value. Execution does. This final chapter addresses how to translate understanding into action, how to build your specific bridge from current state to exit.

Start with Current State

Bridge building begins with honest assessment. Where is the business today? Not where leadership wishes it were, not where the investment thesis assumed it would be, but where it actually stands.

Calculate the current equity value using the formula from the opening of this book: Operating Earnings multiplied by Multiple, minus Net Debt. Be precise. Use trailing twelve-month operating earnings, adjusted for anything non-recurring. Use a realistic multiple based on comparable transactions. Include all debt. This is your starting point.

Then assess performance across each arena. How is revenue growing? What is the margin trajectory? What acquisition opportunities exist? How efficiently does the business convert earnings to cash? What would a buyer think of the business today?

Be unflinching in this assessment. Every weakness you identify is an opportunity. Every challenge you acknowledge can be addressed. The problems you do not see are the ones that persist.

Define the Target

What equity value do you need to achieve? Work backward from required returns. If the investment requires a certain multiple of invested capital, calculate the exit equity value needed to deliver it. This becomes the target.

Then decompose the target into bridge components. How much must operating earnings grow? What multiple is achievable? How much debt will be paid down? Express the target not as a single number but as specific achievements across each bridge.

Test whether the target is achievable. Does the required earnings growth match what comparable businesses achieve? Does the target multiple align with how similar businesses are valued? Does the debt paydown timeline match cash generation capability? Ambitious targets motivate. Impossible targets demoralize. Find the line between them.

Map the Gap

The gap between current state and target defines the required value creation. Express this gap in bridge terms. If current operating earnings are fifteen million and the target is twenty-five million, the operating earnings bridge must create ten million. If the current multiple is six and the target is eight, the enterprise value bridge must deliver two turns of expansion.

Then break down each bridge into components. For operating earnings, how much will come from revenue growth versus margin expansion? For enterprise value, how much from earnings improvement versus multiple expansion? For equity value, how much from business improvement versus debt reduction?

This decomposition reveals where value creation must happen. If the plan requires margin expansion but margins are already at peer levels, something must change. If the plan requires multiple expansion but the business has structural discount factors, those factors must be addressed. The gap analysis exposes required breakthroughs.

Select Your Gambits

With the gap defined, select the gambits that will close it. Return to the forty gambits in Part Three. For each component of the gap, identify the gambits that address it.

If revenue growth is required, which revenue gambits fit? If the business has pricing power, consider the Pricing Ratchet. If customer expansion is possible, consider the Expansion Loop. If mix improvement is achievable, consider the Mix Elevator. Select the gambits whose preconditions match your situation.

If margin expansion is required, which margin gambits fit? If overhead is bloated, consider Zero-Based Rebuild. If procurement is fragmented, consider Procurement Concentration. If unit economics are unclear, consider Unit Economics Rewrite. Match gambits to specific margin opportunities.

Continue through each bridge component. Build a portfolio of gambits that collectively close the gap. Then pressure test: can this portfolio realistically deliver the required value? Is the organization capable of executing these gambits? Is the timeline realistic?

Build the Waterfall

Combine everything into a waterfall that shows how current equity value becomes target equity value. Start with current operating earnings. Add the contribution of each gambit. Arrive at target operating earnings. Apply the target multiple. Arrive at target enterprise value. Subtract projected net debt. Arrive at target equity value.

The waterfall makes value creation tangible. It shows exactly how the gap will be closed. It assigns specific contribution to each gambit. It creates accountability for results.

Review the waterfall critically. Does each gambit contribution seem achievable? Are the combined contributions realistic or do they require everything to go perfectly? Is there cushion for initiatives that underperform?

Build multiple scenarios: base case with reasonable assumptions, upside case where gambits outperform, and downside case where execution challenges emerge. Understand the range of outcomes. Plan for contingencies.

Execute with Discipline

The plan means nothing without execution. Gambits do not execute themselves. They require leadership attention, resource allocation, and organizational commitment.

Assign clear ownership for each gambit. One executive owns each initiative. That owner is accountable for executing the sequence, delivering the results, and reporting progress. Shared ownership means no ownership.

Allocate resources explicitly. Gambits require investment: people, technology, consulting support, or capital. Identify resource requirements for each gambit. Budget for them. Do not assume gambits will execute with existing resources unless that is genuinely true.

Create the rhythm of execution. Monthly reviews where owners report progress. Quarterly deep dives on each gambit. Annual refresh of the overall plan. The rhythm maintains focus and creates accountability.

Be willing to adjust. Plans change. Some gambits will outperform. Others will underperform. New opportunities will emerge. Old assumptions will prove wrong. The best operators adjust continuously while maintaining focus on the ultimate objective.

The Bridge You Build

At exit, the bridge becomes visible. Buyers see the transformation: revenue grown, margins expanded, cash generated, risks mitigated, capabilities built. They see the waterfall: from entry value to exit value, each component documented and defensible.

But the bridge you build is not just financial. It is organizational. A business that has successfully executed multiple gambits has developed capability: discipline, execution muscle, and performance culture. That capability is itself valuable. It signals to buyers that the business can continue to improve.

The bridge you build is also personal. Operating partners who develop pattern recognition, who learn to diagnose constraints and select appropriate responses, build expertise that transfers. Each successful engagement builds capability for the next.

Value creation is not magic. It is pattern recognition plus disciplined execution. The patterns are in this book. The execution is up to you.

PART FIVE

THE SELECTION ENGINE

From Forty Patterns to Five That Matter

Chapter 13

The Constraint Assessment

Forty gambits is not a menu. It is an arsenal. And no one deploys an entire arsenal at once.

The difference between operators who create value and those who create chaos is selection discipline. The best operating partners do not ask which gambits look attractive. They ask which gambits fit the constraints. Every portfolio company operates within boundaries: time remaining before exit, cash available to invest, talent capacity to execute, data maturity to measure, customer concentration that limits risk tolerance, and debt pressure that restricts flexibility.

This chapter provides the diagnostic framework to assess those constraints before selecting gambits. Get this wrong, and you will pursue patterns that the organization cannot execute, that the balance sheet cannot support, or that the timeline cannot accommodate.

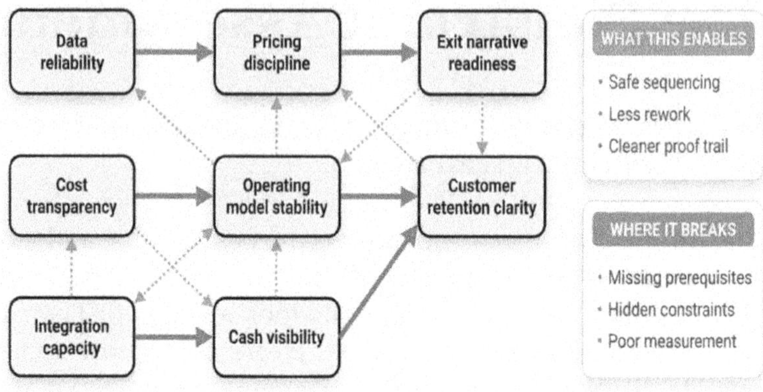

The Six Constraint Dimensions

Before opening the gambit library, assess the portfolio company across six dimensions. Each dimension either enables or disqualifies certain patterns.

Constraint One: Time Remaining

How many months remain before the target exit window? This is the master constraint. A gambit that requires eighteen months to show results cannot be selected if exit is planned in twelve months.

Short runway (under twelve months): Only fast-impact gambits qualify. Pricing Ratchet, Working Capital Sprint, Cash Visibility System, and Risk Mitigation Package. Avoid anything requiring sustained execution or buyer proof periods.

Medium runway (twelve to twenty-four months): Most gambits become viable. Can execute medium-impact patterns and show results before exit. This is the optimal window for margin gambits, synergy capture, and technology automation.

Long runway (over twenty-four months): Full gambit library available. Can pursue business model transformation, platform roll-ups, recurring revenue conversion, and other patterns requiring sustained execution and proof periods.

Constraint Two: Cash Available

How much cash can the company invest in value creation initiatives without straining operations or violating covenants? Some gambits are cash-light. Others require significant capital.

Cash-constrained: Focus on gambits that release cash or require minimal investment. Working Capital Sprint, Pricing Ratchet, Zero-Based Rebuild, Bad Revenue Exit. Avoid technology infrastructure builds, acquisition programs, or major system implementations.

Moderate cash: Can fund one or two capital-intensive gambits if sequenced properly. May pursue process automation, system upgrades, or capability tuck-ins if prioritized against other uses.

Cash-rich: Full range of investment-heavy gambits available. Platform roll-ups, data infrastructure builds, technology-enabled service model transformations, and major digital product enhancements all become viable.

Constraint Three: Talent Capacity

Does the organization have the leadership talent and execution bandwidth to pursue additional initiatives beyond running the core business? Gambits require attention. Attention is finite.

Talent-thin: Leadership team is stretched running operations. Cannot absorb major initiatives without external support or talent additions. Either add capability first (Management Depth Build) or select only gambits that can be consultant-led or require minimal management bandwidth.

Talent-adequate: Team can handle two to three initiatives alongside operations if properly prioritized. Select gambits carefully and sequence to avoid overwhelming any single function.

Talent-deep: Strong bench with capacity for initiative leadership. Can pursue multiple gambits in parallel with dedicated owners for each. This is the ideal state but rare.

Constraint Four: Data Maturity

Can the company measure what matters? Some gambits require sophisticated data infrastructure. Others can execute with basic financials.

Data-poor: Limited visibility into unit economics, customer behavior, or operational performance. Must either build data capability first (Cash Visibility System, Data Infrastructure Build) or select gambits that do not require granular measurement. Avoid advanced analytics, dynamic pricing, or precision segmentation until foundation exists.

Data-adequate: Basic operational and financial metrics available. Can execute most gambits with existing measurement capability. May need targeted improvements for specific initiatives.

Data-rich: Comprehensive data infrastructure with reliable metrics across functions. Can pursue advanced gambits like analytics-driven pricing, customer segmentation, predictive maintenance, and sophisticated performance management.

Constraint Five: Customer Concentration Risk

How much revenue depends on a small number of customers? High concentration limits the gambits you can pursue without risking catastrophic customer loss.

High concentration (top customer over twenty percent): Extreme caution on any gambit that could trigger customer defection. Pricing Ratchet may be dangerous if applied to concentrated customers. Service Model Surgery or product changes require careful customer consultation. Prioritize Concentration Reduction before aggressive commercial gambits.

Moderate concentration (top five customers over forty percent): Commercial gambits possible but require customer-by-customer analysis. Some customers can absorb pricing changes. Others cannot. Segment the approach.

Low concentration (diversified base): Full range of commercial gambits available. Can pursue aggressive pricing, service model changes, or portfolio rationalization without existential customer risk.

Constraint Six: Debt Pressure

How much leverage does the company carry, and how close is it to covenant limits? High debt pressure constrains both investment capacity and risk tolerance.

High pressure (near covenants or tight coverage): Prioritize gambits that generate cash and protect earnings. Working Capital Sprint, Debt Paydown Accelerator, and defensive margin gambits. Avoid anything that creates short-term earnings volatility or requires investment that could trigger covenant issues.

Moderate pressure (comfortable headroom): Most gambits available but must monitor impact on coverage ratios. Short-term earnings dips from transformation initiatives may be acceptable if trajectory improves.

Low pressure (deleveraged or equity-heavy): Full flexibility to pursue investment-heavy gambits, accept short-term earnings pressure, or fund acquisitions. The constraint shifts from debt to other dimensions.

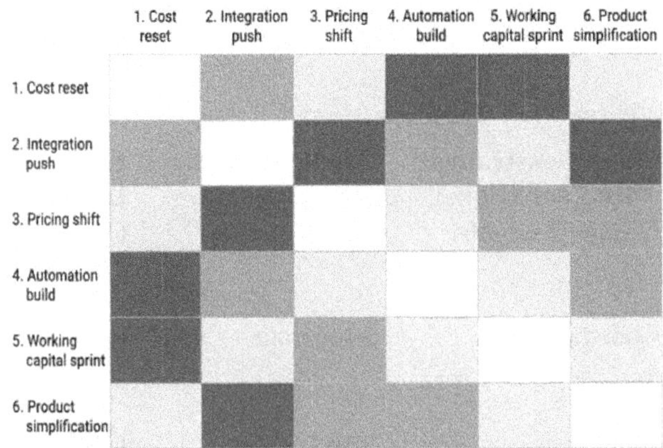
Conflict Matrix: Combinations That Collide
Resource collision map
1. Cost reset
2. Integration push
3. Pricing shift
4. Automation build
5. Working capital sprint
6. Product simplification
1. Cost reset
2. Integration push
3. Pricing shift
4. Automation build
5. Working capital sprint
6. Product simplification
WHAT THIS ENABLES
• Avoiding self-inflicted friction
WHERE IT BREAKS
• Conflicting incentives
• Bandwidth overload
• Customer disruption

The Constraint Card

Before selecting gambits, complete a simple assessment card. For each dimension, mark the current state. The combination of constraints determines which gambits are viable.

Dimension	Short/Constrained/ Thin/Poor/High	Medium/Moderate/Adequate	Long/Rich/ Deep/Low
Time Remaining	Under 12 months	12-24 months	Over 24 months
Cash Available	Constrained	Moderate	Rich
Talent Capacity	Thin	Adequate	Deep
Data Maturity	Poor	Adequate	Rich
Customer Concentration	High	Moderate	Low
Debt Pressure	High	Moderate	Low

A company with short time, constrained cash, thin talent, poor data, high concentration, and high debt pressure has a very different gambit menu than one with long runway and resources. The constraint card forces honest assessment before the excitement of gambit selection begins.

Disqualifier Gates Template

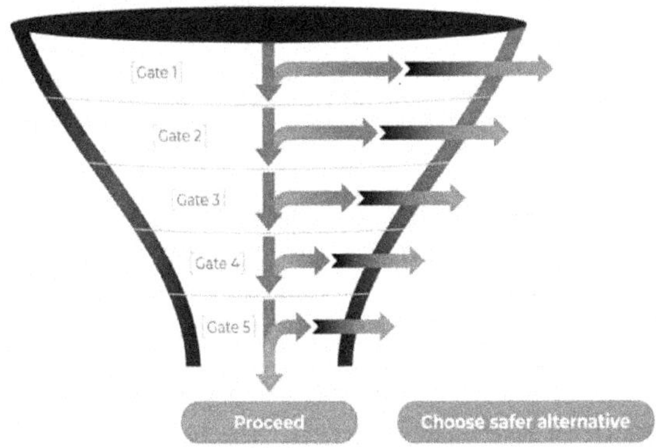

Constraint Radar: What Limits You Right Now

Honest constraint-first planning

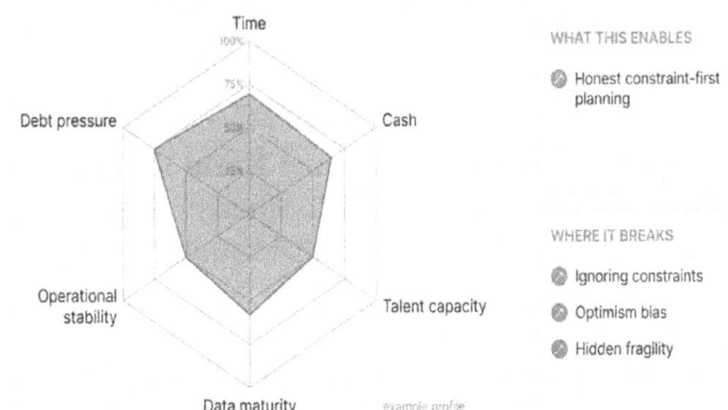

Disqualifiers: When Not to Pursue a Gambit

Some constraint combinations create absolute disqualifiers. These are not judgment calls. They are hard stops.

Do not pursue Platform Roll-Up if time is short or talent is thin. Acquisitions require integration bandwidth and time to prove synergies.

Do not pursue Recurring Revenue Conversion if time is short or debt pressure is high. Model transitions create short-term revenue and earnings dips that cannot be absorbed under these constraints.

Do not pursue aggressive Pricing Ratchet if customer concentration is high and those customers lack pricing tolerance. The risk of losing a major customer exceeds the benefit of the price increase.

Do not pursue Data Infrastructure Build or Technology Debt Remediation if cash is constrained and time is short. These are foundation investments that require resources and take time to yield returns.

Do not pursue Service Model Surgery or Organizational Flattening if talent is thin. Major organizational changes require strong leadership to execute without destabilizing operations.

Do not pursue Cross-Sell Fuse or Expansion Loop if data maturity is poor. These gambits require customer segmentation, behavior analysis, and targeting precision that data-poor organizations cannot provide.

The constraint assessment is not about limiting ambition. It is about matching ambition to reality. A gambit that fails due to constraint mismatch does not just waste resources. It damages credibility, demoralizes the organization, and consumes time that could have been spent on patterns that fit.

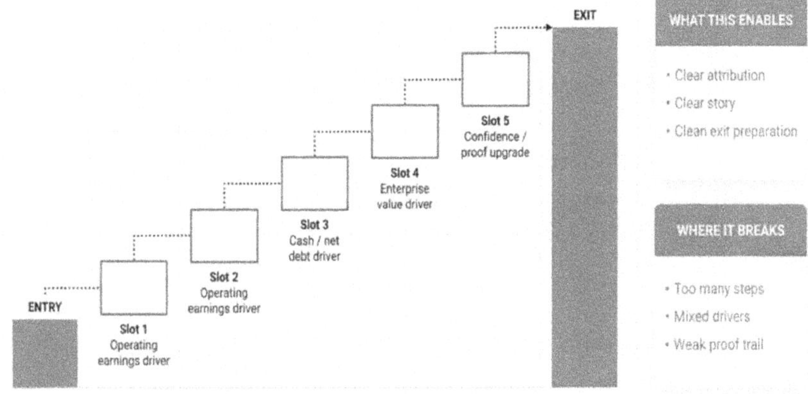

Chapter 14

Fit Score and Dependency Logic

Constraints tell you which gambits to exclude. Fit scoring tells you which to prioritize. Dependency logic tells you the order.

Once the constraint assessment eliminates gambits that do not fit the situation, the remaining options must be ranked. The goal is a short list of five to seven gambits that will receive concentrated execution. More than seven, and attention fragments. Fewer than five, and you may leave value on the table.

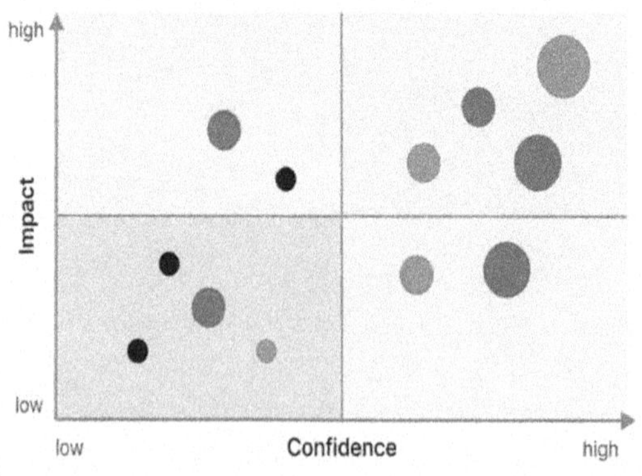

The Fit Score: Impact Times Confidence Times Speed

For each gambit that passes the constraint filter, score it on three dimensions. The product of these scores determines fit.

Impact: Bridge Contribution

How much value will this gambit create if executed successfully? Measure impact in terms of bridge contribution: dollars of operating earnings improvement, points of multiple expansion, or dollars of debt reduction.

- High impact (score 3): Material effect on equity value. Moves one or more bridge components by five percent or more.
- Medium impact (score 2): Meaningful contribution but not transformative. Moves bridge components by two to five percent.
- Low impact (score 1): Incremental improvement. Less than two percent effect on bridge components.

Confidence: Execution Probability

How certain are you that the organization can execute this gambit? This is not about whether the gambit works in theory. It is about whether it will work in this organization with this team under these conditions.

- High confidence (score 3): Team has executed similar initiatives before. Prerequisites are in place. Low execution risk.
- Medium confidence (score 2): Team has related experience but not identical. Some prerequisites may be missing. Moderate execution risk.

- Low confidence (score 1): New territory for the organization. Significant prerequisites missing. High execution risk.

Speed: Time to Bridge Impact

How quickly will this gambit affect the value bridge? Speed matters because it determines when value is captured and demonstrated to buyers.

- Fast (score 3): Bridge impact within six months.
- Medium (score 2): Bridge impact within six to eighteen months.
- Slow (score 1): Bridge impact beyond eighteen months.

Calculating the Fit Score

Multiply the three scores: Impact times Confidence times Speed. The maximum score is 27 (3 x 3 x 3). The minimum is 1 (1 x 1 x 1). Rank the surviving gambits by fit score. The top five to seven become your active portfolio.

Example: A Pricing Ratchet gambit might score: Impact 3 (significant margin contribution expected), Confidence 3 (company has pricing power and team has done this before), Speed 3 (results visible within one quarter). Fit score: 27. This goes to the top of the list.

A Platform Roll-Up might score: Impact 3 (transformative value creation), Confidence 2 (team is new to integration), Speed 1 (results take two or more years). Fit score: 6. This ranks lower and may be deferred unless the long runway permits.

The Dependency Map

Fit scores determine which gambits to pursue. Dependencies determine the order. Some gambits require others first. Ignoring dependencies leads to execution failure.

Data Dependencies

Several gambits cannot execute without data infrastructure. The dependency chain:

Cash Visibility System or Data Infrastructure Build must precede: Unit Economics Rewrite, Pricing Ratchet (if data-driven), Conversion Rebuild, Retention Firewall (churn analysis), and any analytics-intensive gambit.

Data Infrastructure Build must precede: Machine-Supported Analysis Program, advanced Process Automation, and technology-enabled service transformations.

Process Dependencies

Automation amplifies existing processes. If processes are broken, automation makes them faster at being wrong.

Process discipline and standardization must precede: Process Automation Wave, Standardization Program (across acquisitions), and technology-enabled service delivery.

Platform Dependencies

Acquisition programs require platform stability before adding complexity.

Platform operational stability must precede: Platform Roll-Up, Adjacency Expansion, Capability Tuck-In. Integration bandwidth must exist before acquisition velocity increases.

Cash Dependencies

Investment-heavy gambits require cash. Cash-generating gambits may need to come first.

Working Capital Sprint, Cash Conversion Engine, or asset monetization must precede (if cash-constrained): Technology infrastructure builds, acquisition programs, major automation investments.

Talent Dependencies

Complex gambits require leadership capability that may not exist.

Management Depth Build must precede (if talent is thin): Major organizational transformations, multi-site integrations, aggressive growth programs, and any initiative requiring leadership bandwidth the current team cannot provide.

Sequencing Rules

With dependencies mapped, sequence the selected gambits according to these principles.

Rule One: Enabling gambits before dependent gambits. If Gambit A requires Gambit B, start B first. Build data before analytics. Build platform before acquisitions. Build cash before investments.

Rule Two: Fast gambits early. Quick wins create momentum, demonstrate capability, and fund subsequent initiatives. Pricing Ratchet, Working Capital Sprint, and Zero-Based Rebuild often lead the sequence.

Rule Three: Proof gambits before exit. Any gambit intended to affect exit valuation must be complete, and results demonstrable, at least twelve months before exit. Buyers discount claims without track records.

Rule Four: No more than two major transformations per function simultaneously. Sales cannot absorb Pricing Ratchet, Conversion Rebuild, and Channel Redesign at once. Sequence or combine where possible.

Rule Five: Reserve bandwidth for problems. No plan survives contact with reality. Build slack into the sequence for unexpected challenges, market shifts, and execution setbacks.

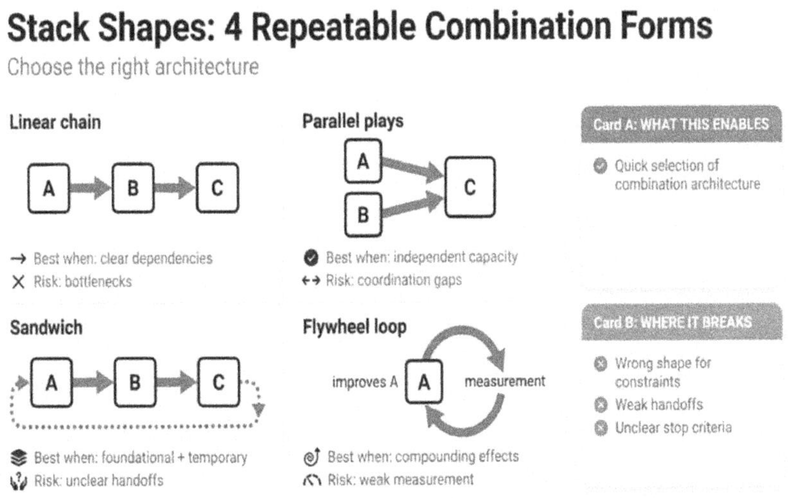

The Gambit Portfolio

The output of this process is a gambit portfolio: five to seven patterns, ranked by fit score, sequenced by dependency and timing. This is the tactical layer of the value creation plan.

Document the portfolio clearly:

For each gambit: name, fit score components, target bridge impact, owner, start date, expected impact date, dependencies.

For the portfolio: total expected bridge impact (operating earnings delta, multiple delta, debt delta), phasing across the hold period, critical path dependencies.

This document becomes the tactical backbone of the value creation plan. It translates the theoretical forty gambits into the specific five to seven that this company will execute to build its bridge from entry to exit.

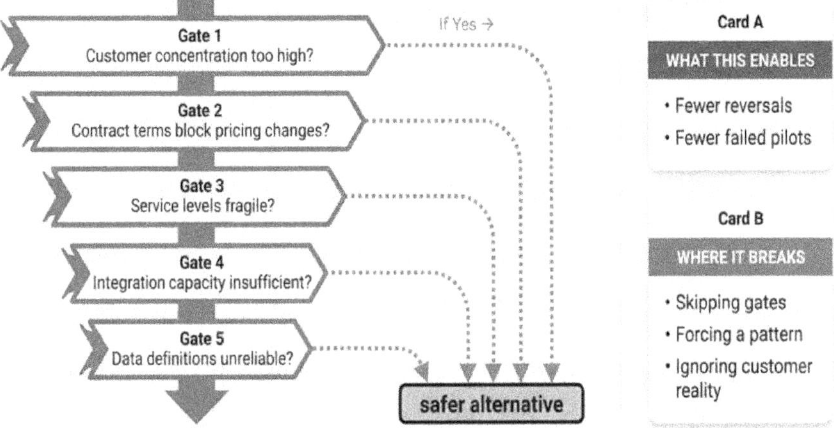
Disqualifier Gates: When Not to Run a Pattern
Fewer reversals, fewer failed pilots
Gate 1
Customer concentration too high?
Gate 2
Contract terms block pricing changes?
Gate 3
Service levels fragile?
Gate 4
Integration capacity insufficient?
Gate 5
Data definitions unreliable?
If Yes →
safer alternative
Card A
WHAT THIS ENABLES
• Fewer reversals
• Fewer failed pilots
Card B
WHERE IT BREAKS
• Skipping gates
• Forcing a pattern
• Ignoring customer reality

Chapter 15

Proof Before Narrative

Stories do not survive diligence. Evidence does.

Every gambit has a Proof section for a reason. Proof is not documentation. It is the currency of exit valuation. Buyers pay for what they can verify. Claims without evidence become deductions, earnouts, or deal killers.

This chapter provides the evidence index: what buyers expect to see for each type of gambit, what they will challenge, and the minimum standard to clear diligence.

The Evidence Standard

Buyer-grade evidence meets three tests. Fail any one, and the evidence is discounted.

Verifiable: The data can be traced to source systems, audited financials, or third-party validation. Self-reported metrics without verification are discounted.

Sustained: The improvement has persisted across multiple periods, not just one quarter. One-time gains are treated as one-time. Sustained performance is capitalized.

Attributed: The improvement can be connected to specific actions, not just market conditions or timing. Buyers want to know the improvement came from something replicable.

Evidence Index by Gambit Category

Revenue Gambits (Gambits 1-8)

Key artifacts buyers expect:

Price realization bridge: Shows average selling price movement over time, net of discounts and allowances. Buyer challenge: Did volume hold or did price gains cause volume loss? Minimum standard: Twelve months of stable or improving volume alongside price increases.

Revenue mix analysis: Shows margin contribution by product, customer segment, or channel over time. Buyer challenge: Is the mix shift intentional or accidental? Minimum standard: Clear strategy documentation plus three or more periods of consistent direction.

Customer retention cohort analysis: Shows retention rates by customer cohort, demonstrating that improvements are systemic. Buyer challenge: Are retention gains real or is it just a favorable vintage? Minimum standard: Improving retention across multiple cohorts.

Conversion funnel metrics: Shows conversion rates at each stage of the sales process. Buyer challenge: Is the improvement in leads or conversion? Minimum standard: Attribution to specific sales effectiveness initiatives with before and after comparison.

Margin Gambits (Gambits 9-16)

Key artifacts buyers expect:

Cost waterfall: Shows cost structure at entry and current state, with each reduction initiative isolated. Buyer challenge: Are cost reductions sustainable or will they creep back? Minimum standard: Structural changes (contracts, headcount, footprint) not just temporary freezes.

Procurement savings log: Shows specific vendor renegotiations, unit cost reductions, and annualized savings. Buyer challenge: Are savings actually flowing to the income statement? Minimum standard: Savings verified in financial statements, not just projected.

Unit economics dashboard: Shows fully-loaded cost per unit, customer, or transaction over time. Buyer challenge: Does the company actually know its unit economics? Minimum standard: Methodology documented, data sources verified, trend consistent.

Organizational chart comparison: Shows structure at entry and current, demonstrating headcount and layer changes. Buyer challenge: Did quality or capability suffer? Minimum standard: Performance metrics stable or improving alongside restructuring.

Acquisition Gambits (Gambits 17-22)

Key artifacts buyers expect:

Synergy tracker: Shows projected synergies at deal close versus achieved synergies, by category. Buyer challenge: Did you actually capture what you projected? Minimum standard: At least eighty percent of cost synergies realized and visible in financials.

Integration completeness checklist: Shows status of integration workstreams: systems, organization, processes. Buyer challenge: Is this really one company or still a holding company? Minimum standard: Critical systems integrated, one reporting structure, unified go-to-market.

Pro forma financials: Shows combined entity performance versus standalone projections. Buyer challenge: Is the combined entity performing better than the sum of parts? Minimum standard: Clear evidence of value creation from combination.

Cross-sell revenue attribution: Shows revenue generated from selling acquired products to platform customers or vice versa. Buyer challenge: Is this real new revenue or just relabeling? Minimum standard: Clear customer-level attribution showing products sold that would not have been purchased otherwise.

Cash and Debt Gambits (Gambits 23-28)

Key artifacts buyers expect:

Cash conversion dashboard: Shows operating cash flow as percentage of operating earnings over time. Buyer challenge: Is cash conversion sustainable or one-time? Minimum standard: Twelve months of conversion ratio at target level.

Working capital trend: Shows days sales outstanding, days inventory, days payable over time. Buyer challenge: Was improvement from genuine efficiency or from stretching payables unsustainably? Minimum standard: Improvement across all three metrics without vendor relationship damage.

Thirteen-week cash forecast accuracy: Shows forecast versus actual cash position over time. Buyer challenge: Does the company actually manage cash well? Minimum standard: Forecast accuracy within five percent consistently.

Covenant compliance history: Shows covenant metrics over time with headroom calculation. Buyer challenge: Is debt manageable? Minimum standard: No breaches, comfortable headroom, proactive lender communication documented.

Multiple Expansion Gambits (Gambits 29-34)

Key artifacts buyers expect:

Recurring revenue percentage trend: Shows percentage of recurring or contracted revenue over time. Buyer challenge: Is this really recurring or just relabeled transactional? Minimum standard: Revenue recognized as recurring meeting accounting standards, with retention data to support.

Customer concentration remediation chart: Shows top customer percentage declining over time. Buyer challenge: Did diversification come from new customer growth or large customer decline? Minimum standard: Diversification from growth, not attrition, with large customer revenue stable.

Management depth documentation: Shows organizational structure, succession plans, and tenure of leadership. Buyer challenge: Will the business perform without the founder or key person? Minimum standard: Demonstrated delegation, successors identified for critical roles, key person not required for daily operations.

Earnings quality report: Third-party validation of earnings quality and adjustments. Buyer challenge: Are the earnings real? Minimum standard: Clean earnings quality report with minimal adjustments and no surprises.

Technology Gambits (Gambits 35-40)

Key artifacts buyers expect:

Automation impact quantification: Shows labor cost reduction or throughput improvement from automation initiatives. Buyer challenge: Did automation actually reduce cost or just shift it? Minimum standard: Headcount reduction or productivity gain verified in financial statements.

System reliability metrics: Shows uptime, incident frequency, and resolution time before and after technology improvements. Buyer challenge: Is the technology a strength or a risk? Minimum standard: Reliability at or above industry benchmarks.

Technology debt assessment: Shows current state of technical infrastructure with any remaining debt identified and remediation planned. Buyer challenge: What hidden technology investments will I need to make? Minimum standard: Honest assessment with critical debt remediated and remaining items quantified.

Product usage and adoption metrics: Shows customer engagement with digital products or technology-enabled services. Buyer challenge: Are customers actually using and valuing the technology? Minimum standard: Usage metrics trending positively with correlation to retention or expansion.

Building the Proof Package

Proof is not assembled at exit. It is built throughout the hold period. Every gambit execution should generate evidence as a byproduct of the work itself.

Document baselines before launching gambits. You cannot show improvement without a starting point. Capture the before state rigorously.

Track metrics monthly, not just at milestones. Continuous tracking shows trajectory, not just endpoints. Buyers value trends.

Connect actions to outcomes explicitly. Document what was done and when. Create the link between initiative and result.

Use third parties where credibility matters. For significant claims, consider sell-side earnings quality analysis, technical diligence, or customer references. External validation carries more weight.

Anticipate the challenge. For each proof artifact, know what a skeptical buyer will question and have the answer ready.

The proof package is not a presentation. It is a data room. It is the foundation beneath the narrative. Get it right, and the exit narrative writes itself. Get it wrong, and no story will save the valuation.

THE PREGAME SCOUTING REPORT

A Diagnostic Before You Design the Play

No coach designs a game plan without scouting. Before selecting gambits, you must know what you are working with: the strengths to leverage, the weaknesses to address, the constraints that will shape every decision you make.

This Scouting Report is a structured diagnostic. It assesses your portfolio company across seven dimensions that determine which gambits are viable, which are urgent, and which will fail before they start. Complete it honestly. The score is not the point. The conversation that happens when your leadership team discovers their scores differ by two or three points tells you more about readiness than any single metric.

Use this before Part Three. Use it again at the midpoint of your hold. Use it twelve months before exit. Each time, the pattern of strengths and gaps will guide gambit selection.

The Seven Dimensions

A weakness in any single dimension constrains the entire system.

1. Leadership Bandwidth Do senior leaders have capacity to absorb new ways of working, or is the team already running at maximum just to keep operations stable?

2. System Maturity Are core processes predictable and documented, or does the organization operate through improvisation and heroics?

3. Operational Stability Is performance consistent period to period, or does it vary significantly based on who is working, which shift is running, or what fire needs fighting?

4. Data Hygiene Do teams trust the data they see? Are definitions consistent? Could systems support three times current volume without breaking?

5. Financial Engine Quality Are earnings truly underwritable? Is revenue mix attractive? Does cash conversion match the profitability story?

6. Cultural Cohesion Is there openness to structured change, or does the organization resist new approaches, hoard information, and operate in silos?

7. Organizational Capacity Is there room to absorb new initiatives, or would any additional effort overwhelm existing capability?

The Diagnostic: Twenty-Five Questions

For each question, score 1 to 5:

- **1** = Not true at all
- **3** = Partially true or inconsistent
- **5** = Consistently and demonstrably true

Section A: Financial Engine (Questions 1-5)

#	Question	Score
1	**Earnings are underwritable.** We can show a clear, explainable trajectory with bridges that separate structural performance from one-offs and accounting effects.	
2	**Revenue mix is attractive.** We understand revenue by segment, product, and geography. We are managing concentration and increasing the share of recurring or resilient streams.	
3	**Cash conversion matches the story.** Working capital and capital expenditure are under control. Cash generation aligns with reported earnings.	
4	**The value bridge is clear.** We can summarize how revenue growth, margin expansion, capital efficiency, debt reduction, and multiple expansion have contributed to equity value on one page.	
5	**Financial information is buyer-ready.** Definitions are stable, reconciliations tight, and adjustments documented. An earnings quality review would be confirmation, not cleanup.	

Section A Total: ___ / 25

Section B: Operational Throughput (Questions 6-10)

#	Question	Score
6	**We could handle three times current volume.** Systems, processes, and team capacity could absorb significant growth without breaking.	
7	**We know where throughput is constrained.** Bottlenecks are identified, measured, and actively managed.	
8	**Operating rhythm is embedded.** Monthly and quarterly reviews happen on schedule with real decisions, not just updates.	
9	**Quality issues are prevented upstream.** We catch problems early rather than fixing them after they reach customers.	
10	**The operating model is simple enough to teach.** A new leader could understand how we work within thirty days.	

Section B Total: ___ / 25

Section C: Commercial Engine (Questions 11-15)

#	Question	Score
11	**Growth is grounded in evidence.** We have cohort data, pipeline coverage, and conversion metrics that support our growth projections.	

#	Question	Score
12	**We manage pricing with discipline.** Price realization is tracked, discounting is governed, and we capture value for value delivered.	
13	**We know which customers create value.** Customer-level profitability is understood. We invest in profitable relationships and address unprofitable ones.	
14	**Retention is a managed process.** We track churn by cohort, understand drivers, and have systematic programs to improve retention.	
15	**We can articulate our competitive moat.** The answer to "why will this business continue to win?" is clear, specific, and supported by evidence.	

Section C Total: ___ / 25

Section D: Digital and Data Backbone (Questions 16-20)

#	Question	Score
16	**Core system architecture is a strength.** Systems are integrated, not fragmented. Data flows without manual intervention.	
17	**We have a single source of truth.** Key metrics are defined once and used consistently across the organization.	
18	**Data is clean enough to support analytics.** We could implement advanced analytics or machine-supported decision tools without major data remediation.	

#	Question	Score
19	**Data governance is simple, owned, and followed.** We know who owns key data domains, how they are defined, and how quality is monitored.	
20	**A buyer's technology team would leave confident.** If specialists reviewed our architecture, processes, and backlog, they would see coherence, not patches.	

Section D Total: ___ / 25

Section E: Talent and Leadership (Questions 21-25)

#	Question	Score
21	**The leadership system outlives individual leaders.** Succession plans exist, the bench is adequate, and the company is not dependent on irreplaceable people.	
22	**Organizational capacity is protected.** We monitor bandwidth and change load. We adjust initiatives rather than push until the system cracks.	
23	**Role clarity prevents duplication and drift.** Accountabilities are documented, non-overlapping, and understood. Issues do not fall between chairs.	
24	**Actual culture matches stated values.** Behaviors on the ground align with the disciplines in our playbook. There is no gap between what we say and what we do.	

#	Question	Score
25	**Leadership behaves as one system under pressure.** When results wobble, key stakeholders converge on priorities and reinforce discipline rather than fragmenting into competing agendas.	

Section E Total: ___ / 25

Interpreting the Scouting Report

Grand Total: ___ / 125

Score Ranges

Range	Interpretation
100-125	Strong position. Full gambit library available. Focus on high-impact, reinforcing combinations.
75-99	Solid foundation with gaps. Address weak dimensions before pursuing gambits that depend on them.
50-74	Significant constraints. Prioritize foundation-building gambits. Limit active initiatives to three.
Below 50	Fundamental issues. Focus on stabilization before value creation. Some gambits are not viable.

Section-Level Analysis

The section totals reveal where constraint binds tightest:

Section A below 15: Financial engine issues will compress multiple regardless of operational improvement. Prioritize earnings quality, cash conversion, and bridge documentation.

Section B below 15: Operational instability limits execution capacity. Gambits requiring organizational change will struggle. Prioritize process discipline before transformation.

Section C below 15: Commercial engine weakness limits revenue gambits. Pricing Ratchet, Expansion Loop, and Conversion Rebuild require this foundation.

Section D below 15: Data constraints eliminate analytics-dependent gambits. Machine-supported analysis, dynamic pricing, and precision segmentation are not viable. Build data infrastructure first.

Section E below 15: Talent and leadership gaps limit everything. Complex initiatives will fail. Consider Management Depth Build before other gambits.

Constraint-to-Gambit Mapping

Use the diagnostic to eliminate gambits that do not fit your situation:

If This Section Scores Below 15...	These Gambits Are High-Risk
Financial Engine	Exit Narrative Construction, Multiple Expansion gambits
Operational Throughput	Platform Roll-Up, Process Automation, Standardization Program
Commercial Engine	Pricing Ratchet, Expansion Loop, Cross-Sell Fuse, Conversion Rebuild
Digital Backbone	Machine-Supported Analysis Program, Data Infrastructure Build, Technology-Enabled Service Model
Talent and Leadership	Service Model Surgery, Organizational Flattening, Synergy Capture System

Using the Scouting Report

Before Gambit Selection: Complete the diagnostic with your leadership team. Discuss where scores diverge. Use the constraint mapping to eliminate gambits that do not fit.

At Midpoint: Repeat the diagnostic. Compare to baseline. Adjust the gambit portfolio based on what has improved and what remains constrained.

Twelve Months Before Exit: Run the diagnostic through a buyer's lens. Every question a buyer will ask during diligence is embedded in these twenty-five questions. Gaps discovered now can be addressed. Gaps discovered in diligence become discounts.

The best operators do not select gambits based on what looks attractive. They select based on what fits the constraints. The Scouting Report reveals those constraints before you commit resources to patterns that cannot succeed in your specific situation.

Scout before you plan. Then plan with precision.

BONUS MATERIAL

From Forty Patterns to Five That Matter

The VALUE CREATION FINANCE TOOLKIT

This toolkit is the financial backbone behind the Gameplan method. It converts the most useful private equity finance concepts into compact, card-style reference pages you can actually use inside a portfolio. Each card is designed like a small whiteboard: it defines the concept, explains why it matters to equity value, gives the core formula and drivers, and flags the common traps that create "paper value" instead of real value.

Use these cards to sanity-check a plan, pressure-test assumptions, and keep every operational move anchored to the only outcomes that ultimately matter: EBITDA quality, free cash flow, net debt, and enterprise value.

What you will find inside

1) Core value math

The bridge logic behind every story.

- Enterprise Value and Equity Value
- Value bridges and attribution discipline
- The levers that move equity value (earnings, net debt, multiple)
- What counts as a real delta versus noise

2) Cash and working capital mechanics

Where plans succeed or die quietly.

- Cash conversion cycle mechanics
- Working capital releases vs snapbacks
- Free cash flow construction and reconciliation
- Debt paydown impact on equity value
- 13-week cash visibility and liquidity risk

3) Unit economics and pricing

How revenue turns into operating earnings.

- Contribution margin and variable profit
- Price-volume-mix discipline
- Discount governance and price realization
- Cohorts, retention, expansion, and revenue quality proof

4) Return logic

How value creation shows up in returns.

- IRR and MOIC intuition (what actually drives each)
- Scenario thinking and sensitivity discipline

- Value creation attribution: what drove the outcome, when, and how repeatable it is

5) Deal and portfolio pragmatics
The board-grade realities that shape execution.

- Covenant awareness and headroom management
- Liquidity planning and refinancing readiness
- Exit readiness evidence and proof packs
- Buyer-grade documentation expectations

How to use the toolkit in practice
Use it as a bridge-first checklist

Before you approve an initiative, force it through three questions:

1. **Where does it show up on the bridge?** (earnings, net debt, multiple, or a mix)
2. **What is the mechanism?** (what changes operationally, not just financially)
3. **What proof will a buyer accept?** (what gets believed, what gets discounted)

Use it to prevent "fake progress"

Cards are written to surface the traps that create temporary wins, reversals, or non-repeatable gains:

- one-off working capital releases
- savings that do not land in financials
- pricing changes hidden by discounting
- narratives that outrun evidence
- multiple expansion that is assumed, not earned

Use it to standardize language across the portfolio

If you want fewer debates and faster decisions, insist on consistent definitions:

- "EBITDA improvement" means the same thing everywhere
- "Free cash flow" is reconciled the same way everywhere
- "Price realization" is measured the same way everywhere
- "Proof artifact" is stored, versioned, and auditable

Card 01: Equity Value Bridge

Translating operational results into equity outcomes

Enterprise Value (EV) equals EBITDA × exit multiple. Equity Value is EV minus net debt.

(1) Growing EBITDA through revenue/margin: **Improving sales performance and operational efficiency to increase earnings before interest, taxes, depreciation, and amortization.**

(2) Expanding exit multiple via growth outlook and quality: **Demonstrating strong future growth potential and high business quality to command a higher valuation multiple.**

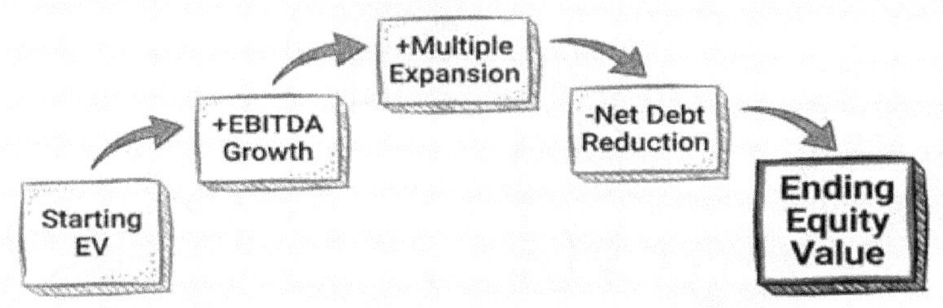

(3) Deleveraging via free cash flow: **Using generated cash to pay down debt, increasing the equity portion of the enterprise value.**

Value Creation Finance Toolkit

Card 02: LBO Return Decomposition

Breaking down multiple on invested capital (MOIC)

$$\text{MOIC} = \frac{\text{Final Equity Value} + \text{Cumulative Distributions}}{\text{Initial Equity Investment}}$$

Four 4 components of value creation is:

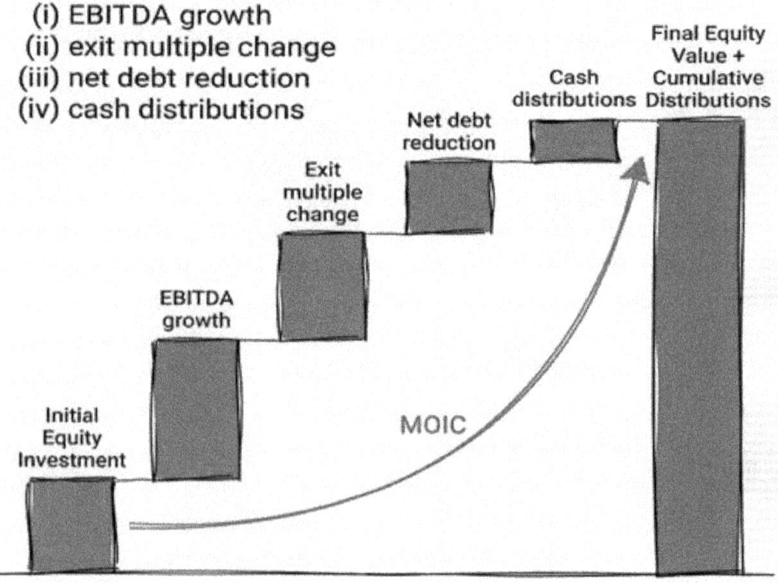

Operational improvements drive majority of value.

Value Creation Finance Toolkit

Card 03: Internal Rate of Return (IRR)

Measuring return with the time value of money

IRR is the discount rate making NPV of cash flows equal zero.

$$NPV = \sum \frac{\text{Cash Flow}_t}{(1+IRR)^t} = 0$$

- capital calls (outflows) and distributions (inflows)
- highly sensitive to timing
- same MOIC can yield different IRRs

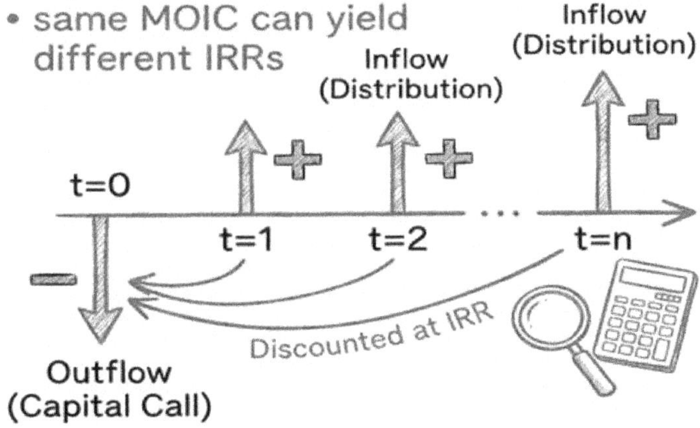

Value Creation Finance Toolkit

'Card 04: MOIC vs IRR Tension

High multiple or high speed?

- MOIC = total return.
- IRR = speed of returns.
- Key: Quick flip = high IRR + modest MOIC.
- Longer hold = high MOIC + lower IRR.

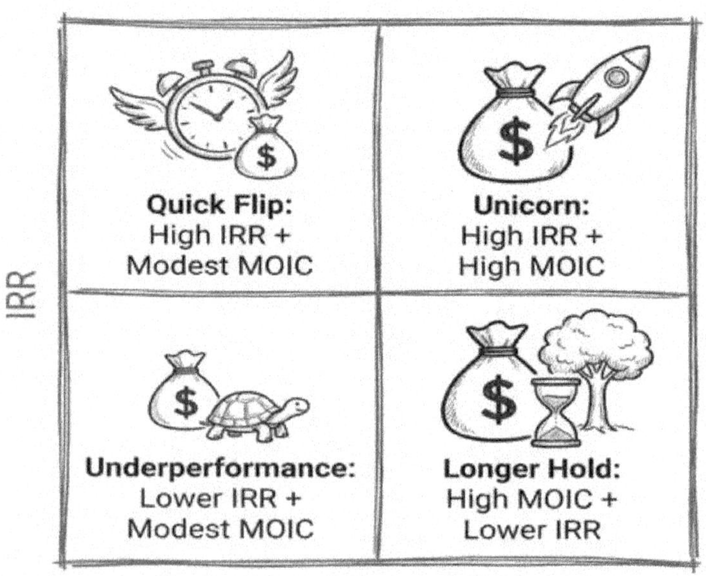

Objective: maximise both through disciplined execution.

Value Creation Finance Toolkit

Card 05: Distributions to Paid-In (DPI)'

The cash that has been returned

DPI measures realised cash returns.

$$\text{DPI} = \frac{\text{Total Distributions}}{\text{Paid-In Capital}}$$

- captures cash from dividends/recaps/sales
- high DPI early improves IRR
- balance reinvestment with timely returns

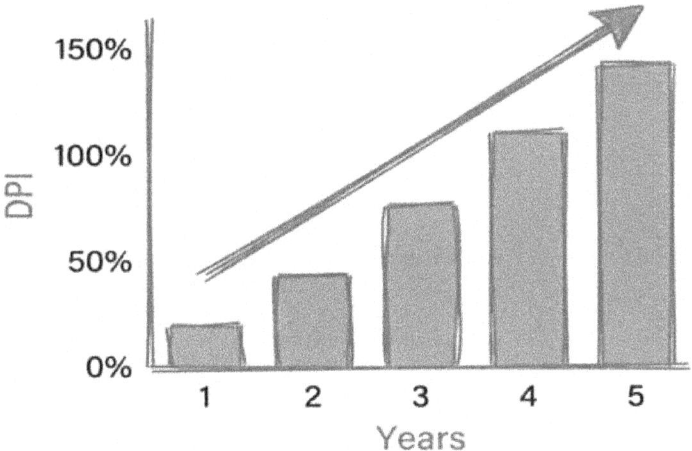

Value Creation Finance Toolkit

Card 06: Total Value to Paid-In (TVPI)

Realised plus unrealised value

TVPI is the ratio of total value (distributions + current NAV) to paid-in capital.

$$\text{TVPI} = \frac{\text{Distributions} + \text{Net Asset Value}}{\text{Paid-In Capital}}$$

- captures realised returns and fair value
- quality of NAV depends on valuation methods
- NAV must reflect true enterprise value

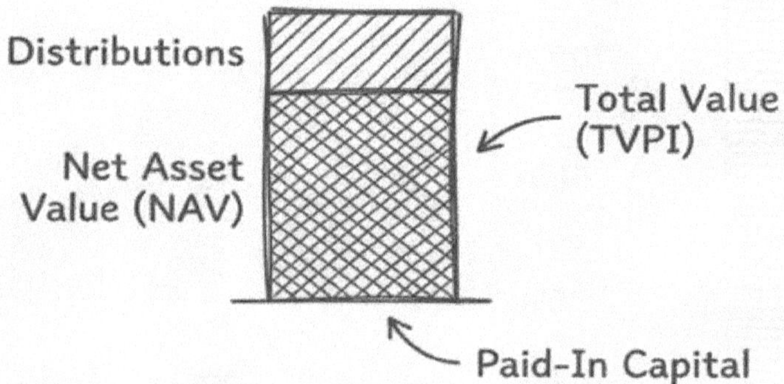

Value Creation Finance Toolkit

Card 07: Residual Value to Paid-In (RVPI)

The unrealised component of value

RVPI measures the unrealised portion of the investment.

$$RVPI = \frac{\text{Net Asset Value}}{\text{Paid-In Capital}}$$

- high RVPI + low DPI appropriate early in fund life
- over time RVPI converts to DPI
- RVPI growth supported by operational performance
- quality of earnings validates unrealised value

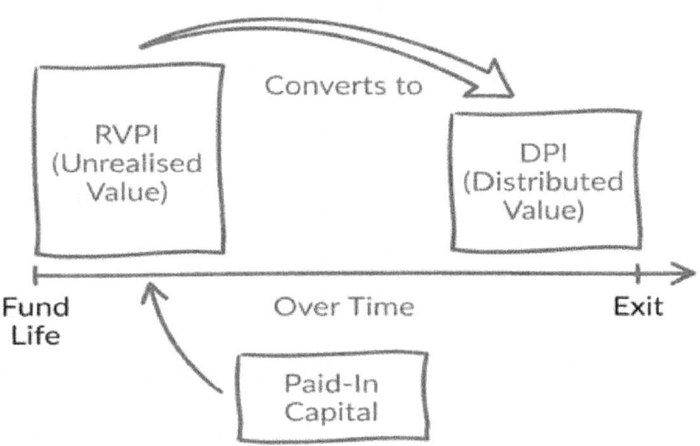

Value Creation Finance Toolkit

Card 08: Fund Economics Snapshot

Fees and carry fundamentals

Management fees and carried interest shape net return to investors.

(1) Management Fees:

- ✓ Based on committed capital during investment period, then on invested cost or NAV.
- – Fee offsets may reduce drag.

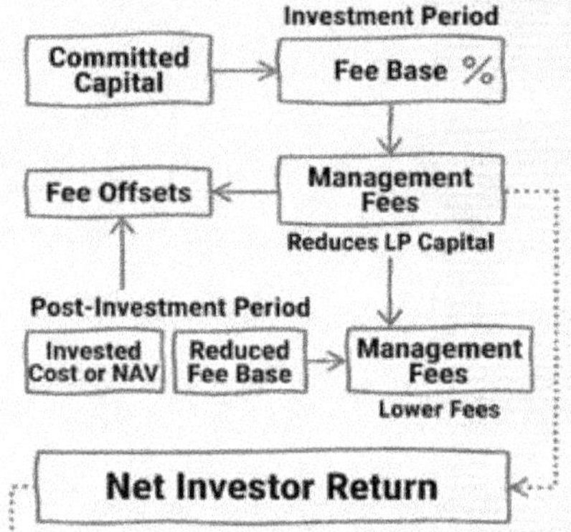

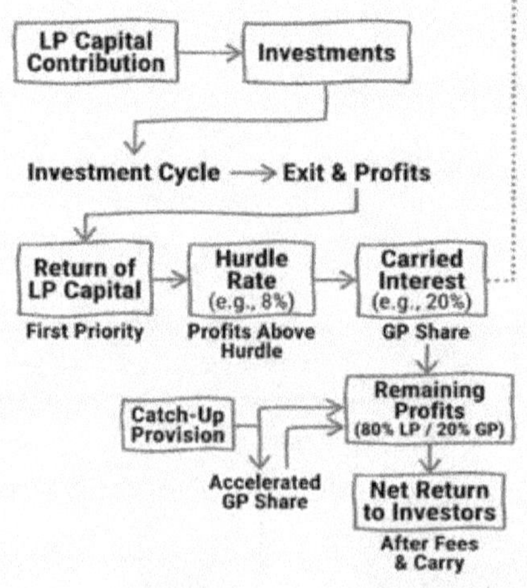

(2) Carried Interest:

- ✓ Often 20% of profits above hurdle.
- ✓ Accrues after LPs recover capital.
- ✓ Catch-up provisions accelerate GP share.

Value Creation Finance Toolkit

Card 09: Management Fee Drag

Understand the compounding cost of fees

Management fees paid annually as % of commitments or AUM. Over time, fees reduce invested capital and compound against gross returns.

At 2% fee for 5 years, fees can exceed 10% of committed capital.

- fees step down post-investment period
- calculated on invested capital or NAV
- monitor fee drag for efficiencies

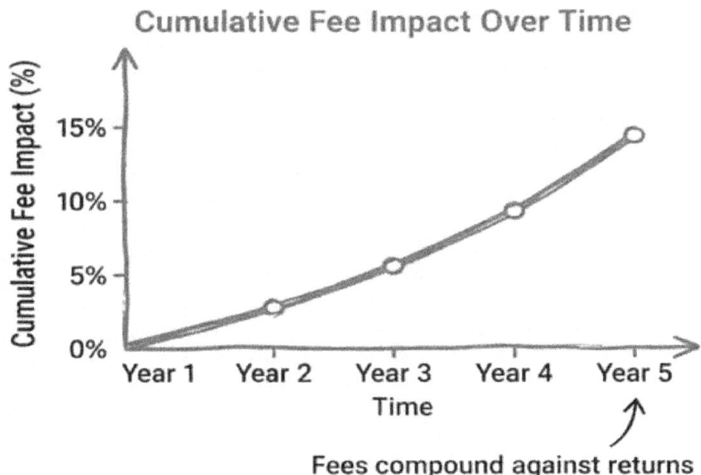

Value Creation Finance Toolkit

Card 10: Carry and Hurdle Basics

How profits are shared

Carried interest is the portion of profits allocated to GP after returning capital and preferred return (hurdle) to LPs.

Typical: 8% preferred return → 80/20 split of profits

- Catch-up provision allows GP higher share after hurdle until reaching negotiated %
- Clawback ensures GP returns excess carry if later investments underperform
- Aligns incentive with portfolio exits

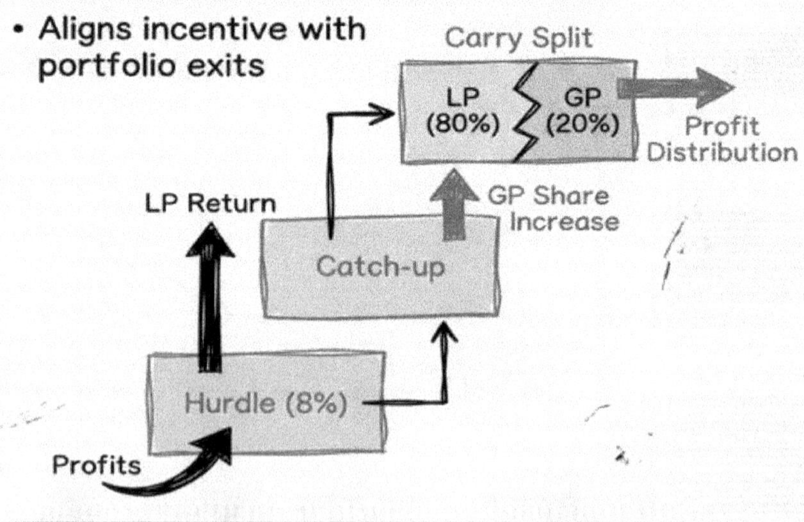

Value Creation Finance Toolkit

Card 11: European Waterfall (Whole-of-Fund)

Priority of cash flows to LPs

In a European waterfall, GP does not receive carry until entire fund has returned capital and preferred return to investors.

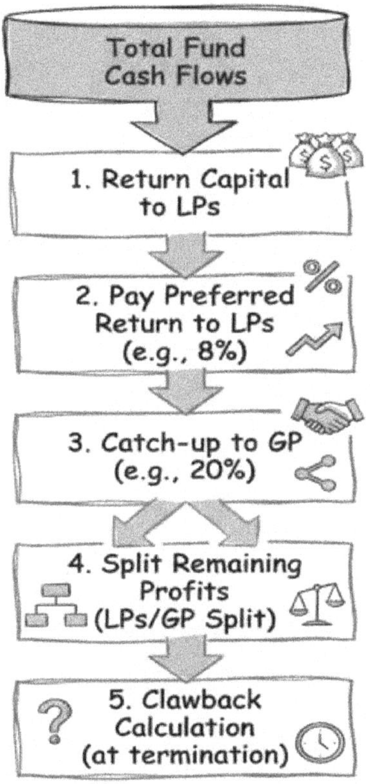

Total Fund Cash Flows

1. Return Capital to LPs

2. Pay Preferred Return to LPs (e.g., 8%)

3. Catch-up to GP (e.g., 20%)

4. Split Remaining Profits (LPs/GP Split)

5. Clawback Calculation (at termination)

(1) Return capital contributions to LPs

(2) Pay accrued preferred return to LPs (e.g., 8%)

(3) Allocate catch-up distributions to GP until negotiated share (e.g., 20%)

(4) Split remaining profits between LPs and GP according to carry split

(5) Conduct clawback calculation at fund termination

Value Creation Finance Toolkit

Card 12: American Waterfall (Deal-by-Deal)

Carry at the deal level

In an American or deal-by-deal waterfall, GP may receive carry as individual deals are realised rather than waiting for whole fund to return capital.

This accelerates carry but increases risk of clawback if later deals underperform.

Cash flow order:

- Capital and preferred return paid first, then GP catch-up, then carry split.

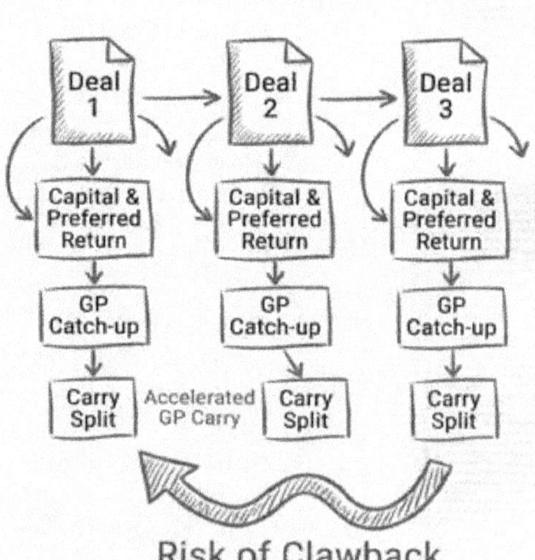

Note: Excess distributions may be held in escrow to cover potential future clawback.

Value Creation Finance Toolkit

Card 13: Catch-Up Logic

Accelerating GP share after the hurdle

Catch-up provision determines how quickly GP receives its share of profits after preferred return is met.

Example: with 8% preferred return and 20% carry, all distributions after hurdle may go entirely to GP until cumulative share reaches 20% of profits. Thereafter, profits split 80/20.

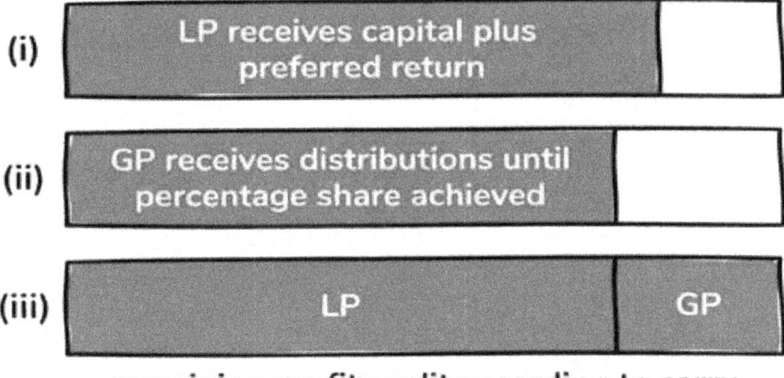

Catch-up balances LP protection with GP incentives.

Value Creation Finance Toolkit

Card 14: Clawback Explained

Preventing over-payment of carried interest

Clawback provision requires GP to **return a portion of carry** if later fund results **reduce total profits** below the level at which GP was previously paid.

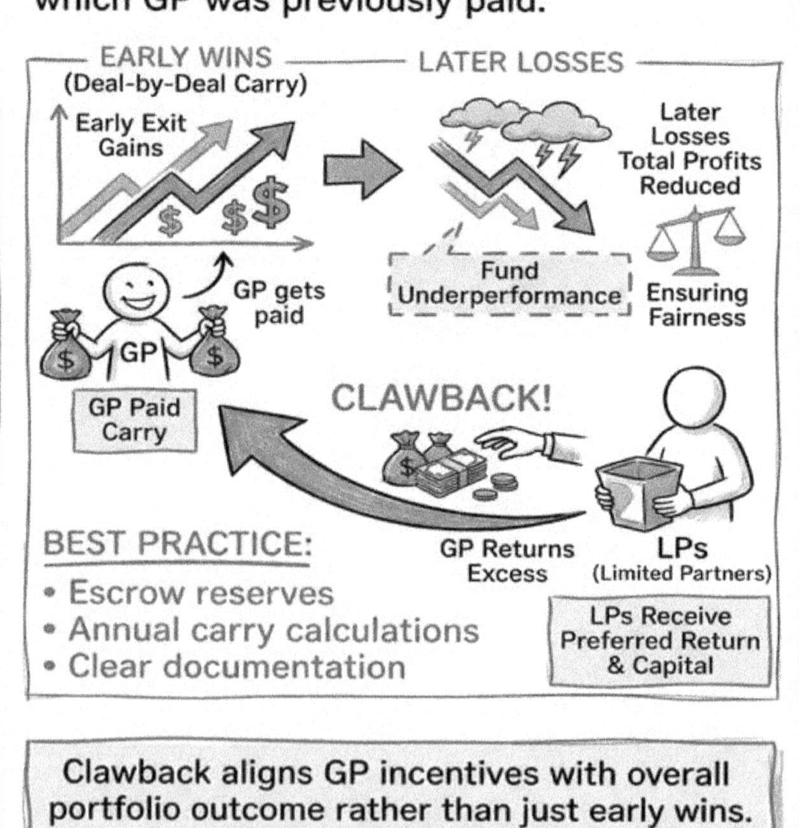

Value Creation Finance Toolkit

Card 15: Recycling Capital

Reinvesting early proceeds for more deployment

Recycling provisions allow fund to reinvest proceeds from realised investments or fees without counting them as distributions. This can increase invested capital and amplify gross returns without additional commitments.

Key consideration:
Rey considerration: Recycling temporarily depresses DPI by increasing the denominator (paid-in capital).

- *Balance benefits of additional deployment against liquidity preferences and fund duration constraints*
- *Clearly document what qualifies for recycling (realisation proceeds, fees)*
- *Ensure transparency with LPs*

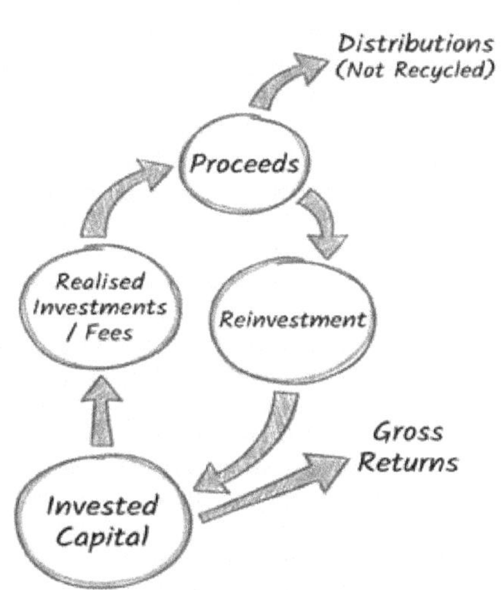

Value Creation Finance Toolkit

Card 16: Subscription Line Financing

Short-term credit for convenience and IRR optics

Subscription line (capital call facility) is a short-term credit line secured by uncalled investor commitments. It allows fund to delay calling capital, pay deal expenses quickly and streamline cash management.

Key consideration:

From portfolio perspective, facility may improve IRR because paid-in capital is called later. Nevertheless, interest cost and potential dilution of LP returns must be disclosed.

Best practice:

report returns with and without effect of subscription lines, avoid overusing facility to not distort economic reality.

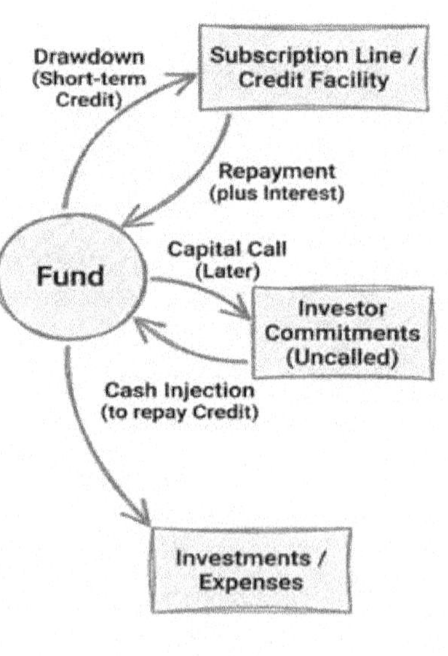

Value Creation Finance Toolkit

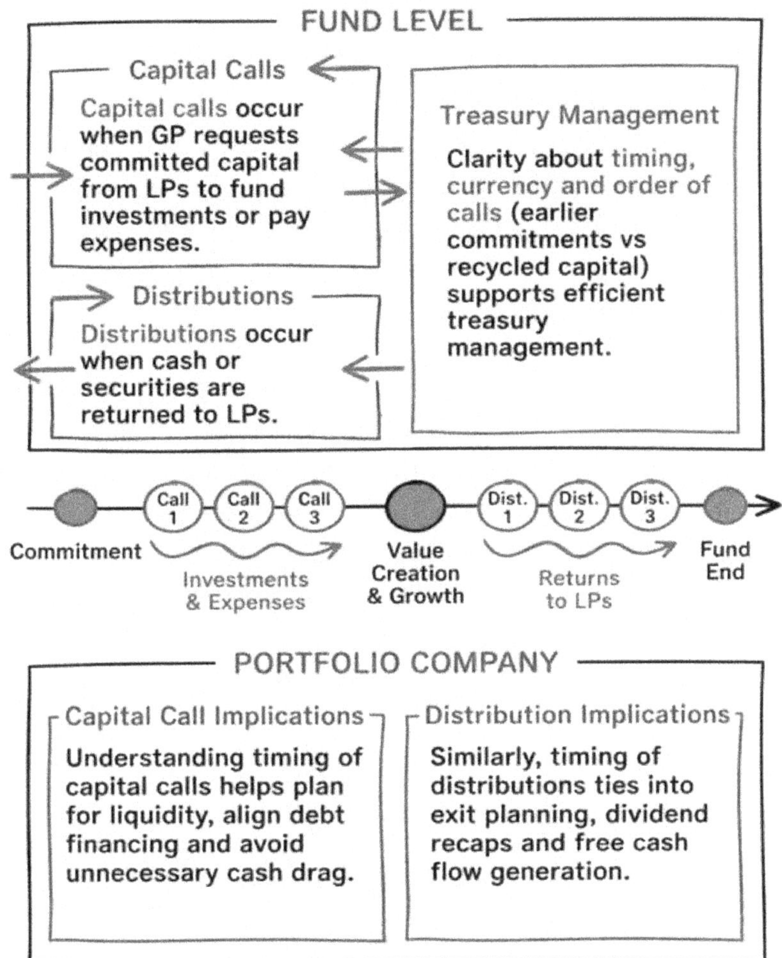

Value Creation Finance Toolkit

Card 18: GP Commitment

Demonstrating alignment

GP commitment is the portion of capital contributed by the general partner, typically 1-5% of total commitments. A meaningful GP commitment aligns interests between GP and LP, as GP stands to lose their own capital if returns underperform.

In portfolio context: GP commitment assures management that sponsor has skin in the game, fostering trust and long-term partnership. However, commitment should not be financed through back-to-back loans that reduce its effectiveness.

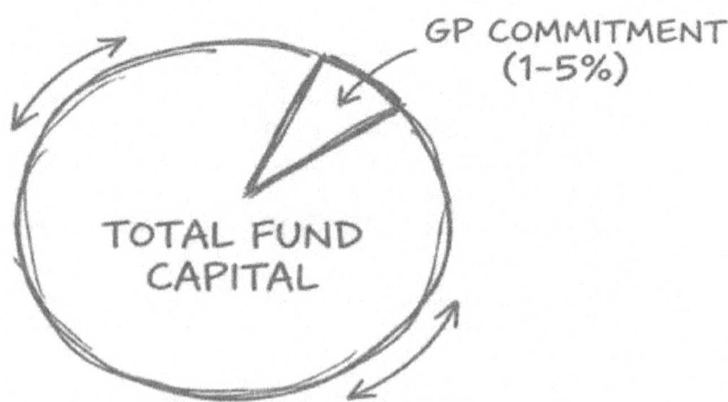

Value Creation Finance Toolkit

Card 19: LPAC & Governance Triggers

Oversight mechanisms that protect value

Limited Partner Advisory Committee (LPAC) reviews conflicts of interest, valuation methodologies and fund policy exceptions.

- Typical triggers for LPAC consultation:

- Typical triggers for LPAC consultation: (i) related-party transactions, (ii) material deviations from valuation policy, (iii) changes in control at portfolio companies, (iv) GP key-key-person events.

For portfolio teams: Engaging with LPAC ensures transparency and can expedite approvals for items like recycling, co-investments or follow-on capital. Effective governance strengthens relationships with investors and reduces friction at exit.

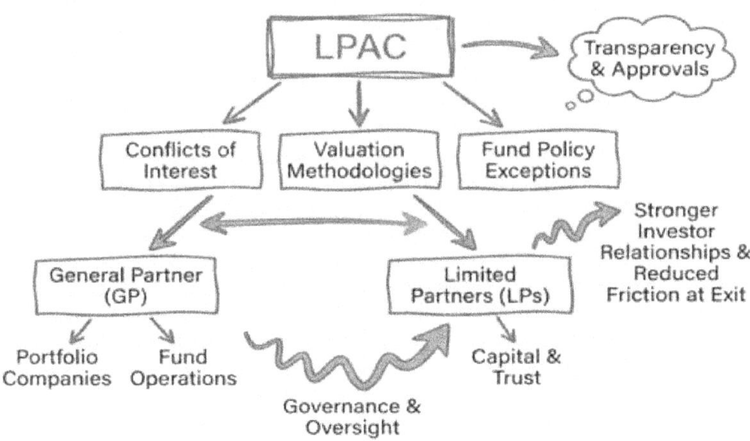

Value Creation Finance Toolkit

Card 20: Sources & Uses Table

Mapping capital flows at deal close

Sources and uses schedule summarises capital required to complete a transaction and where that capital comes from. Typical uses include: equity purchase price, refinancing of existing debt, transaction fees, cash to balance sheet. Sources include: equity from sponsors, debt facilities, rollover equity from sellers, sometimes mezzanine or vendor notes.

USES (Where Capital Goes)	SOURCES (Where Capital Comes From)
Equity Purchase Price: $100M	Sponsor Equity: $60M
Refinancing of Existing Debt: $50M	Debt Facilities (Senior/Junior): $80M
Transaction Fees (Advisory, Legal, etc.): $5M	Rollover Equity from Sellers: $15M
Cash to Balance Sheet (Working Capital): $10M	Mezzanine / Vendor Notes: $10M
TOTAL USES: $165M	TOTAL SOURCES: $165M

Creating clear sources and uses table helps all stakeholders understand capital structure at closing and ensures sufficient funds allocated to working capital.

Value Creation Finance Toolkit

Card 21: Enterprise Value vs Equity Value

Avoiding a common valuation mistake

Enterprise Value (EV) measures total value of company to all capital providers. It equals market value of equity plus net debt (debt minus cash) plus non-core liabilities and minus non-core assets. Equity Value is the portion of EV attributable to shareholders after satisfying debt obligations and adjusting for working capital.

Key distinction: Operational improvements impact EV (profitability, growth, risk). Financing decisions affect equity value (leverage, cash management).

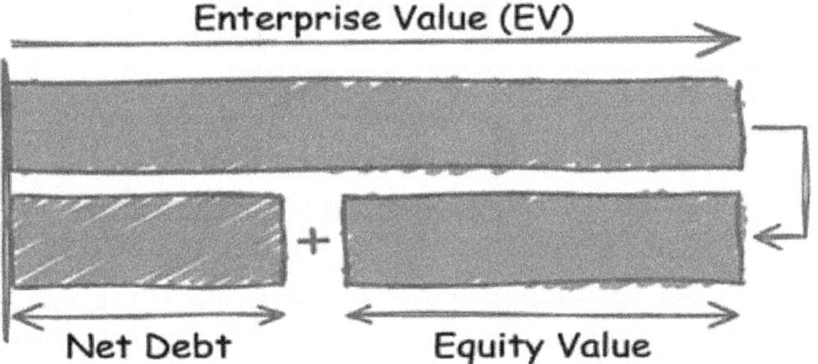

Value Creation Finance Toolkit

Card 22: Entry Multiple & EBITDA Quality

You buy sustainable cash earnings, not just EBITDA

Entry multiple (Price / EBITDA) depends on quality of underlying earnings. Adjustments to reported EBITDA include removal of non-recurring items, normalisation of extraordinary expenses or income, and addition of run-rate benefits.

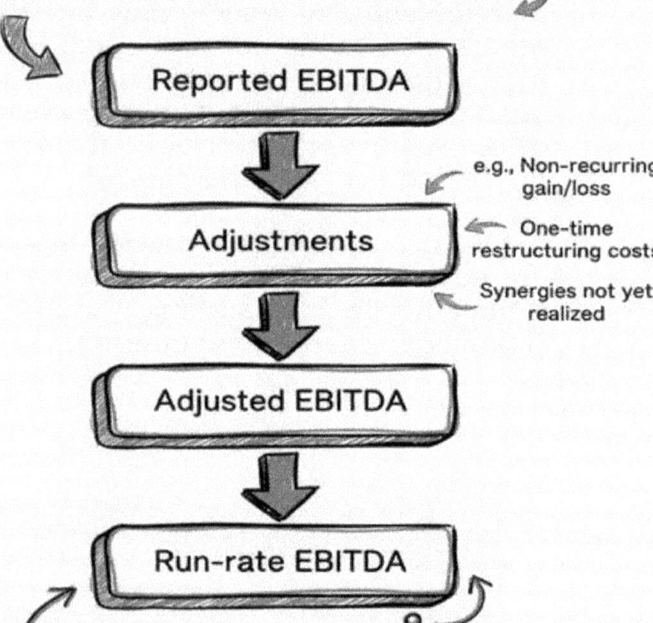

Higher-quality EBITDA reduces risk of overpaying and provides stronger foundation for future value creation. Focus on operational dillligence and quality of earnings analyses analyses to derive realistic entry multiple.

Value Creation Finance Toolkit

Card 23: Quality of Earnings (QoE)

Making adjusted EBITDA defendable

Quality of Earnings analysis validates the sustainability and accuracy of reported earnings. It examines revenue recognition policies, expense classifications, working capital trends, and one-time items.

(1) Revenue quality:

- timing, customer concentration, contract terms

(2) Cost structure:

- fixed vs variable, normalised run-rate

(3) Working capital:

- sustainable levels, cash conversion

(4) Non-recurring items:

- add-backs and adjustments

QoE report provides confidence in EBITDA used for valuation and value creation planning.

Value Creation Finance Toolkit

Card 24: Working Capital Normalization

Adjusting for sustainable operating levels

Working capital normalisation adjusts balance sheet to reflect sustainable operating levels. It removes timing distortions, seasonal peaks, and one-off events to determine true cash requirement.

Net Working Capital = (Accounts Receivable + Inventory) - Accounts Payable

Key adjustments:

- seasonality
- payment terms changes
- inventory build-up/draw down
- prepayments

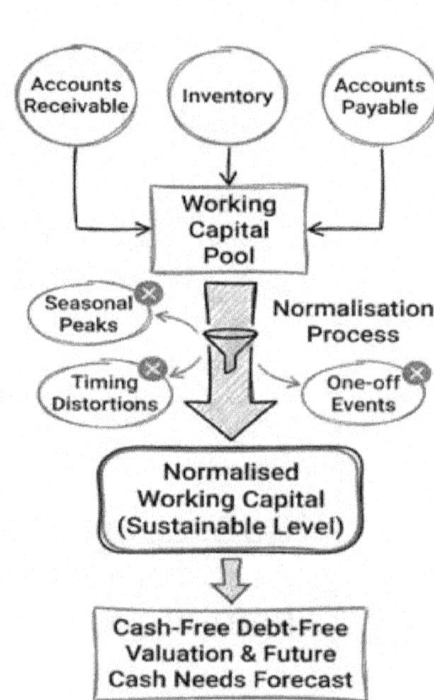

Normalised working capital informs cash-free debt-free valuation and helps forecast future cash needs.

Value Creation Finance Toolkit

Card 25: Cash Conversion Cycle (CCC)

Measuring operational efficiency

Cash Conversion Cycle measures how quickly company converts inventory and receivables into cash. Shorter cycle = better cash generation.

CCC = Days Inventory Outstanding + Days Sales Outstanding – Days Payable Outstanding.

Components: DIO (inventory turnover), DSO (receivables collection), DPO (payables extension).

Improving CCC through faster collections, inventory management, and supplier terms enhances free cash flow and reduces working capital drag.

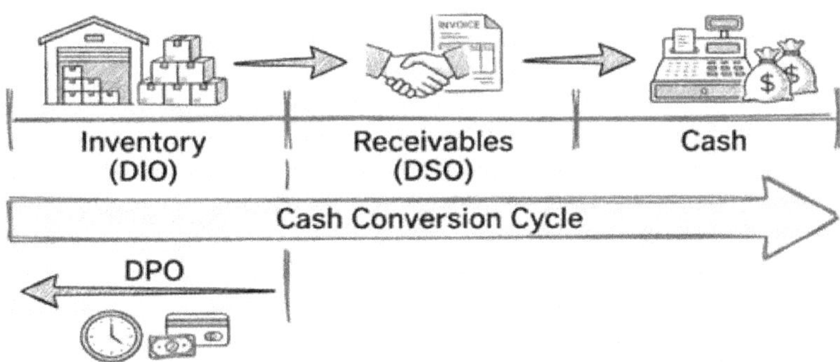

Value Creation Finance Toolkit

Card 26: Free Cash Flow to Firm (FCFF)

Cash available to all capital providers

Free Cash Flow to Firm represents cash generated by operations available to all investors (debt and equity holders) before financing decisions.

FCFF = EBIT(1-Tax Rate) + Depreciation - CapEx - ΔNet Working Capital

Key components:

- operating profit after tax, add back non-cash charges, subtract capital investments and working capital increases.

FCFF is used for enterprise valuation (DCF) and measures ability to service debt, pay dividends, and reinvest in growth.

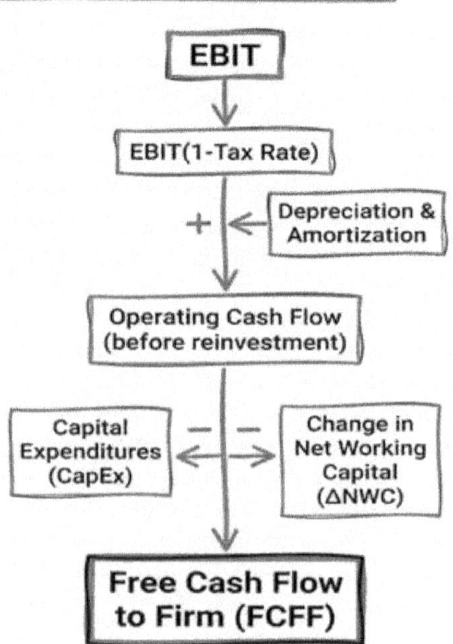

Value Creation Finance Toolkit

Card 27: Net Debt Definition

The true leverage position

Net Debt is total debt minus cash and cash equivalents. It represents the actual debt burden after accounting for liquid assets that could immediately repay debt.

Net Debt = Total Debt (Short-term + Long-term) - Cash & Cash Equivalents

Adjustments may include: debt-like items (pension liabilities, lease obligations), excess cash vs operating cash needs, restricted cash exclusions.

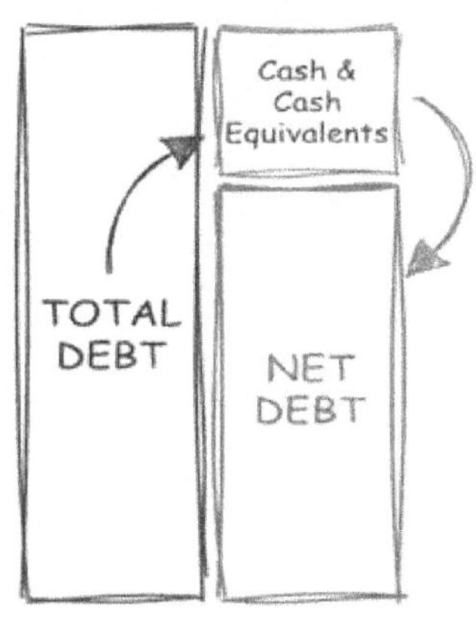

Net Debt is used in enterprise value calculations and leverage ratios. Lower net debt improves equity value and financial flexibility.

Value Creation Finance Toolkit

Card 28: Leverage Ratio

Measuring debt relative to earnings

Leverage ratio measures total debt or net debt relative to EBITDA. It indicates how many years of earnings would be required to repay all debt.

Leverage Ratio = Net Debt / EBITDA

Typical ranges: 3-5x for buyouts, lower for growth equity, higher for stable cash flow businesses.

High leverage amplifies equity returns but increases financial risk. Deleveraging through EBITDA growth and debt paydown improves credit profile and exit valuation. Lenders impose maximum leverage covenants.

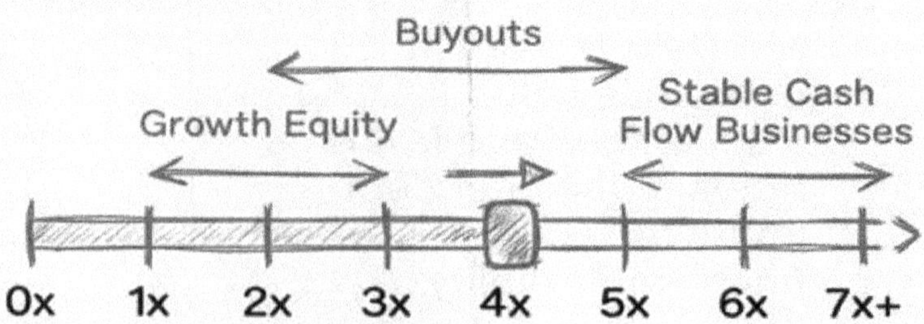

Value Creation Finance Toolkit

Card 29: Interest Coverage

Ability to service debt obligations

Interest Coverage ratio measures company ability to pay interest expense from operating earnings. Higher coverage = lower default risk.

$$\text{Interest Coverage} = \frac{\text{EBITDA}}{\text{Interest Expense}}$$

Typical thresholds: >3x comfortable, 2-3x moderate risk, <2x distress signal. Alternative: **EBIT / Interest Expense** (excludes non-cash items).

Strong interest coverage provides cushion for operational volatility and supports higher leverage. Lenders monitor this ratio closely as covenant metric.

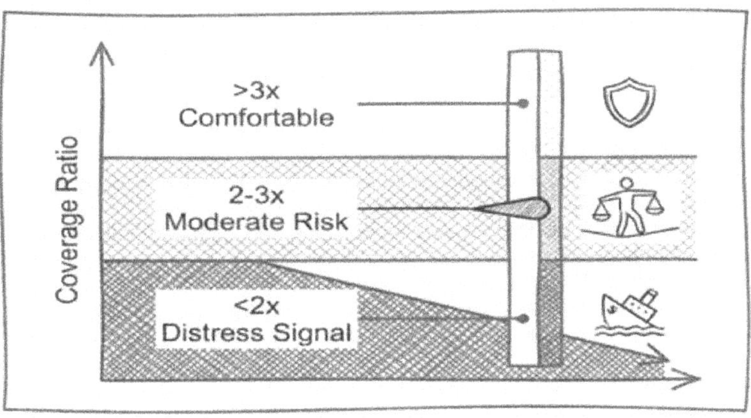

Value Creation Finance Toolkit

Card 30: Covenant Headroom

Managing financial flexibility

Covenant headroom is the buffer between actual financial metrics and covenant thresholds in debt agreements. Adequate headroom prevents technical default and preserves operational flexibility.

Common covenants:

- Maximum leverage ratio (Net Debt/EBITDA)
- Minimum interest coverage (EBITDA/Interest)
- Minimum liquidity
- CapEx limits

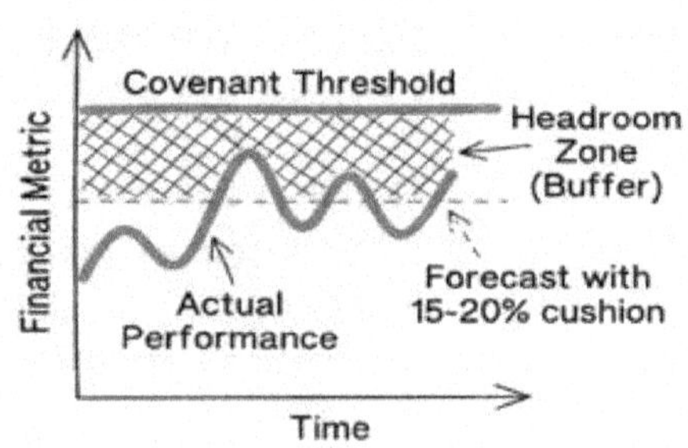

Monitoring covenant headroom allows proactive management of capital structure. Breaching covenants triggers lender consent requirements, fee increases, or acceleration. Build 15-20% cushion into forecasts.

Value Creation Finance Toolkit

Card 31: Weighted Average Cost of Capital (WACC)

Discount rate for enterprise valuation

- WACC is the blended cost of all capital sources (debt and equity), weighted by their proportion in the capital structure. It represents the minimum return required by all investors.

WACC = (E/V) × Cost of Equity + (D/V) × Cost of Debt × (1-Tax Rate).

Where E = market value of equity, D = market value of debt, V = E + D.

WACC is used as discount rate in DCF valuation. Lower WACC increases enterprise value. Optimal capital structure minimizes WACC.

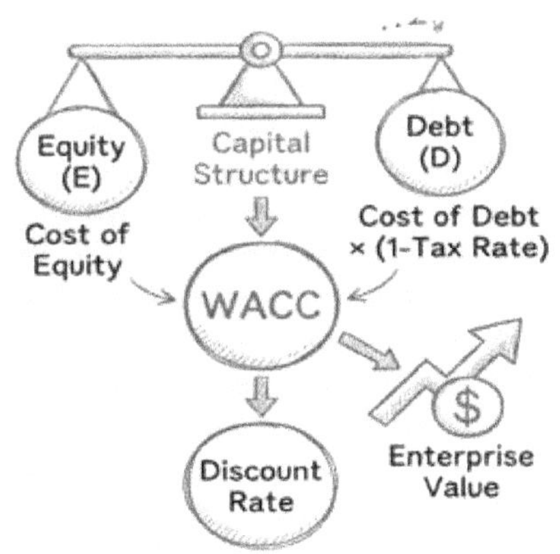

Value Creation Finance Toolkit

Card 32: Cost of Equity Using CAPM

Expected return for equity investors

Capital Asset Pricing Model (CAPM) estimates cost of equity based on risk-free rate, market risk premium, and company-specific risk (beta).

> Cost of Equity = Risk-Free Rate + Beta × Market Risk Premium

Components: **Risk-free rate** (government bonds), **Beta** (volatility vs market, typically 1.0–2.0 for PE-backed companies), **Market risk premium** (historical equity return above risk-free, ~5-7%).

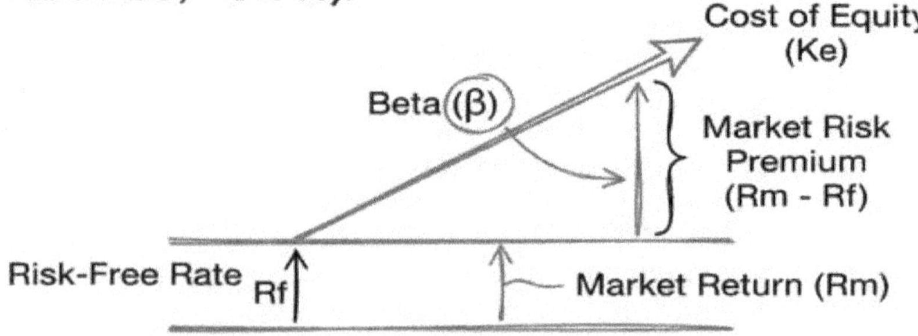

- Higher beta = higher cost of equity.
- Used in WACC calculation and equity valuation.

Value Creation Finance Toolkit

Card 33: After-Tax Cost of Debt

Effective cost of borrowing

After-tax cost of debt reflects the tax deductibility of interest expense, which reduces the effective cost of borrowing.

After-Tax Cost of Debt =
Interest Rate × (1 – Tax Rate)

Example: 8% interest rate with 25% tax rate = 8% × (1-0.25) = 6% after-tax cost.

- Tax shield makes debt cheaper than equity.
- After-tax cost of debt is used in WACC calculation.
- Higher tax rates increase value of debt tax shield.

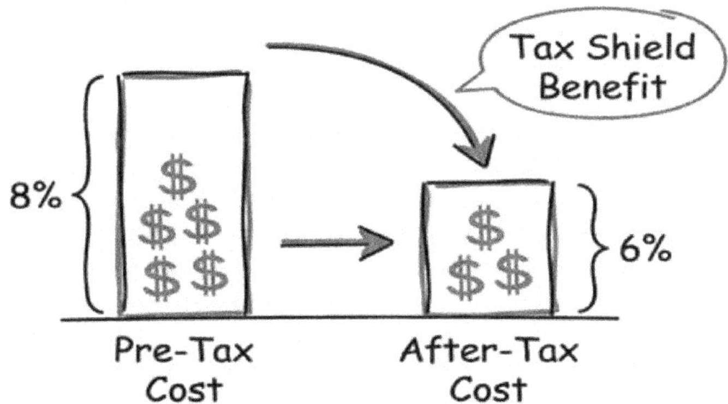

Value Creation Finance Toolkit

Card 34: DCF Terminal Value

Capturing value beyond the forecast period

Terminal Value represents the present value of all future cash flows beyond the explicit forecast period. It typically accounts for 60-80% of total enterprise value.

Two methods:

- (1) Perpetuity Growth: Terminal Value = Final Year FCF × $\frac{(1+g)}{(WACC-g)}$

  where g = long-term growth rate (2-3%)

- (2) Exit Multiple: Terminal Value = Final Year EBITDA × Exit Multiple

Terminal value is discounted back to present using WACC. Assumptions about growth rate and exit multiple significantly impact valuation.

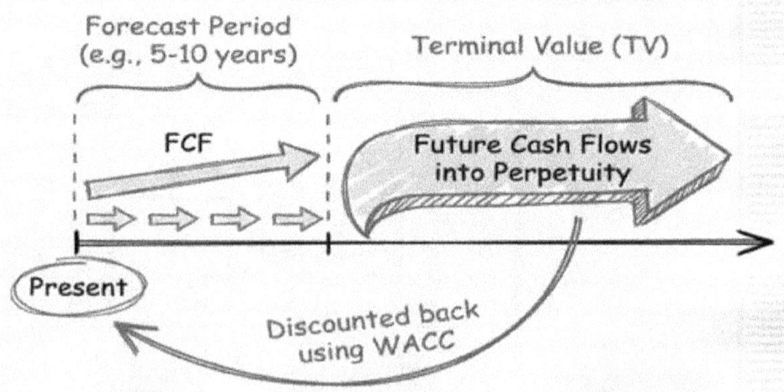

Value Creation Finance Toolkit

Card 35: Multiple-Based Valuation

Benchmarking value against peers

Multiple-based valuation estimates enterprise value by applying comparable company multiples to target company metrics.

- Common multiples: EV/EBITDA (most common for PE), EV/Revenue (for high-growth or negative EBITDA), P/E ratio (public markets).

> Enterprise Value = EBITDA × Comparable Multiple

Select peer companies with similar size, growth, margins, and industry. Adjust for differences in quality, risk, and growth prospects.
Cross-check with DCF valuation.

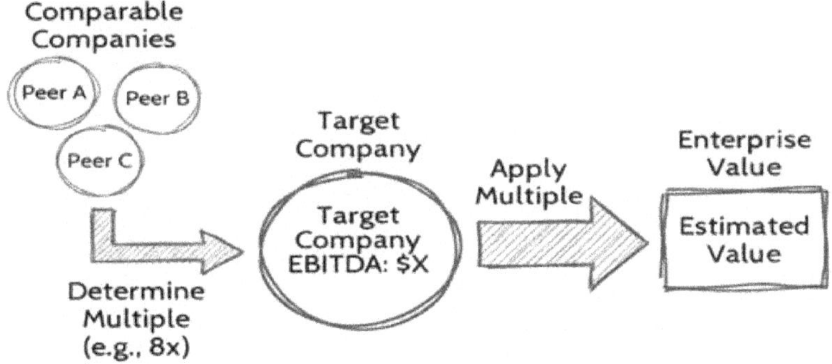

Value Creation Finance Toolkit

Card 36: Trading vs Transaction Comps

Two approaches to comparable valuation

Trading comps use public company multiples based on current market prices. Transaction comps use multiples from recent M&A deals in the sector.

Trading Comps	Transaction Comps
• Based on public market valuations • Reflect minority stakes • Lower multiples (no control premium) • Liquid markets	• Based on actual deal prices • Include control premium • Higher multiples • Reflect strategic value and synergies

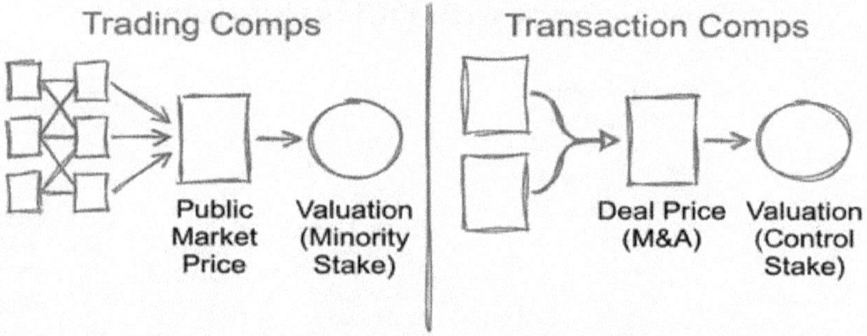

Trading Comps
Public Market Price
Valuation (Minority Stake)

Transaction Comps
Deal Price (M&A)
Valuation (Control Stake)

Transaction comps are more relevant for PE buyouts. Trading comps provide market reality check. Use both for triangulation.

Value Creation Finance Toolkit

Card 37: EBITDA vs Cash Flow

Understanding the difference

EBITDA is an accounting measure of operating profitability. Cash Flow measures actual cash generated or consumed.

EBITDA excludes:	Cash Flow includes:
• taxes • interest • CapEx • working capital changes	• all cash movements • actual tax paid • capital investments • working capital requirements

Cash Flow = EBITDA - Taxes - CapEx - ΔWorking Capital - Interest

EBITDA is used for valuation multiples. Cash Flow determines debt service capacity and distributions. High EBITDA with poor cash conversion signals working capital or CapEx issues.

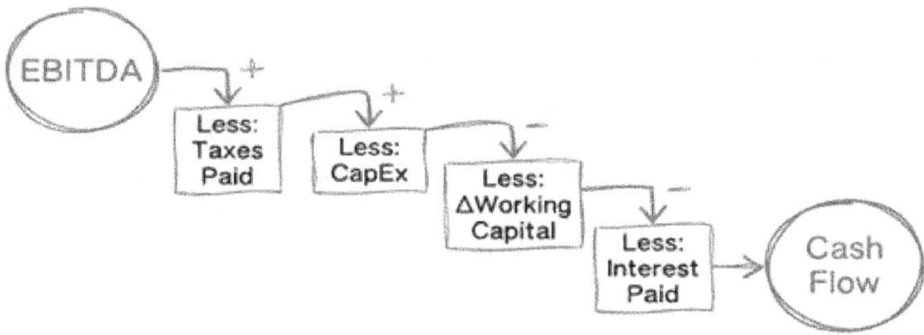

Value Creation Finance Toolkit

Card 38: Tax Shield Value

Quantifying the benefit of debt

Tax shield is the reduction in taxable income from interest expense deductibility. It creates value by reducing corporate taxes.

> Annual Tax Shield = Interest Expense × Tax Rate.
> Present value of tax shield = Annual Tax Shield / Cost of Debt (perpetuity assumption)

Example: $10M interest expense, 25% tax rate = $2.5M annual tax savings.

- Tax shield increases with higher leverage and tax rates.
- Supports use of debt in LBO structures.
- Changes in tax policy affect optimal capital structure.

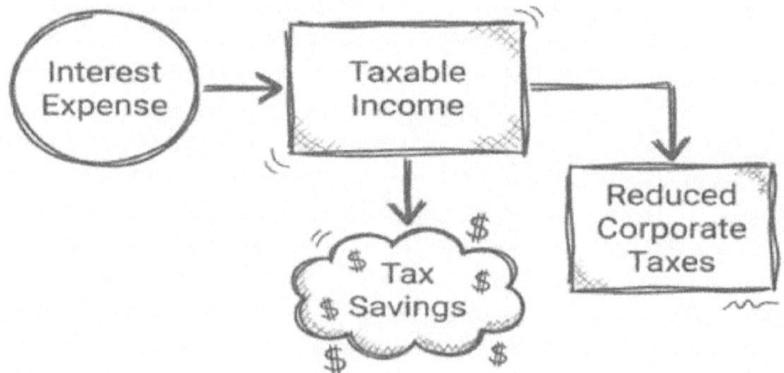

Value Creation Finance Toolkit

Card 39: Dividend Recapitalisation

Extracting value before exit

Dividend recapitalisation (recap) involves taking on additional debt to pay a dividend to equity holders, returning capital while maintaining ownership.

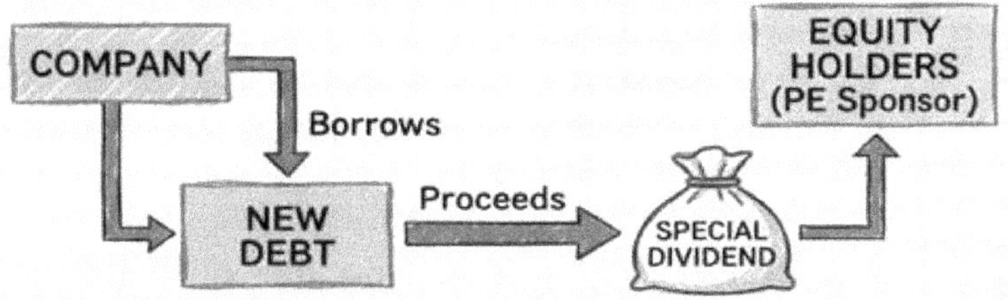

Increases leverage ratio, no change in equity ownership.

Mechanics:

- company borrows new debt
- uses proceeds to pay special dividend to PE sponsor
- increases leverage ratio
- no change in equity ownership

Benefits:

- accelerates cash returns (improves IRR and DPI)
- proves business model and debt capacity
- retains upside exposure

Risks:

- higher leverage reduces financial flexibility
- increases covenant risk
- may limit growth investments

Typically done 2-3 years into hold period after operational improvements.

Value Creation Finance Toolkit

Card 40: Refinancing Debt

Optimizing the capital structure

Refinancing replaces existing debt with new debt at better terms (lower rates, extended maturity, increased flexibility).

Reasons to refinance:

- Lower interest rates reduce cash interest burden,
- Extend maturity pushes out repayment and reduces refinancing risk,
- Remove or loosen covenants for operational flexibility,
- Upsize facility to fund growth or dividend recap.

Process:

- Negotiate new debt terms with existing or new lenders,
- Use proceeds to repay old debt,
- Pay refinancing fees and prepayment penalties.

Refinancing is common 12-24 months after acquisition once operational improvements are demonstrated. Improves cash flow and equity returns.

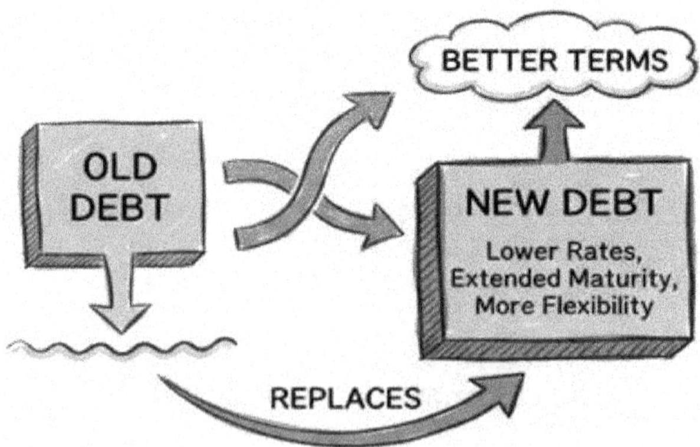

Value Creation Finance Toolkit

Card 41: Value Creation Attribution

Decomposing sources of return

Value creation attribution breaks down total return into specific drivers to understand what created value.

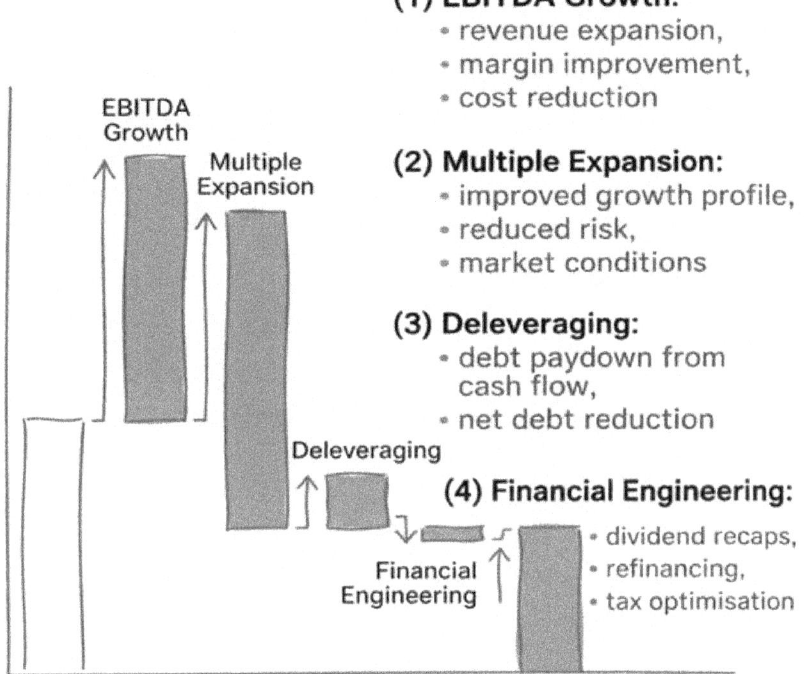

Attribution analysis guides future value creation priorities and validates investment thesis.

Operational improvements typically drive 50-70% of total value in successful deals.

Value Creation Finance Toolkit

Card 42: Hold Period Mathematics

Mathematics

Time impacts returns differently

Hold period affects IRR and MOIC differently. Longer holds can increase MOIC but reduce IRR due to time value of money.

Key relationships: MOIC = cumulative multiple regardless of time, IRR = annualised return sensitive to timing, shorter hold with 3x MOIC may yield higher IRR than longer hold with 4x MOIC.

$$IRR = \left(\frac{\text{Ending Value}}{\text{Beginning Value}}\right)^{(1/\text{Years})} - 1$$

Optimal hold period balances maximising total value (MOIC) with) with speed of returns (IRR).

Market conditions, operational readiness, and fund life influence exit timing.

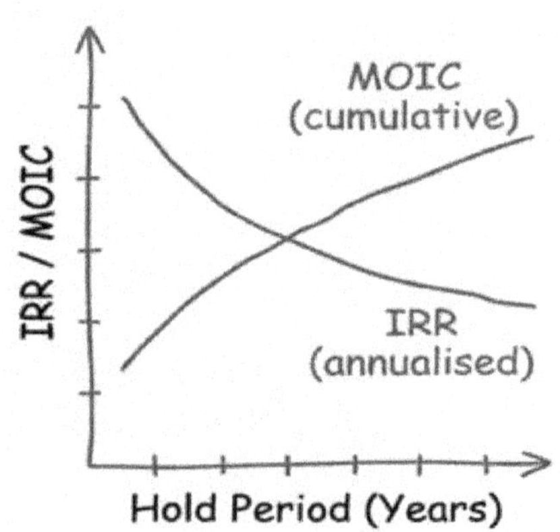

Value Creation Finance Toolkit

Card 43: Sensitivity Grid

Testing assumptions systematically

Sensitivity grid (or table) shows how enterprise value or IRR changes when two key variables are adjusted simultaneously.

Common variable pairs include:

- exit multiple **vs** EBITDA growth
- leverage **vs** interest rate
- revenue growth **vs** margin

Structure: one variable on rows (e.g., exit multiple 6x-10x), second variable on columns (e.g., EBITDA $10M-$20M), cells show resulting IRR or equity value.

Sensitivity analysis identifies which assumptions drive valuation most and helps assess downside risk. Darker shading or color coding highlights acceptable return zones.

Example: IRR Sensitivity Grid (%)

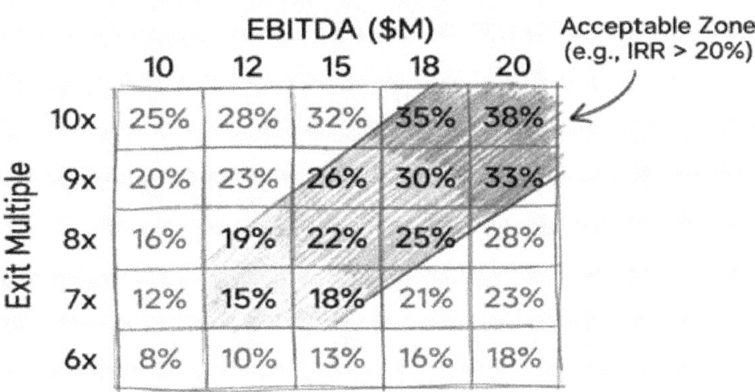

Exit Multiple \ EBITDA ($M)	10	12	15	18	20
10x	25%	28%	32%	35%	38%
9x	20%	23%	26%	30%	33%
8x	16%	19%	22%	25%	28%
7x	12%	15%	18%	21%	23%
6x	8%	10%	13%	16%	18%

Value Creation Finance Toolkit

Card 44: Scenario Analysis

Planning for multiple futures

- Scenario analysis models returns under different business outcomes: base case, upside case, downside case.

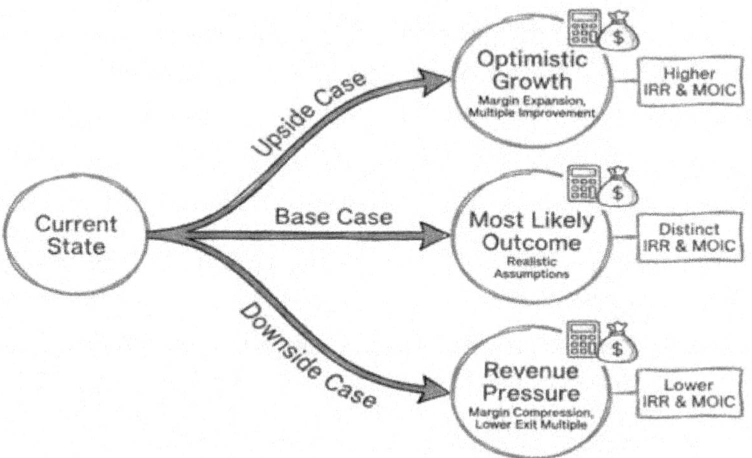

- Base Case - most likely outcome based on realistic assumptions. Produces distinct IRR and MOIC.
- Upside Case - optimistic growth, margin expansion, multiple improvement. Produces distinct IRR and MOIC.
- Downside Case - revenue pressure, margin compression, lower exit multiple. Produces distinct IRR and MOIC.

Scenario analysis supports investment committee decisions, risk assessment, and portfolio monitoring. Probability-weighted scenarios estimate expected returns.

- Downside protection (e.g., asset coverage, cash flow stability) is critical.

Value Creation Finance Toolkit

Card 45: Capital Stack Map

Visualising the financing structure

Capital stack illustrates layers of financing from most senior (lowest risk, lowest return) to most junior (highest risk, highest return).

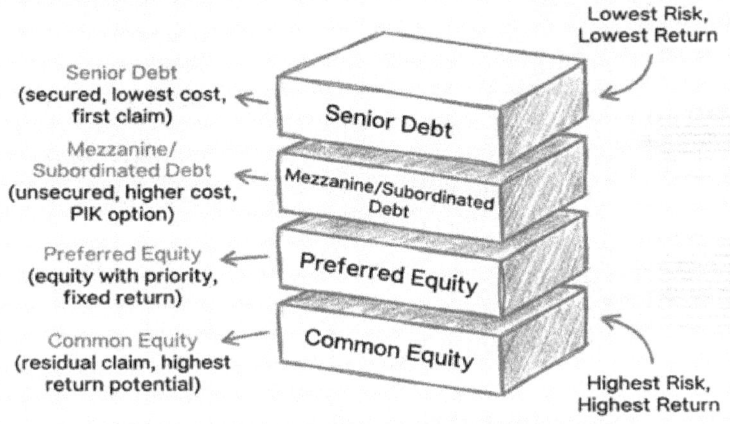

Each layer has different risk/return profile, seniority in liquidation, and cost of capital. Optimising capital stack balances cost, flexibility, and control.

Value Creation Finance Toolkit

Card 46: Mezzanine & PIK Instruments

Flexible subordinated financing

Mezzanine debt sits between senior debt and equity in the capital stack. PIK (Payment-In-Kind) allows interest to be paid with additional debt rather than cash.

Characteristics
- Unsecured or subordinated
- Higher interest rate (10-15%)
- Often includes equity warrants or kickers
- PIK toggle reduces cash burden during growth phase
- Used to bridge financing gap without diluting equity.

Risks
- Increases total leverage
- Higher cost than senior debt
- Compounds if PIK interest accrues.

Mezzanine financing supports larger buyouts and growth investments while preserving equity ownership. Exit typically requires refinancing or repayment from sale proceeds.

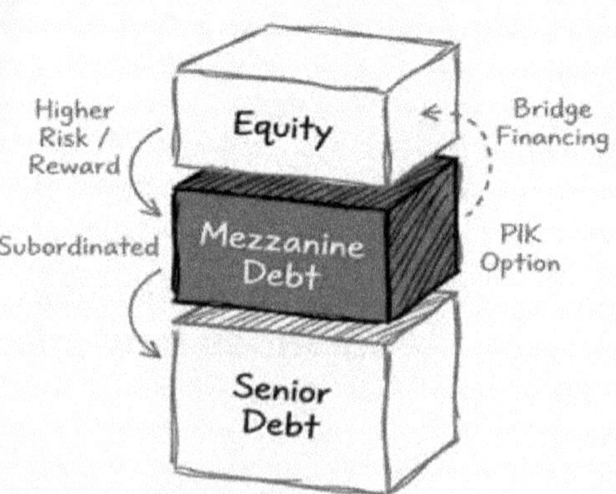

Value Creation Finance Toolkit

Card 47: Unitranche Financing

Simplified debt structure

Unitranche combines senior and subordinated debt into a single facility with blended pricing and unified documentation.

Benefits:

- Single lender relationship simplifies negotiations
- Faster execution than syndicated deals
- Fewer covenants and more flexibility
- Blended rate between senior and mezz (typically 7-10%)

Structure:

- One credit agreement
- One set of covenants
- Single agent
- Priority waterfall within lender group (first-out vs last-out tranches)

Unitranche popular for mid-market deals where speed and simplicity outweigh cost savings from separate facilities. Provides operational flexibility with less administrative burden.

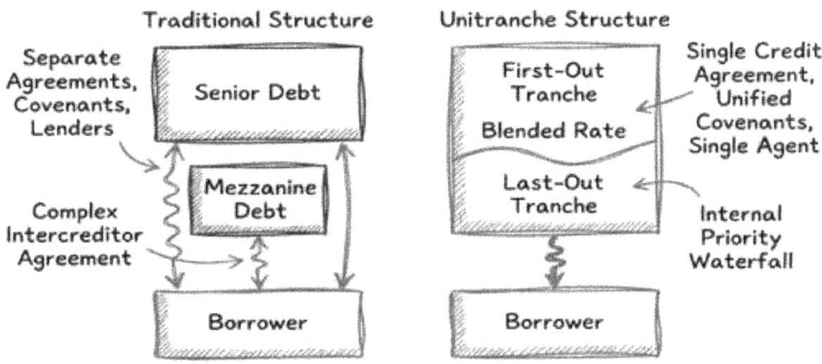

Value Creation Finance Toolkit

Card 48: Working Capital Release & Equity Value

Unlocking trapped cash

Working capital release occurs when improvements in cash conversion cycle free up cash that flows to equity holders.

Mechanisms:

- accelerate receivables collection (reduce DSO)
- optimise inventory levels (reduce DIO)
- extend payables terms (increase DPO)
- eliminate excess working capital

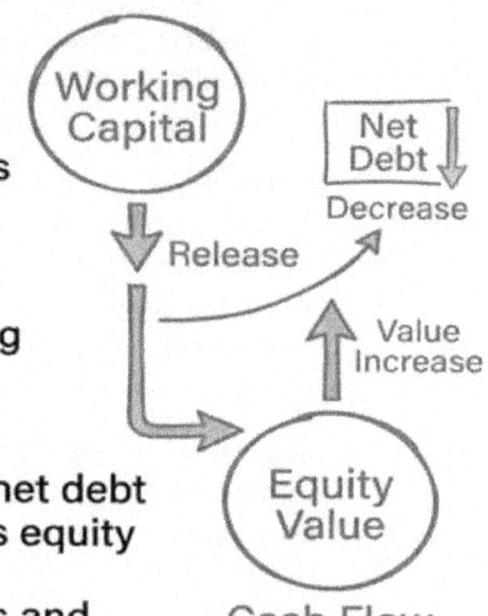

Impact on equity value:

- released cash reduces net debt
- lower net debt increases equity value dollar-for-dollar
- improves leverage ratios and financial flexibility

$$\Delta \text{Equity Value} = \Delta \text{Working Capital}$$

(if used to pay down debt)

Working capital optimisation is a quick value creation lever. Typical release: 5-15% of revenue depending on industry and starting efficiency.

Value Creation Finance Toolkit

Card 49: Audit-Ready Exit Finance Pack

Preparing for buyer due diligence

Exit finance pack is a comprehensive set of financial materials prepared for prospective buyers during exit process.

Checklist Diagram

Core components:

- (1) Historical financials (3-5 years audited)
- (2) Quality of Earnings report
- (3) Quality of Earnings report
- (3) Adjusted EBITDA bridge with normalisation
- (4) Working capital analysis and normalisation
- (5) Net debt schedule and debt payoff amounts
- (6) CapEx history and maintenance vs growth split
- (7) Management projections with sensitivities
- (8) Customer and revenue concentration analysis

Well-prepared finance pack accelerates buyer diligence, supports valuation, reduces re-trading risk, and demonstrates professionalism. Start preparation 6-12 months before exit.

Value Creation Finance Toolkit

Card 50: Risk-Adjusted Performance

Returns in context of risk taken

Risk-adjusted performance measures returns relative to volatility or downside risk, providing better comparison across investments.

Common metrics:
Sharpe Ratio = (Return - Risk-Free Rate) / Standard Deviation
(penalises total volatility)

Sortino Ratio = (Return - Target) / Downside Deviation
(penalises only downside volatility)

Public Market Equivalent (PME) = PE returns vs public market benchmark

In PE context:
- assess whether higher returns justify illiquidity and concentration risk
- compare fund performance to public equity alternatives
- evaluate consistency of returns across vintage years

Risk-adjusted metrics help LPs allocate capital across asset classes and evaluate GP skill vs market beta. Strong risk-adjusted returns indicate disciplined underwriting and value creation.

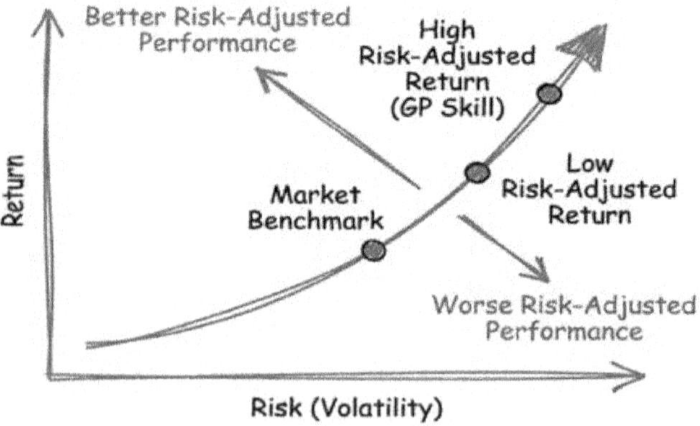

Value Creation Finance Toolkit

APPENDIX A

THE ANTI-PATTERN LIBRARY

Value Destruction Disguised as Value Creation

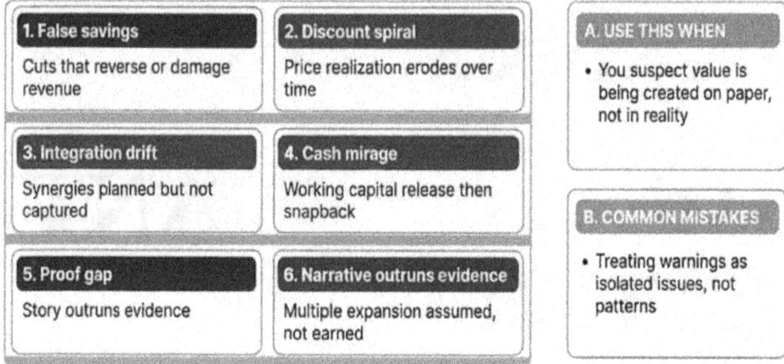

Not every pattern that improves one bridge component creates net value. Some patterns look like value creation in the short term but destroy value over the hold period. They move operating earnings up while simultaneously compressing the exit multiple or increasing net debt in ways that more than offset the earnings gain.

These are anti-patterns: value destruction disguised as value creation.

Experienced operators recognize anti-patterns before they execute them. They understand that the three bridges interact. Aggressive moves on one bridge can undermine the others. A dollar of operating earnings created by destroying future growth potential is worth less than a dollar of operating earnings from sustainable improvement. Sometimes much less.

This appendix catalogs the most common anti-patterns. Each entry describes what the pattern looks like, why it seems attractive, which bridge component it harms, the early warning signs, and what to do instead. Recognize these before someone proposes them in your operating review.

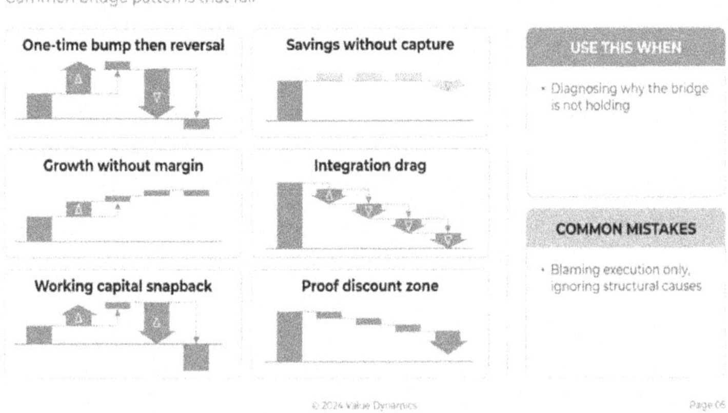

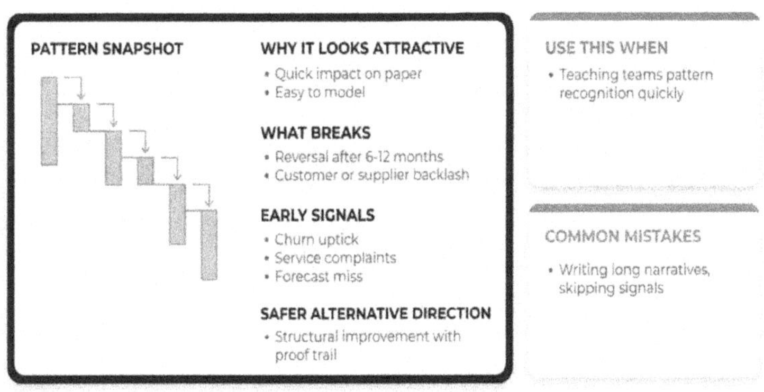

Anti-Pattern 1: The False Margin

The Pattern: Aggressive cost cutting that improves margins in the short term but breaks the growth engine. Marketing spend slashed, sales capacity reduced, product development frozen, customer service degraded. Operating earnings rise temporarily while the foundation for future revenue erodes.

Why It Looks Attractive: Immediate and visible impact on operating earnings. Easy to execute because cutting requires no innovation or market risk. Creates a short-term narrative of operational discipline. The damage to growth potential is invisible in the first few quarters.

Bridge Damage: Operating earnings rise temporarily (positive). Revenue growth stalls or declines (negative, appears later). Exit multiple compresses as buyers see a shrinking business with limited growth potential (negative, significant). Net effect: equity value declines despite higher margins.

Early Warning Signs: Cost cuts target revenue-generating functions first. No corresponding investment in remaining revenue capacity. Pipeline metrics weaken before revenue does. Customer acquisition cost rises as marketing efficiency drops. Sales team bandwidth saturates. New product launches postponed indefinitely.

What To Do Instead: Cut costs in non-revenue-generating overhead first. Protect customer-facing capacity and product investment. Set minimum thresholds for marketing and development spend as a percentage of revenue. Measure cost efficiency, not just cost reduction. Accept slower margin expansion if it preserves growth trajectory.

Anti-Pattern 2: The Discount Spiral

The Pattern: Sales heroics that sacrifice price for volume. Discounting to close deals, extending promotional pricing indefinitely, competing on price rather than value. Revenue grows while margins erode and price expectations reset downward permanently.

Why It Looks Attractive: Revenue hits targets. Sales team appears productive. Customer count grows. Market share metrics look strong. The margin damage is attributed to other factors or expected to recover. Nobody wants to report a missed quarter.

Bridge Damage: Revenue grows (positive, temporary). Operating earnings decline as margin compresses (negative). Exit multiple compresses as buyers see commoditized pricing and lack of pricing power (negative). Net effect: equity value stagnates or declines despite revenue growth.

Early Warning Signs: Average selling price declining while volume rises. Discount approval frequency increasing. Sales team blaming competitive pricing for every deal. Renewal pricing below original contract value. Promotions extended past intended end dates. Customers delaying purchases to wait for discounts.

What To Do Instead: Implement discount governance with approval thresholds. Tie sales compensation to margin, not just revenue. Invest in value articulation and differentiation. Accept slower volume growth to protect price realization. Train sales team to sell value, not process discounts.

Anti-Pattern 3: The Integration Mirage

The Pattern: Acquisitions pursued without integration muscle. Companies bought and loosely held together as a portfolio rather than combined into an operating entity. Synergies projected but never captured. Platform complexity grows without corresponding value creation.

Why It Looks Attractive: Revenue grows with each acquisition. Pro forma operating earnings increase. The deal thesis sounds compelling. Integration work is hard and unglamorous compared to deal making. Leadership attention moves to the next acquisition before the last one is integrated.

Bridge Damage: Revenue grows (positive). Operating earnings grow less than expected as synergies fail to materialize (disappointing). Net debt increases to fund acquisitions (negative). Exit multiple compresses as buyers see a holding company, not an integrated platform, and discount accordingly (negative, significant). Net effect: equity value lower than sum of parts.

Early Warning Signs: Synergy tracker showing projected versus achieved with large gaps. Multiple ERP systems, CRM systems, and processes still running. Acquired companies operating as separate units with minimal coordination. Cross-sell revenue negligible. Corporate overhead growing to manage complexity. Integration team disbanded before work complete.

What To Do Instead: Complete integration before next acquisition. Build dedicated integration capability. Tie deal team compensation to synergy realization, not deal close. Set integration completeness criteria that must be met before new deals approved. Slow acquisition pace to match integration capacity.

Anti-Pattern 4: The Dashboard Lie

The Pattern: Metrics that lag reality by weeks or months. Operating reviews based on data that no longer reflects current conditions. Decisions made on stale information. Problems visible in the business but invisible in the dashboard until too late to address.

Why It Looks Attractive: Dashboards exist. Reports are generated. Leadership reviews them regularly. The process looks disciplined. Nobody wants to admit the data is stale or that they do not actually know current performance. The effort to fix it seems expensive.

Bridge Damage: All bridge components at risk because corrective action is delayed. Operating earnings damaged when problems surface too late. Multiple compressed when buyers discover data quality issues in diligence. Net debt may rise if cash position is not visible. Net effect: preventable value destruction from delayed response.

Early Warning Signs: Operating review metrics do not match what people see on the floor. Month-end close takes more than five business days. Flash reports required to supplement formal reports. Leaders make decisions then ask for data to support them. Surprises at quarter end that were visible in operations weeks earlier.

What To Do Instead: Invest in data infrastructure that enables real-time or near-real-time visibility. Prioritize leading indicators over lagging. Define data freshness requirements for each metric. Fix the data foundation before building more dashboards on broken inputs. Accept that data capability is infrastructure, not overhead.

Anti-Pattern 5: The Synergy Fiction

The Pattern: Projected synergies that appear in deal models and board presentations but never materialize in financial statements. Cost synergies that require actions nobody is willing to take. Revenue synergies that assume customer behavior with no evidence. Savings claimed on paper while actual costs remain.

Why It Looks Attractive: Synergies justify acquisition prices. Deal models require them to show returns. Leadership commits to them in board meetings. Admitting they will not materialize means admitting the deal was overpriced. Easier to project than to execute.

Bridge Damage: Operating earnings flat or grow less than projected (negative versus plan). Net debt higher than planned because earnings do not support paydown (negative). Exit multiple compressed when buyers verify that projected synergies did not materialize and discount future projections accordingly (negative). Net effect: deal destroys value relative to standalone growth.

Early Warning Signs: Synergy targets not assigned to specific owners with timelines. No integration budget allocated to capture synergies. Synergy tracking shows projected but no achieved column. Revenue synergies based on cross-sell assumptions without pilot data. Cost synergies require headcount reductions that leadership is reluctant to execute.

What To Do Instead: Haircut synergy projections before deal close. Require named owners and specific milestones for each synergy line. Track achieved versus projected monthly from day one. Fund integration properly. Accept that revenue synergies are harder than cost synergies and plan accordingly.

Anti-Pattern 6: The Extraction Trap

The Pattern: Financial engineering that extracts cash from the business faster than it can be replenished. Sale-leasebacks that convert equity to rent obligations. Dividend recapitalizations that add debt without adding capability. Short-term cash extraction that starves the business of investment capacity.

Why It Looks Attractive: Returns cash to investors quickly. Improves early IRR metrics. Creates immediate liquidity. The long-term burden on the business is someone else's problem if exit happens soon. The constraint on future investment is not visible in current results.

Bridge Damage: Net debt increases or debt-equivalent obligations increase (negative, significant). Operating earnings may appear stable initially but constrained by fixed rent or interest (negative over time). Exit multiple compressed as buyers see inflexible cost structure and limited investment capacity (negative). Net effect: equity value lower than if business retained flexibility.

Early Warning Signs: Cash extracted exceeds cash generated by operations. Lease obligations rising faster than revenue. Debt paydown deferred to fund distributions. Investment requests denied due to cash constraints. Covenant headroom shrinking. Business cannot fund normal capital needs without additional financing.

What To Do Instead: Limit extraction to sustainable free cash flow. Maintain investment capacity for value-creating initiatives. Model total obligations including lease equivalents. Preserve operational flexibility. Accept lower early returns for sustainable value creation.

Anti-Pattern 7: The Promotion Spiral

The Pattern: Revenue gambits that destroy unit economics. Loss-leader promotions that attract customers who never convert to profitable relationships. Customer acquisition at any cost. Volume growth celebrated while contribution margin turns negative.

Why It Looks Attractive: Top-line growth looks impressive. Customer counts rise. Market share appears to grow. Leadership believes unprofitable customers will become profitable. The narrative of growth obscures the math of contribution margin.

Bridge Damage: Revenue grows (positive, visible). Operating earnings decline as promotion costs exceed margin contribution (negative, significant). Net debt may increase to fund losses (negative). Exit multiple collapses when buyers see negative unit economics and customer quality issues (negative, severe). Net effect: value destruction accelerates with scale.

Early Warning Signs: Promotion costs growing faster than revenue. Customer lifetime value calculations require heroic assumptions. Promotional customers showing low retention. Gross margin declining while revenue grows. Cash burn rate increasing. Team unable to articulate path to profitable unit economics.

What To Do Instead: Set customer acquisition cost limits tied to lifetime value. Measure contribution margin at customer level. End promotions that attract unprofitable customer segments. Accept slower growth with positive unit economics. Prove profitable customer acquisition before scaling.

Anti-Pattern 8: The Talent Drain

The Pattern: Cost reductions that push out institutional knowledge. Compensation cuts that trigger departure of key performers. Reorganizations that create uncertainty and drive voluntary attrition. Short-term savings that leave the business unable to execute its value creation plan.

Why It Looks Attractive: People cost is the largest expense in most businesses. Headcount reductions create immediate savings. High performers are expensive. The knowledge walking out the door is invisible on financial statements. Remaining team says they can absorb the work.

Bridge Damage: Operating earnings improve initially from lower compensation (positive, temporary). Execution capacity declines as key people leave (negative, delayed). Growth initiatives stall without talent to execute (negative). Exit multiple compressed when buyers see weak bench and key person risk (negative). Net effect: short-term savings, long-term value destruction.

Early Warning Signs: Voluntary attrition rising, especially among high performers. Compensation below market for critical roles. Key person dependencies increasing. Recruitment declining to fill openings. Projects delayed due to resource constraints. Institutional knowledge undocumented and walking out the door.

What To Do Instead: Identify critical roles and talent before restructuring. Pay to retain key performers. Document institutional knowledge. Build bench strength before it is needed. Accept higher compensation costs for roles that drive value creation. Cut roles, not capability.

Anti-Pattern 9: The Quality Fade

The Pattern: Cost reductions that degrade product or service quality in ways customers eventually notice. Cheaper inputs, reduced testing, eliminated features, slower service. Margins improve while customer satisfaction erodes and churn accelerates.

Why It Looks Attractive: Direct cost savings are immediate and visible. Quality degradation is gradual and invisible in financial metrics until customers leave. Leadership believes customers will not notice or will not care. The gap between quality cut and churn spike creates a false sense of safety.

Bridge Damage: Operating earnings improve initially from lower costs (positive, temporary). Customer retention declines as quality issues compound (negative, delayed but significant). Revenue eventually declines as churn exceeds acquisition (negative). Exit multiple collapses when buyers see quality metrics and customer complaints (negative, severe). Net effect: margin gains overwhelmed by revenue and multiple destruction.

Early Warning Signs: Customer satisfaction scores declining. Support ticket volume rising. Product return rates increasing. Negative reviews appearing. Customer complaints about things that used to work. Quality team raising concerns that are dismissed. Cost savings initiatives targeting product or service delivery.

What To Do Instead: Define quality floors that cost reduction cannot breach. Monitor customer satisfaction as a leading indicator. Test cost reductions with customer segments before broad rollout. Protect product and service elements that drive customer loyalty. Accept lower margins if quality preservation requires it.

Anti-Pattern 10: The Channel Conflict

The Pattern: Channel expansion that cannibalizes existing revenue rather than capturing new customers. Direct sales competing with distribution partners.

Online channels undercutting retail. New channels capturing share from existing channels rather than expanding the market.

Why It Looks Attractive: New channel shows growth. Direct channel margins are higher than partner channels. Leadership wants to own the customer relationship. The cannibalization is attributed to market dynamics rather than internal competition.

Bridge Damage: Total revenue flat or grows less than channel investments suggest (disappointing). Operating earnings may improve slightly from channel mix but not enough to justify investment (marginal). Distribution partners reduce support or exit, limiting market access (negative). Exit multiple affected if buyers see channel strategy dysfunction (negative). Net effect: investment in cannibalization rather than growth.

Early Warning Signs: New channel growth offset by existing channel decline. Partner complaints about pricing or competition. Customer migration between channels rather than new customer acquisition. Total addressable market not expanding despite channel investment. Channel profitability declining across all channels due to competition.

What To Do Instead: Design channel strategy to expand market access, not redistribute existing customers. Differentiate channel offerings to reduce direct competition. Set pricing policies that protect partner margins where partners add value. Measure incremental revenue from new channels, not just channel revenue. Align incentives across channels toward total market growth.

Recognizing Anti-Patterns in Your Organization

Anti-patterns rarely announce themselves. They arrive disguised as operational discipline, growth initiatives, or financial optimization. They survive because the short-term metrics look good and the long-term damage is attributed to other causes.

The test for any proposed initiative: trace its effects through all three bridges. If operating earnings rise but exit multiple or growth trajectory suffers, reconsider. If cash extraction improves early returns but constrains future investment, reconsider. If cost reduction creates savings but destroys capability, reconsider.

Value creation is not a single bridge. It is the interaction of all three. Anti-patterns optimize one at the expense of the others. True gambits improve the whole.

APPENDIX B

INDUSTRY ADAPTERS

Rules of Translation by Business Archetype

Industry Overlays:
Same Bridge, Different Reality

Adapt patterns to business model constraints

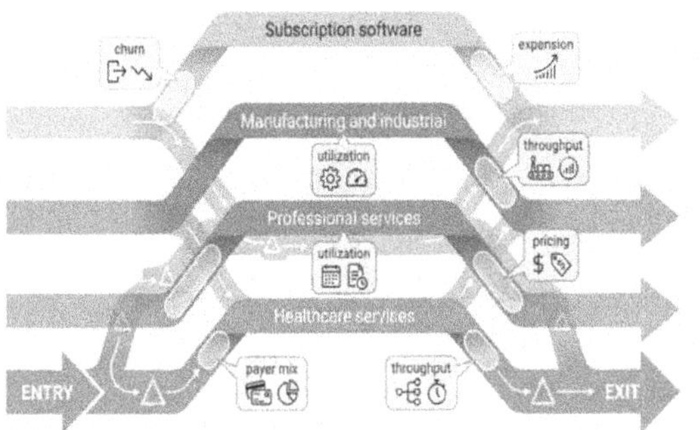

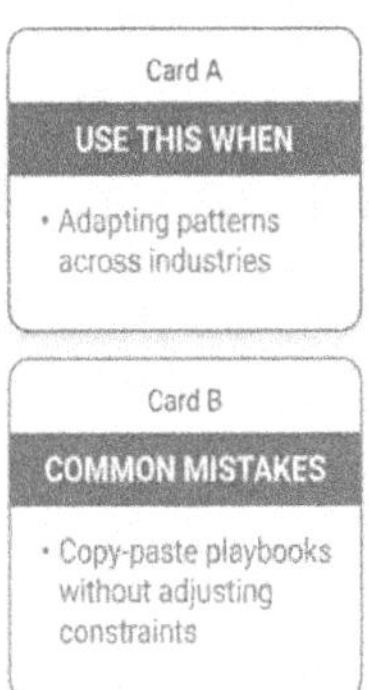

The forty gambits apply across industries, but they apply differently. A Pricing Ratchet in software-as-a-service works differently than in manufacturing. A Platform Roll-Up in healthcare services follows different rules than in distribution. The bridges remain the same. The translation changes.

This appendix provides quick adapters for six common business archetypes. Each adapter covers four elements: what changes in bridge logic, which gambits are most reliable, which gambits are most dangerous, and what evidence buyers demand most.

These are rules of translation, not new content. The gambits remain the same. The application shifts.

Industry Adapter Cards

Fast-fit pattern selection by business model

Subscription software

WHAT TYPICALLY WORKS
- Churn reduction
- Expansion revenue
- Pricing discipline

WHAT IS RISKY
- Forced upsells
- Feature bloat

PROOF BUYERS EXPECT
- Cohort retention
- Net revenue retention

Manufacturing and industrial

WHAT TYPICALLY WORKS
- Throughput improvement
- Procurement savings
- Utilization gains

WHAT IS RISKY
- Deferred maintenance
- Quality slip

PROOF BUYERS EXPECT
- Unit cost trend
- Capacity utilization

USE THIS WHEN

- Selecting patterns with faster fit

Professional services

WHAT TYPICALLY WORKS
- Utilization improvement
- Pricing realization
- Leverage model

WHAT IS RISKY
- Talent churn
- Client concentration

PROOF BUYERS EXPECT
- Billable utilization
- Revenue per professional

Healthcare services

WHAT TYPICALLY WORKS
- Payer mix improvement
- Throughput optimization
- Cost per episode

WHAT IS RISKY
- Quality metrics slip
- Regulatory exposure

PROOF BUYERS EXPECT
- Payer mix trend
- Cost per case

COMMON MISTAKES

- Ignoring business model economics

Archetype 1: Software as a Service

Bridge Logic Differences

Multiple dominates. Subscription software companies trade on revenue multiples, not earnings multiples. Growth rate and retention metrics drive valuation more than current profitability. Net revenue retention above one hundred percent can justify premium multiples even with operating losses. The exit multiple bridge component often contributes more to equity value than operating earnings improvement.

Most Reliable Gambits

Retention Firewall (churn reduction flows directly to revenue and multiple), Expansion Loop (net revenue retention expansion), Value Packaging Reset (pricing tier optimization), Recurring Revenue Conversion (if transitioning from perpetual licenses), Platform Roll-Up (consolidation plays common and rewarded).

Most Dangerous Gambits

Zero-Based Rebuild (cutting customer success or product investment destroys growth and multiple), Bad Revenue Exit (revenue decline severely penalized even if margin improves), Organizational Flattening (thin teams cannot support enterprise customers requiring support and customization).

Buyer Evidence Priorities

Logo retention and net revenue retention by cohort, annual recurring revenue growth trend, customer acquisition cost payback period, lifetime value to customer acquisition cost ratio, gross margin (target seventy percent or higher), rule of forty compliance (growth rate plus operating margin).

Archetype 2: Professional Services

Bridge Logic Differences

People are the product. Utilization and bill rates drive operating earnings directly. Key person risk affects multiple significantly. Recurring revenue (retainer models, managed services) commands premium multiples over project-based revenue. Leverage ratio (junior to senior staff) determines scalability.

Most Reliable Gambits

Pricing Ratchet (rate card increases and utilization optimization), Mix Elevator (shift to higher-margin service lines), Management Depth Build (reduce key person dependence), Recurring Revenue Conversion (move project work to retainers), Concentration Reduction (diversify client base).

Most Dangerous Gambits

Organizational Flattening (destroying leverage ratio hurts margin), Platform Roll-Up without cultural integration (talent leaves post-acquisition), Process Automation (automating away billable hours without replacing revenue), Zero-Based Rebuild (underinvesting in talent development and retention).

Buyer Evidence Priorities

Utilization rates by role, effective bill rate trends, client concentration and tenure, employee retention especially senior staff, pipeline coverage, recurring revenue percentage, revenue per professional.

Archetype 3: Manufacturing

Bridge Logic Differences

Operating earnings improvements are highly credible and valued. Asset efficiency drives returns. Working capital intensity affects cash conversion significantly. Multiple expansion requires demonstrating end market stability or growth, proprietary capability, or aftermarket revenue streams. Capacity utilization affects both margin and growth potential.

Most Reliable Gambits

Throughput Unlock (capacity and yield improvement), Procurement Concentration (material cost reduction), Working Capital Sprint (inventory and receivables optimization), Unit Economics Rewrite (product line profitability), Process Automation (labor productivity improvement).

Most Dangerous Gambits

Pricing Ratchet without market power (customers switch to competitors), Footprint Rationalization without capacity planning (cannot serve demand surge), Bad Revenue Exit of products that cover fixed costs (stranding overhead), Platform Roll-Up without operational integration (missed synergies).

Buyer Evidence Priorities

Gross margin by product line, capacity utilization, equipment age and condition, working capital as percentage of revenue, customer concentration, backlog coverage, capital expenditure requirements, environmental and safety compliance.

Archetype 4: Healthcare Services

Bridge Logic Differences

Regulatory complexity affects multiple significantly. Payer mix (commercial versus government) drives margin quality. Physician or clinician relationships are key person risks. Reimbursement rate changes can materially affect earnings. Platform scale creates leverage with payers and referral sources.

Most Reliable Gambits

Platform Roll-Up (scale creates payer leverage and referral density), Mix Elevator (shift to higher-acuity or better-reimbursed services), Revenue Cycle Optimization (reducing days in accounts receivable), Standardization Program (consistent clinical and operational protocols across sites), Management Depth Build (reduce physician dependence).

Most Dangerous Gambits

Zero-Based Rebuild that affects clinical quality (regulatory and reputational risk), Pricing Ratchet above contracted rates (payer relationships), Process Automation that removes clinical judgment (liability exposure), Organizational Flattening that removes clinical leadership layers (quality governance).

Buyer Evidence Priorities

Payer mix and rate trends, same-store volume growth, physician or clinician retention, days in accounts receivable, compliance history, patient satisfaction scores, referral source concentration, clinical quality metrics.

Archetype 5: Distribution

Bridge Logic Differences

Low margins magnify importance of operating leverage. Working capital intensity is high, making cash conversion critical. Supplier relationships and exclusive rights drive competitive position. Logistics efficiency directly affects margin. Technology enablement (e-commerce, inventory management) increasingly differentiates.

Most Reliable Gambits

Working Capital Sprint (inventory turns critical in low-margin business), Procurement Concentration (supplier rebates and terms), Platform Roll-Up (density creates logistics efficiency), Process Automation (warehouse and logistics productivity), Footprint Rationalization (optimize warehouse network).

Most Dangerous Gambits

Pricing Ratchet (customers have alternatives, margin is already thin), Bad Revenue Exit (fixed cost absorption critical), Service Model Surgery that slows delivery (customers expect speed), Technology investments without clear productivity return (technology for its own sake).

Buyer Evidence Priorities

Gross margin by product category, inventory turns, days sales outstanding, supplier concentration and terms, customer retention, fill rate and delivery performance, technology platform maturity, private label or proprietary product mix.

Archetype 6: Consumer and Retail

Bridge Logic Differences

Brand strength affects both margin and multiple. Same-store sales growth is critical signal. Real estate strategy (owned versus leased, location quality) significantly affects flexibility and risk. Consumer trends can shift rapidly, making growth trajectory uncertain. Omnichannel capability increasingly required.

Most Reliable Gambits

Value Packaging Reset (pricing architecture and promotion optimization), Mix Elevator (category and product mix improvement), Retention Firewall (loyalty programs and customer lifetime value), Digital Product Enhancement (e-commerce and omnichannel), Footprint Rationalization (exit underperforming locations).

Most Dangerous Gambits

Zero-Based Rebuild that cuts marketing (brand requires constant investment), Platform Roll-Up without brand strategy (portfolio confusion), Extraction Trap via sale-leaseback (inflexible real estate costs), Quality Fade (customers notice immediately in consumer products).

Buyer Evidence Priorities

Same-store sales trend, customer acquisition cost and lifetime value, brand awareness and consideration metrics, gross margin by category, e-commerce penetration and growth, store-level four-wall profitability, lease expiration schedule, inventory turnover.

APPENDIX C

THE DEPENDENCY MATRIX

What Must Come Before What

Not all gambits can execute in parallel. Some require others first. Attempting a gambit without its prerequisites leads to execution failure, wasted resources, and lost time.

This matrix maps the major dependency chains. Read it as: the gambits in the left column require or strongly benefit from completion of the enabling gambits listed to the right before they can succeed.

Case Evidence Card

Build credibility without a long casebook

STARTING CONDITION

[Describe the initial state, challenge, or problem]

PATTERN APPLIED

[Identify the specific methodology, solution, or pattern used]

BRIDGE IMPACT (QUALITATIVE)

EVIDENCE ARTIFACTS

- Cohort retention data
- Margin bridge
- Cash conversion cycle
- Customer feedback log
- Quality of earnings audit

WHAT NEARLY BROKE IT

[Highlight the key risk, obstacle, or near-failure point]

TRANSFERABILITY NOTE

[Mention how this can be applied to other contexts or clients]

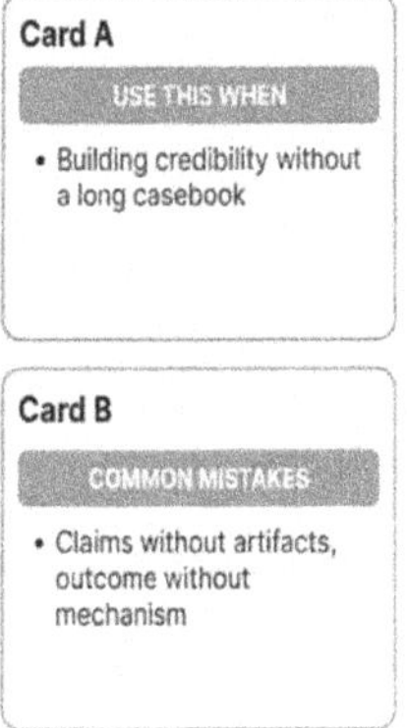

Chain One: Data Foundation

These gambits cannot succeed without data infrastructure in place first.

Enabling Gambit: Data Infrastructure Build (Gambit 36), Cash Visibility System (Gambit 27)

Dependent Gambits:

• AI Deployment Program (Gambit 37) requires clean, accessible data

• Unit Economics Rewrite (Gambit 11) requires product and customer-level cost data

• Conversion Rebuild (Gambit 7) requires funnel and conversion data

• Retention Firewall (Gambit 5) requires churn analysis and customer behavior data

• Pricing Ratchet (Gambit 1) benefits significantly from price elasticity and customer segment data

Chain Two: Process Discipline

Automation and standardization amplify existing processes. Broken processes automated are still broken, just faster.

Enabling Actions: Process mapping, standardization, and optimization

Dependent Gambits:

• Process Automation Wave (Gambit 35) requires processes worth automating

• Standardization Program (Gambit 22) requires understanding which process is best

• Technology-Enabled Service Model (Gambit 40) requires service processes that work manually first

Chain Three: Platform Stability

Acquisition programs require a stable platform before adding complexity. Integration bandwidth must exist before acquisition velocity increases.

Enabling Actions: Platform operational stability, integration capability, management bandwidth

Dependent Gambits:

• Platform Roll-Up (Gambit 17) requires platform that can absorb and integrate acquisitions

• Adjacency Expansion (Gambit 18) requires stable core before extending

• Capability Tuck-In (Gambit 21) requires bandwidth to integrate the capability

• Cross-Sell Fuse (Gambit 20) requires integrated sales motion to execute

Chain Four: Cash Availability

Investment-heavy gambits require cash. In cash-constrained situations, cash-generating gambits must precede cash-consuming ones.

Enabling Gambits: Working Capital Sprint (Gambit 23), Cash Conversion Engine (Gambit 24), Debt Paydown Accelerator (Gambit 26)

Dependent Gambits (when cash-constrained):

• Data Infrastructure Build (Gambit 36) requires investment

• Technology Debt Remediation (Gambit 38) requires investment

• Process Automation Wave (Gambit 35) requires capital for automation technology

• Acquisition gambits (Gambits 17-22) require acquisition capital

Chain Five: Talent Capability

Complex gambits require leadership capability. When capability is thin, building it must precede demanding initiatives.

Enabling Gambit: Management Depth Build (Gambit 31)

Dependent Gambits (when talent-thin):

• Service Model Surgery (Gambit 13) requires leadership to manage transformation

• Organizational Flattening (Gambit 14) requires capable leaders who can span larger teams

• Synergy Capture System (Gambit 19) requires integration leadership

• Major growth initiatives require bandwidth beyond running operations

Using the Dependency Matrix

Before sequencing your selected gambits, trace each one through these dependency chains. Ask: does this gambit require data, process discipline, platform stability, cash, or talent that does not yet exist? If so, the enabling action or gambit must come first or in parallel.

Dependencies are not optional. They are prerequisites. Ignoring them does not accelerate execution. It guarantees failure.

The gambit portfolio that respects dependencies executes. The one that ignores them creates motion without progress.

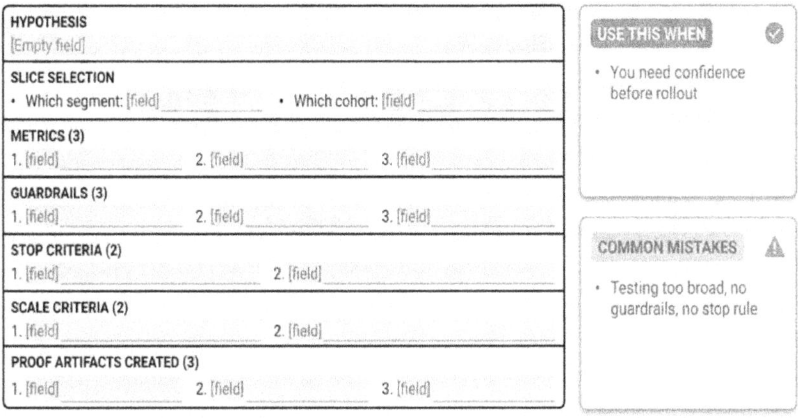
Sandbox Test Canvas
Build confidence before rollout
HYPOTHESIS
[Empty field]
SLICE SELECTION
• Which segment: [field]
• Which cohort: [field]
METRICS (3)
1. [field] 2. [field] 3. [field]
GUARDRAILS (3)
1. [field] 2. [field] 3. [field]
STOP CRITERIA (2)
1. [field] 2. [field]
SCALE CRITERIA (2)
1. [field] 2. [field]
PROOF ARTIFACTS CREATED (3)
1. [field] 2. [field] 3. [field]
USE THIS WHEN
• You need confidence before rollout
COMMON MISTAKES
• Testing too broad, no guardrails, no stop rule

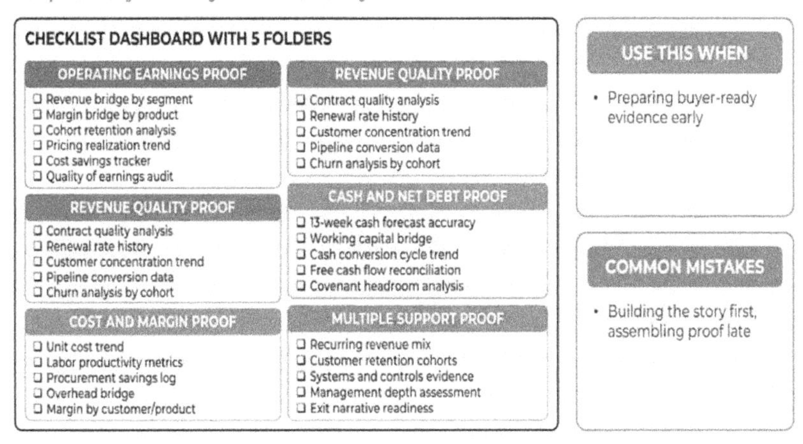
Exit Proof Pack Builder
Prepare buyer-ready evidence early
CHECKLIST DASHBOARD WITH 5 FOLDERS
OPERATING EARNINGS PROOF
❑ Revenue bridge by segment
❑ Margin bridge by product
❑ Cohort retention analysis
❑ Pricing realization trend
❑ Cost savings tracker
❑ Quality of earnings audit
REVENUE QUALITY PROOF
❑ Contract quality analysis
❑ Renewal rate history
❑ Customer concentration trend
❑ Pipeline conversion data
❑ Churn analysis by cohort
REVENUE QUALITY PROOF
❑ Contract quality analysis
❑ Renewal rate history
❑ Customer concentration trend
❑ Pipeline conversion data
❑ Churn analysis by cohort
CASH AND NET DEBT PROOF
❑ 13-week cash forecast accuracy
❑ Working capital bridge
❑ Cash conversion cycle trend
❑ Free cash flow reconciliation
❑ Covenant headroom analysis
COST AND MARGIN PROOF
❑ Unit cost trend
❑ Labor productivity metrics
❑ Procurement savings log
❑ Overhead bridge
❑ Margin by customer/product
MULTIPLE SUPPORT PROOF
❑ Recurring revenue mix
❑ Customer retention cohorts
❑ Systems and controls evidence
❑ Management depth assessment
❑ Exit narrative readiness
USE THIS WHEN
• Preparing buyer-ready evidence early
COMMON MISTAKES
• Building the story first, assembling proof late

APPENDIX D

TOOLS & WORKSHEETS

A systematic Planning Method

Starting Condition

Printable worksheet

Problem statement

[Write here]

Symptoms checklist

- ☐ [Symptom 1]
- ☐ [Symptom 2]
- ☐ [Symptom 3]
- ☐ [Symptom 4]
- ☐ [Symptom 5]
- ☐ [Symptom 6]
- ☐ [Symptom 7]
- ☐ [Symptom 8]

Constraint notes

First measurement to confirm

Private Equity Gameplan Tools

Constraint Assessment

Printable worksheet

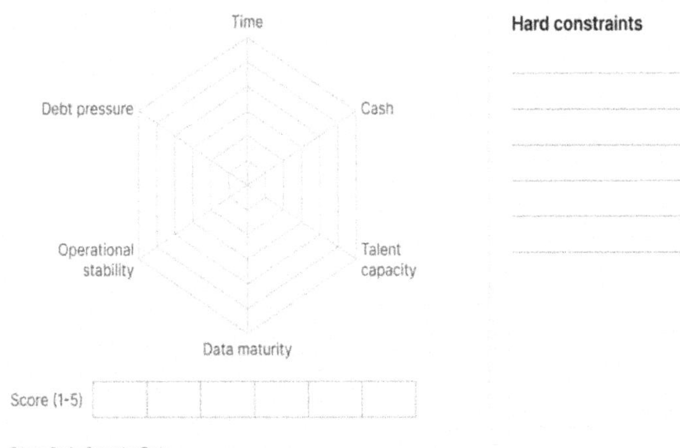

Private Equity Gameplan Tools

Fit Scoring

Printable worksheet

A. Candidate list

Candidate name	Impact (1-5)	Confidence (1-5)	Speed (1-5)	Notes

B. Disqualifiers

- [ ] [Disqualifier 1]
- [ ] [Disqualifier 2]
- [ ] [Disqualifier 3]
- [ ] [Disqualifier 4]
- [ ] [Disqualifier 5]

C. Top 2 picks

[Pick 1]

[Pick 2]

Private Equity Gameplan Tools

Shortlist

Printable worksheet

A. Top 5 candidates

Name	Bridge target	Time	Owner	Notes

B. Trade-off statement per candidate

1.
2.
3.
4.
5.

C. Decision log

Date	Decision	Reason

Private Equity Gameplan Tools

Proof Register

Printable worksheet

Operating Earnings Proof					
	Artifact	Owner	Where stored	Status	Notes
☐					
☐					
☐					

Cash and Net Debt Proof					
	Artifact	Owner	Where stored	Status	Notes
☐					
☐					
☐					

Multiple Support Proof					
	Artifact	Owner	Where stored	Status	Notes
☐					
☐					
☐					

Private Equity Gameplan Tools

Evidence Gap

Printable worksheet

A. What we claim

[Claim 1]

[Claim 2]

[Claim 3]

B. What we can prove today

[Proof 1]

[Proof 2]

[Proof 3]

C. What buyers will ask for

[Ask 1]

[Ask 2]

[Ask 3]

D. Proof plan

Artifact	Source	Build steps	Deadline

Private Equity Gameplan Tools

Sandbox Test

Printable worksheet

Hypothesis		Slice selection
[Write here]		[Write here]

Metric 1	Metric 2	Metric 3
[Write here]	[Write here]	[Write here]

Guardrail 1	Guardrail 2	Guardrail 3
[Write here]	[Write here]	[Write here]

Stop criteria	Scale criteria
[Write here] [Write here]	[Write here] [Write here]

Proof artifacts produced
[Write here] [Write here] [Write here]

Private Equity Gameplan Tools

Sequence Builder

Printable worksheet

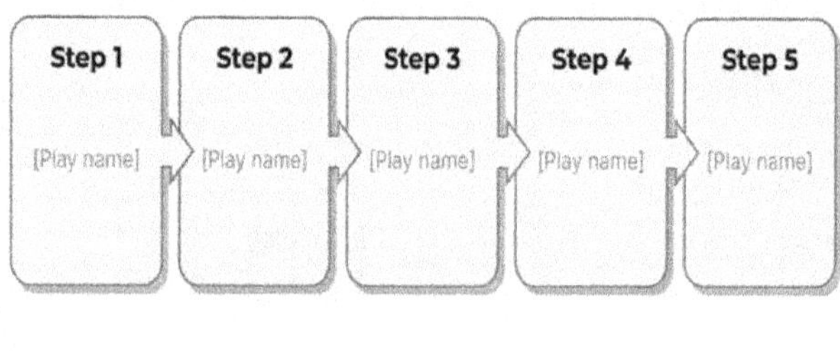

Dependencies

- ☐ [Dependency 1]
- ☐ [Dependency 2]
- ☐ [Dependency 3]
- ☐ [Dependency 4]
- ☐ [Dependency 5]

Conflicts to watch

- ☐ [Conflict 1]
- ☐ [Conflict 2]
- ☐ [Conflict 3]
- ☐ [Conflict 4]
- ☐ [Conflict 5]

Keep steps explainable on the bridge.

Integration Readiness

Printable worksheet

A Integration capacity

- [ ] [Capacity item 1]
- [ ] [Capacity item 2]
- [ ] [Capacity item 3]
- [ ] [Capacity item 4]
- [ ] [Capacity item 5]
- [ ] [Capacity item 6]

B Systems alignment

- [ ] [System item 1]
- [ ] [System item 2]
- [ ] [System item 3]
- [ ] [System item 4]
- [ ] [System item 5]
- [ ] [System item 6]

C People/process alignment

- [ ] [People item 1]
- [ ] [People item 2]
- [ ] [People item 3]
- [ ] [People item 4]
- [ ] [People item 5]
- [ ] [People item 6]

D Synergy tracking plan

Synergy	Owner	Target

Private Equity Gameplan Tools

Exit Readiness

Printable worksheet

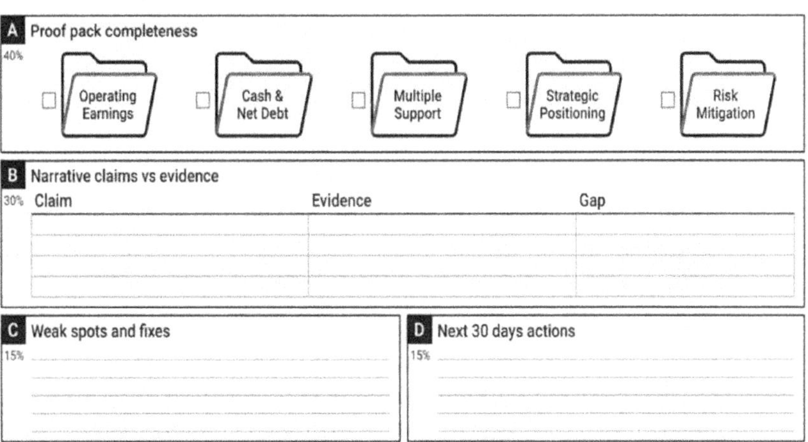

Afterword

This book completes a trilogy.

The Private Equity Quarterback addressed the WHO question: what kind of leader succeeds in private equity environments, how operating partners think, and how to navigate the unique dynamics of sponsor-backed leadership.

The Private Equity Coach addressed the HOW question: the governance systems, meeting cadences, accountability structures, and operating rhythms that enable value creation.

This book, The Private Equity Gameplan, addresses the WHAT question: the specific tactical patterns that change numbers on the value bridge.

Together, the three books form a complete system. You need the right leadership approach (Quarterback) operating through the right systems (Coach) executing the right tactics (Gameplan). Missing any element undermines the others.

But here is what the books cannot provide: experience. Pattern recognition develops through reps. Judgment develops through decisions. Confidence develops through results. Books accelerate learning. They cannot replace it.

So use this book as a reference, not a recipe. Return to it when facing specific challenges. Let it prompt questions rather than dictate answers. Adapt the gambits to your specific situation. Develop your own variants. Build your own pattern library.

The gambits in this book work. I have seen them work across dozens of portfolio companies, multiple fund cycles, and various economic conditions. But they work because skilled operators adapted them to specific situations, executed them with discipline, and adjusted when reality diverged from plan.

Value creation is ultimately about people making decisions. The bridge does not build itself. Leaders build it, one decision at a time, one gambit at a time, one day at a time. The goal of this book is to make those decisions better.

The best operating partners I know share certain characteristics. They are endlessly curious about how businesses work. They see patterns others miss. They maintain calm under pressure. They execute with discipline but adapt with speed. They care about results and about the people who deliver them.

If you have read this far, you probably share those characteristics. You are investing in your craft. You are building your pattern library. You are preparing for the next challenge.

The field needs more people like you. Private equity's impact depends on the quality of operating work. Better operators build better businesses. Better businesses create better outcomes for employees, customers, and investors alike.

So go build your bridge. Pick your gambits. Execute with discipline. Create value that matters.

The game is on.

Mohamad Chahine

2025

www.ingramcontent.com/pod-product-compliance
Ingram Content Group UK Ltd.
Pitfield, Milton Keynes, MK11 3LW, UK
UKHW022029190726
13853UKWH00005B/2173